RICHARD SAWYER'S

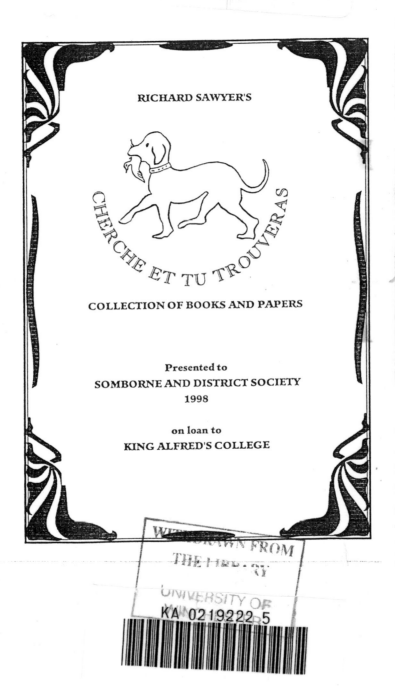

CHERCHE ET TU TROUVERAS

COLLECTION OF BOOKS AND PAPERS

Presented to
SOMBORNE AND DISTRICT SOCIETY
1998

on loan to
KING ALFRED'S COLLEGE

Hampshire Record Series Volume VIII

The Register of William Edington Bishop of Winchester 1346–1366

PART 2

Edited by Dom S. F. Hockey, F.R.Hist.S.

Hampshire Record Office for
Hampshire County Council, 1987

ISSN 0267-9930
ISBN 0 906680 05 0

Printed in England by
Hobbs the Printers of Southampton (1028/87)

Contents

Editorial note

This is the second of the two volumes of Edington's Register. The edition is set out on the same principles as volume 1, with its own index of personal names and placenames. The subject index, however, refers to both volumes. There is also a table of concordance of the foliation of the sixteenth, seventeenth and eighteenth centuries used in both volumes of the manuscript and the pagination employed in this edition.

VARIOUS COMMISSIONS, INQUISITIONS, PROCURATIONS, LICENCES FOR ORATORIES AND OTHER LETTERS WITH THEIR EXECUTION.
MAY 1346—AUGUST 1366

1. LICENCE granted at the request of Margaret countess of Kent for the marriage between Robert de Barnham and Katherine de Weston to take place in any oratory of the said countess in the diocese, but without prejudice to the mother church and preceded by banns.

Southwark, 22 May 1346

2. RECEIPT from Robert de Burton, archdeacon of Winchester, for £20 due annually. For the Easter term.

Southwark, 24 May 1346

3. LICENCE to hear mass in his private oratory with his household granted to John de Purle, of the parish of Sanderstead. Letter to the rector of Sanderstead.

Southwark, 20 May 1346

4. Similar licence granted to Lora Sauvage, residing in the parish of St M. Magdalen, Southwark, to hear mass in her private oratory in bad weather or health. Letter to the prior of Southwark.

Southwark, 27 May 1346

5. Similar licence to Baldwin, rector of Fordingbridge, to celebrate in the rectory oratory with his household, except on solemnities.

6. Similar licence to sir John Darcy junior, to hear mass in his private oratory.

Southwark, 12 June 1346

7. Similar licence to William de Rotherwyk' of the parish of Egham.

Southwark, 12 June 1346

8. GRANT by the bishop to Alan de Killum, king's clerk, by reason of the elevation to the see, of a pension of 10 marks a year payable from the treasury of Wolvesey in two annual payments, beginning next Michaelmas.

Southwark, 14 June 1346

9. MANDATE to Walter atte Brugge of Wanborough, clerk, to enquire into the fruits of benefices vacant in the archdeaconry of Surrey; to sequestrate where required; to enquire into the goods of those dying intestate. The probate of ecclesiastical persons is reserved to the bishop. Walter is appointed sequestrator-general.

Southwark, 5 June 1346

10. COMMISSION to the provost of St Elizabeth and to the dean of Winchester to demand from the justices the delivery from gaol at

Winchester and in the county of Southampton of all imprisoned clerks, acting as the bishop's attorneys.

Southwark, 20 June 1346

11. Similar commission to the dean of Guildford and M. Gilbert rector of the church of Ash, to demand gaol delivery of clerks at Guildford and elsewhere in Surrey.

12. COMMISSION from the apostolic see to the bishop, the archbishop of Canterbury, Edmund bishop of Exeter, the Master of the order of Preachers: to M. William de Appeltre, archdeacon of Stafford, diocese of Lichfield, and Thomas de Asteleye, canons of Lichfield. To investigate the complaint of the prior and brethren of the convent at Derby, that Walter Cawe, perpetual vicar of the church of Hope and William Servelady priest, John de Chadesden' and William Nayl with others have been insulting and molesting the brethren there.

Southwark, 23 June 1346

13. COMMISSION to M. Thomas de Enham to enquire into and punish all excesses and offences of the subjects of the bishop within the diocese and all transgression against his jurisdiction and rights, as well as cases heard before the bishop in his court.

275
Southwark, 15 June 1346

14. APPOINTMENT of M. Thomas de Enham as procurator of the bishop with power to act in his name in all matters where a procurator can legitimately act.

Southwark, 15 June 1346

15. GRANT OF THE OFFICE OF NOTARY by the bishop to Thomas de Finderne, clerk, Coventry and Lichfield diocese, by bull of Clement VI, dated Avignon, 2 January 1346. He will take the oath and receive the pen, ink-pot and chart to invest him in his office [Formula of oath given]. The document was drawn up by John de Beautre, apostolic notary, and sealed by the bishop, attested by John de Beautre, with witnesses: M. Henry de Chaddesden', archdeacon of Stowe, diocese of Lincoln, dean of the court of Canterbury, John de Usk, rector of Burghclere, chancellor of the diocese of Winchester, John de Bosegrove, rector of St Peter the Great, Chichester, and George Vincent.

Southwark, 21 June 1346

16. APPOINTMENT by the bishop of William Jolyf of Leatherhead, clerk, as apparitor, to cite any layman in the archidiaconate of Surrey, or any clerk, even a regular, to appear before the bishop in all cases where a summons is required; to sequestrate the goods of the dead, when a will is declared invalid, or the distribution of the goods entrusted to the bishop, until a settlement is reached.

Southwark, 2 July 1346

17. LICENCE for an oratory granted to John de Burstowe in his house at Horley, to hear mass without prejudice to the mother church. Letter to the vicar of Horley.

Southwark, 25 July 1346

276 18. LICENCE granted to the prior and convent of St Denys, Southampton, for an oratory in honour of St Katherine above the outer gate of the priory and inside the walls, newly constructed, in which to celebrate mass.

Southwark, 13 July 1346

19. MEMORANDUM: the office of notary conferred on Richard de Dorsete, by faculty granted to the bishop by Clement VI. In the presence of John de Beautre and MM. John de Usk of Burghclere, Adam de Wambergh' of Ashbury, diocese of Salisbury, Thomas de Enham and John de Ware.

Southwark, 11 July 1346

20. ABSOLUTION of Richard de Perschore of the suburbs of Winchester from the excommunication imposed at the instance of Walter de Upton' for contumacy.

21. LICENCE granted to Agnes, widow of Roger de Cormailles, of the parish of Kimpton, to hear mass in the oratory of her manor of Shoddesden, within the same parish, except on major feasts. Letter to the rector of Kimpton.

Southwark, 8 July 1346

22. Similar licence to Juliana wife of John Mauduyt, knight, for her oratory in the parish of Grately. Letter to the rector of Grately.

Southwark, 8 July 1346

23. COMMISSION to Benedict, bishop of Cardicensis, to reconcile the graveyard of the church of Portsmouth after bloodshed.

Southwark, 24 July 1346

24. LICENCE granted to Richard de Rechlee, clerk to the prince of Wales, to hear mass in the oratory of the prince at 'Kenyngton', diocese of Winchester.

Southwark, 22 July 1346

25. Similar licence granted to Ralph Consyn of the parish of Crondall for his oratory at Minley within that parish.

Southwark, 28 July 1346

26. MANDATE to order masses, prayers and processions for the king and his army beyond the sea to recover his rights, from Windsor, 3 August.

277

Southwark, 9 August 1346

27. MANDATE to the archdeacon of Winchester to publish and carry out the king's reqest devoutly.

28. Similar mandate to the archdeacon of Surrey.

29. APPOINTMENT of Geoffrey Burgeys to be procurator for the bishop at the court of Rome.

Southwark, 8 August 1346

30. LICENCE granted to John atte Berugh' of the parish of Odiham to hear mass in the oratory of his house in at Stapely in that parish.

Southwark, 12 August 1346

31. Similar licence granted to John Rondulf of Pachelesham of Leatherhead. Letter to the vicar of Leatherhead.

Southwark, 18 August, 1346

278 **32.** LICENCE granted to Elizabeth de Monte Acuto, prioress of Haliwell, to hear mass in the oratory of her manor of Camberwell, when in residence there.

Southwark, 15 September 1346

33. Similar licence to Oliver de Boghun, knight, for his manor of Sherfield [English].

Southwark, 15 September 1346

34. ADMONITION to the abbess and nuns of Nunnaminster. Against scandals which may arise for nuns, proper remedies should be employed. By virtue of obedience to the statutes, there should be excluded from the monastery and not received among the sisters, any beyond the number laid down from of old and any beyond the resources of the house; as, by selling corrodies, or granting them, as they become vacant, or for any other reason than as servants required within the walls, without the special permission of the bishop; no purely secular persons are to stay within the monastery beyond one month. The bishop is to be informed before St Nicholas next of this matter by letter.

Southwark, 20 September 1346

35. Similar document for the abbesses of Romsey and Wherwell.

36. ENQUIRY INTO A PENSION FOR APPROPRIATION of the church of Leatherhead to Leeds priory. John, archbishop of Canterbury has received from pope Clement VI letters directed to the prior and priory of Leeds, order of St Augustine, diocese of Canterbury. King Edward has indicated that in the time of king Edward, his father, because of the siege of the castle of Leeds, the priory which was close to the priory, suffered much loss and the church was in decay through age; they have not been able to complete the reconstruction or maintain their obligations. At the request of queen Isabella, the king's mother, the priory has been granted royal licence to acquire the church of Leatherhead, which is of the king's patronage, for the maintenance of 6 cannons, who will pray daily for the king and queen. The church is assessed at 52 marks in annual value. The pope grants the appropriation, which will take place when the present rector dies or leaves. The vicar's portion will be

279 determined by the archbishop and the vicar will pay the customary dues. The church is in the diocese of Winchester.

Avignon, 14 September 1344

Since the church of Winchester had been accustomed to receive the revenue during the vacancy of the church of Leatherhead, the archbishop, after discussing the matter with the archdeacon of Surrey and with the consent of the prior of Leeds, ordains that the vicar will pay an annual pension of 20s. at Michaelmas at Wolvesey or in the cathedral, in compensation.

Croydon, 21 March 1345

280 37. GRANT OF THE PENSION of 20s. by prior Thomas Perci of the priory of Leeds to the bishop, since the pope has granted them the church of Leatherhead.

Leeds, 23 March 1345

38. RECEIPT for the first payment of the pension of 20s. due for the year 1346.

Southwark, 13 September 1346

39. MANDATE FROM THE ARCHBISHOP FOR THE CONVOCATION OF THE CLERGY, from Ralph, bishop of London, who has received from John, archbishop of Canterbury letters from king Edward requesting all ranks of the clergy to appear at St Paul's, London, Monday after the Trans-
281 lation of St Edward, where he will seek counsel and help for the defence of the kingdom. Lionel, the king's son, guardian of England.

Westminster, 8 September 1346

The archbishop with his suffragans at the meeting of parliament at Westminster, Monday after the Nativity of the BVM (8 September) summons the clergy to the meeting at St Paul's.

Lambeth, 15 September 1346

By authority of this mandate the bishop of London orders the clergy to appear before the archbishop in St Paul's at the date proposed.

London, 17 September 1346

40. EXECUTION OF THE MANDATE. Letter from the bishop in his absence to Adam de Wambergh', commissary-general, to carry out the royal mandate and to forward a list of those cited.

Southwark, 20 September 1346

41. CITATION of the prior and chapter of Winchester to be at St Paul's as required by the mandate from the bishop of London.

Date as above

42. CERTIFICATION to the archbishop that the bishop has cited as required. He could not find the archdeacons of Winchester and Surrey but has ordered the mandate to be carried out. List of names included.

Date as above

282   **43**. COMMISSION to the archdeacon of Surrey, the dean of Guildford and the vicar of Farnham, to discover if there is a benefice vacant or likely to be vacant for the dean of Salisbury to collate or present to Hugh Scovile, poor clerk of Winterborne Whitchurch, diocese of Salisbury, with or without cure of souls—by apostolic provision.
                                        Southwark, 10 June 1346

44. LICENCE for a private oratory granted to Joan de Middleton for her house at Oxenbourn in the parish of East Meon, for a moderate period; at the discretion of the vicar to whom the bishop adresses the licence.
                                        Southwark, 27 October 1346

45. Similar licence to Margaret de Molyns for oratories in her manors of 'Kynteworth', 'Bromlee' and 'Mulle'.
                                        Southwark, 7 November 1346

46. Similar licence to Emma de Braiesfeld for her house in Romsey.
                                        Southwark, 7 November 1346

47. MANDATE to M. Adam de Wambergh' commissary-general in the business concerning fr. Arnald Lym, monk of Hyde, begun by the late bishop, Adam, and now pending before the bishop. Speaking under oath, fr. Arnald replied when questioned that Thomas, now bishop of Ely, while in office as prior of the convent of Preachers in Winchester, handed over to fr. John de Draicote, monk of Hyde, certain apostolic letters by which licence was granted to the said fr. Arnald to return to the said order of Preachers; and that fr. John Blanchwel monk of the same monastery, had received from fr. Arnald a certain public instrument about the renunciation which the same fr. Arnald had made as regards the apostolic letters, by authority of which he was received into the said monastery and order. He believes the letters and the instrument remain in their custody. These documents are necessary for hearing the case. Order to examine John and John, and to seek for information.
                                        Southwark, 17 November 1346

48. LICENCE granted to Roger Gervays for an oratory in his house at Ropley, for his household.
                                        Southwark, 24 November 1346

49. COMMISSION to the perpetual vicar of Camberwell to seek out some bishop for the reconciliation of his church after the shedding of blood.
                                        Southwark, 7 December 1346

283   **50**. COMMISSION entrusted to M. Walter atte Brugg' sequestrator-general for the archdeaconry of Surrey and Robert de Pernycote, rector of Mickleham, diocese of Winchester. Since M. William de Inge, archdeacon of Surrey, by reason of his being often cited to appear and answer charges before the king's justices, which he has repeatedly ignored, to the loss and molestation of the bishop, the bishop orders the sequestration of all mortuaries, *pascalia*, St Swithun's farthings, Peter's pence and other rents and profits belonging in any way to the archdeaconry, excepting those belonging to the church of Farnham and the chapels annexed to the archdeaconry—reserving them in the custody of the bishop.

Southwark, 22 October 1346

51. GRANT OF A FACULTY TO CONSECRATE AN ALTAR in honour of Saints Laurence and Denis in the conventual church of Bermondsey, for Benedict, bishop of Cardicensis; also for portable altars in that church.

Southwark, 31 December 1346

52. MANDATE FROM THE APOSTOLIC SEE to the bishop as protector of the privileges of the Order of Preachers, to the archbishop of Canterbury and the bishop of Exeter, who have delegated the case to the prior to Barnwell and the prior of the conventual order of St Gilbert of Sempringham, near Cambridge, diocese of Ely.

They are to examine the petition of the prior and convent of the order of Preachers of Thetford, diocese of Norwich, complaining that Thomas Carbonel of Ellingham and John, perpetual vicar of Aylsham and Peter, steward of the said vicar of Aylsham, of the same diocese, maliciously and openly imputed fr. John de Fordham, confrater of that same order and convent, with having committed acts of robbery and homicide and other crimes, causing no slight ill-repute and scandal, since his repute among good men has not been defamed. By this imputation he is defamed and the perpetrators are worthy of sentence of major excommunication, according to the constitution of Oxford; hence the convent has sought a remedy from the apostolic see.

Because of excessive business, the bishops have delegated the hearing of the case.

Southwark, 24 July 1346

53. PROBATE of the will of George de Upton, clerk, before John de Usk', vicar-general. The administration of the goods of the deceased in the diocese entrusted of Richard de Hyda, Thomas de Durleye and Philip de Upton, with William de Farlegh' and John de Longeford' as coexecutors.

Southwark, 11 December 1346

54. LICENCE for an oratory granted to Isabella Cormailles for reasons of health at her house called 'Talemache' in the *villula* of Wherwell.

Southwark, 9 February 1347

284 **55.** APPOINTMENT to the office of penitentiary of fr. Richard de Merwell', monk and sacrist of the cathedral church, similar to the earlier appointment, when the bishop was still the 'elect of Winchester' and to fr. Thomas de Berton, fellow-monk (see the beginning of the register).

Southwark, 10 February 1347

56. LICENCE granted for a private oratory to Joan, wife of Guy de Bryan, knight, in her manor of 'Bertegrave' in the parish of Epsom. Letter to the vicar of Epsom.

Southwark, 31 January 1347

57. Similar licence to William de Dale for his house called la Logge in Parkhurst and elsewhere in the Isle of Wight.

Southwark, 15 February 1347

58. NOTIFICATION to the perpetual vicar of Chertsey that the bishop has granted licence to Thomas de Ebesham, priest, to celebrate for one year in the manor of Ham in that parish.

Southwark, 6 March 1347

59. ABSOLUTION of John Cole of Yarmouth, Isle of Wight, from the sentence of excommunication for having laid violent hands on William de Herlaston, rector of Yarmouth.

Esher, 24 March 1347

60. LICENCE to hear mass in his oratories at Wellsworthy, Wade and Budbridge, granted to Henry Romyn and his household.

Southwark, 22 March 1347

61. COMMISSION to M. Adam de Wambergh' commisary-general to find a suitable assistant priest for Robert Jarum, rector of the church of Sherborne St John, now incapacitated by bad health. The bishop awaits the reply.

Southwark, 18 March 1347

62. PROBATE of the will of Robert Talbot, late butler of William, earl of Huntingdon, before the bishop. The administration of his goods within the diocese granted to Henry Talbot, rector of Westmeston, diocese of Chichester, as nominated in the will, for Margery, wife of the late Robert.

Southwark, 11 April 1347

285   **63.** PROBATE of the will of M. John de Bosco, late rector of Brighstone, Isle of Wight, before the bishop. Administration of his goods granted to John de Beautre, rector of the church of Freshwater, Roger de Boys, brother of the said M. John, named as executor in the will. The bishop reserves his rights over the goods through John Talebot coexecutor.

Southwark, 8 April 1347

64. LICENCE for a private oratory granted to John Everard of Durley, parish of Upham, now old and in poor health. Letter to the rector of Upham.

Southwark, 12 April 1347

65. MANDATE to the dean of Winchester, ordering excommunication for those who shall break into the bishop's parks at Marwell and elsewhere, to hunt and carry off game, against the will of the keepers after Michaelmas next, as laid down in the council of Oxford. Offenders should be persuaded to do penance. To be announced at all solemn masses when the people are together in the cathedral and at Twyford,

Waltham, Bishopstoke, the chapel of Owslebury and Durley. The bishop expects a reply before the Sunday of *Jubilate*.

Southwark, 22 March 1347

66. MANDATE CONCERNING AN ABDUCTION from John, archbishop of Canterbury to the bishop concerning the detestable deed perpetrated in the early hours of Good Friday last by a large body of reprobates, who fully armed, entered a manor called Bulmershe, 3 miles from Reading, diocese of Salisbury. Shamelessly, with boats and ladders they carried off the noble lady Margaret, widow of Nicholas de la Beche, knight, dragging her from her bedroom to the hall, carrying her half-naked, with the intention of joining her in matrimony to a certain John de Dalton, knight, of inducing her to consent or with threats of compelling her. Although the lady Margaret declared that she had previously contracted marriage with Gerard del Isle, knight, who was still alive (as we know to be true by evidences and proofs). The perpetrators were deaf to the oath she swore that this was true. They carried her off as she shouted and raised a hue and cry in the countryside, and took her to somewhere remote, where she is still detained against the king's peace. In their violent entry into the manor, they fought those who were trying to prevent the abduction and shamefully killed Michael de Ponynges, uterine brother of Margaret. After the bloodshed, they carried off silver and jewels, as well as the gold rings and precious gems the dead Michael had on his fingers; they removed his belt to take out the gold florins from his purse. The perpetrators of this crime are under sentence of major excommunication by the constitution of the recent provincial council of London, as against the peace of the Church, the king and the realm. The archbishop asks that this crime should not be allowed to go unpunished, lest worse may follow. The sentence of excommunication is to be pronounced in churches and market-places, whenever there is a gathering of the people, as on Sundays and feast-days, until the malefactors seek reconciliation. A certificatory letter is to be returned to the archbishop before the feast of St John Baptist (24 June).

Lambeth, 12 April 1347

286

Order to proclaim the denunciation, with reply before St Alban (22 June).

Southwark, 15 April 1347

67. FINAL HANDING OVER of the church of Leatherhead after its appropriation. According to custom the prior and convent of Leeds were summoned to show to M. Adam de Wanbergh', commissary-general for the archdeaconry of Surrey, by what title they held the church. The priory was declared to be the canonical possessor.

Southwark, 11 February 1347

68. COMMISSION FOR DELIVERY from the gaol of Guildford of all clerks imprisoned in the county of Surrey, entrusted to the dean of Guildford and the rector of St Mary, Guildford.

Southwark, 16 May 1347

287 **69.** LICENCE for an oratory granted to Margery, widow of John de Grymstede, knight, at her manor of Brockenhurst. Letter to the vicar of Boldre.

Southwark, 20 May 1347

70. Similar licence for Nicholas Husee at his house in Froyle. Letter to the rector of Froyle.

Southwark, 23 May 1347

71. LICENCE to choose a suitable chaplain as confessor granted for 2 years to Richard Sweye.

Southwark, 1 June 1347

72. LICENCE granted to John de Alresford' to have mass celebrated in any chapel or oratory within the diocese by a suitable priest.

Southwark, 8 June 1347

73. LICENCE granted to William de Retherwyk' of the parish of Egham to hear mass with his wife in the oratory at his house for one year. Letter to the vicar of Egham.

Southwark, 1 June 1347

74. RECEIPT for 4 marks from John le Dyer of Wyght, perpetual vicar of Highclere, for the term beginning Ladyday 1347, being annual pension from the vicar at the appropriation of the church to the prior and convent of Bisham, diocese of Salisbury.

Southwark, 22 March 1347

75. RECEIPT for a pension of £20 from Robert de Burton' archdeacon of Winchester, for the Easter term.

Southwark, 31 May 1347

76. LICENCE for an oratory at his manor of Segenworth in the parish of Titchfield, granted to William le Waite and his wife in bad weather or in poor health. Letter to the vicar of Titchfield.

Southwark, 16 June 1347

77. MEMORANDUM that fr. Thomas le Couk', prior of Taunton, paid homage to the bishop (formula in French) in the presence of Robert de Hungerford', knight, M. John de Usk chancellor and John de Beautre registrar.

Southwark (no date)

288 **78.** LICENCE granted to Thomas son of Robert Uppehull' of Knoyle, diocese of Salisbury, to study and receive minor orders from any catholic bishop, although he is *nativus noster* of Knoyle and of servile condition.

Southwark, 17 June 1347

79. COMMISSION entrusted to A' de Wambergh' to find a suitable assistant for Robert de Jarum rector of Sherborne, now old and broken down in health, and cannot effectively administer the church and its pastoral work.

Southwark, 4 July 1347

80. MEMORANDUM that fr. Alexander, prior of Winchester cathedral, publicly recognized before the bishop that the tithe of fish from his vivary or pond at Fleet in the parish of Crondall and also the tithe of foals from the mares of the prior, born and reared in that parish, belong to the rector of Crondall. The prior promises in future to pay these tithes of fish and foals to the rector.

Southwark, 28 June 1347

Witnesses: M. John de Usk, chancellor, George de Upton and John de Beautre.

81. LICENCE for an oratory granted to Walter de Okleye, now old and in poor health, to hear mass in his house at Oakley. Letter to the rector of Oakley.

Southwark, 8 July 1347

82. COMMISSION TO EXAMINE THE STATEMENT OF THE EXECUTORS OF A WILL directed to Robert, bishop of Salisbury. Since the task of the administration of the executors of the will of Thomas West, knight, concerns two dioceses, it will be simpler to keep a single statement. Since the greater part of the goods of the deceased are in the diocese of Salisbury, the bishop entrusts the examination of the execution of the will to the bishop of Salisbury, requesting him to carry the matter through.

Southwark, 11 July 1347

83. FACULTY from the bishop to . . . . . . bishop to consecrate three *altaria viatica* in any suitable place within the diocese, when this faculty is presented by Robert de Brighwelle or Thomas de Chibenhurst.

Southwark, 18 June 1347

289 **84.** INSTRUMENT OF AN AGREEMENT drawn up by Peter, apostolic notary, between the prior and convent of Reigate and Roger de Apperdele, concerning a chantry founded by Roger in the church of Reigate and a pension of £4.

1344, 13 October, under Clement VI

Agreement between Roger de Apperdele and John de Pyrie, prior of Holy Cross, Reigate, in the chapter-house there. The prior and convent declared themselves bound to the said Roger by an annual rent of £4, by reason of a chantry in the church of Leatherhead, founded by the said Roger in honour of St Mary the Virgin and for the souls of Roger and his family, to be paid in perpetuity for the maintenance of the chantry. In this the prior and convent expressly submit themselves to the jurisdiction of the Papal Chamber and its auditor.

The prior and chapter have granted and assigned to Roger called Edward, priest, and to his successors as their deputy for celebrating daily in the parish church of Leatherhead at the Lady altar for the souls of Roger de Apperdele and family, receiving a rent of £4 in four quarterly payments. They grant the freedom to levy the £4 from the tenements and tenants in Mickleham, belonging to the manor of Ham, whether free or villeins with all services. The prior grants all this, and if the payment is not forthcoming, they bind all their lands and tenements, also their temporal and spiritual goods to be distrained and coerced. The convent concedes also to Roger and his heirs and to the bishop the right to levy from lands tenements and goods the said £4, or to distrain and drive cattle anywhere in the county of Surrey or beyond, until the said £4 are paid and Roger is satisfied. In case of delayed payment appeal may be made to the Papal Chamber through the auditor for £100.

290   Witnesses: M. Philip de Lond', clerk, and John de Gildeford', *viro litterato*.

In the same year, 25th of the same month of October, in the parish church of St Augustine by Paul's Gate, London, prior John of Reigate showed certain letters and obligations containing the above provisions, signed with the seal of the priory and that of Roger de Apperdele in green wax, in the presence of M. Philip de London', clerk, Thomas de Tymberdon' and others.

Peter de Hakenesse, clerk of the diocese of York, notary apostolic, was present on the date and at the place with the said witnesses and has set it out in the this public form.

85. MANDATE to the dean of Ewell. The bishop has learned with displeasure that W' Douk of Fenny Stratford, chaplain of the chapel of St Mary Magdalen, Kingston, has without any permission asked or given left his benefice and is consuming the revenue of the chapel, which is now without any minister for divine service, causing grave scandal. The bishop, seeking to remedy the situation, orders the dean to try and find the said John in the chapel or the house, to warn him two or three times at a few days' interval between the admonitions, using friends and acquaintances to induce him to return within the time laid down by the canons, and resume residence and attend to the repairs needed for the chapel. The dean will certify the bishop within 20 days.

Southwark, 5 July 1347

86. COMMISSION to M. Walter atte Brugge, sequestrator-general for the county of Surrey. At the time of the death of John, earl of Garenn', he owned much goods in the diocese, which the bishop hears are being removed from the diocese or consumed illicitly. The sequestrator is ordered to sequestrate these goods until the terms of the will are made known and the goods distributed, or used to pay his debts in the deanery of Ewell, or for the poor. To keep them under guard and to report to the bishop before St Laurence (10 August).

Southwark, 19 July 1347

87. PROCURATION on the bishop's departure to visit the tombs of the Apostles Peter and Paul, granted to Elyas Pelegrini, dean of Vigan and to M.M. Robert de Nettleton' and Geoffrey Burgeys, to act in his absence.

London, 1 March 1347

291

88. RECEIPT for 40s., the pension of 20s. per annum from the prior and convent of Reigate for the church of Dorking, for the Ladyday terms of 1347 and 1348.

Southwark, 12 July 1347

89. COMMISSION to M. John de Wolveleye, rector of the church of Arreton [Isle of Wight,] for the compurgation of Walter de Hamme and Matilda widow of Thomas de Hamme, for clearance from the charge of incest, according to the form adjoined.

Southwark, 6 August 1347

The said Walter and Matilda appeared in the parish church of Chertsey, Friday after the Assumption (15 August) and cleared themselves from the charge.

Chertsey, 18 August 1347

90. ACTS of the compurgation held in the manor chapel of Southwark. Walter de Hamme and Matilda, widow of Thomas de Hamme appeared together, willingly, before the bishop and swore to the truth that they had not committed incest, and the bishop demanded that they should clear themselves individually from the accusation.

Date as above

91. COMMISSION addressed to M. Roger de Fulford', professor of civil law, rector of Caerwent, and John de Wolveleye, rector of Arreton, concerning the archdeaconry of Surrey, now vacant by the death of M. William Inge. The emoluments of the archdeaconry now belong to the bishop by custom and by law; it is for him to correct and punish any excesses in the archdeaconry, to deal with wills and their administration. All this he entrusts to the aforesaid.

Southwark,[   ] August 1347

92. COMMISSION to the same to receive the canonical obedience of all rectors, vicars and incumbents of benefices not exempt, whether appropriated or not, to act as required.

Date as above

292

93. PROCURATION granted to the same, since the jurisdiction of the archdeaconry of Surrey rests with the bishop during a vacancy. The said Roger and John are to demand and hold officially all seals and registers of the archdeacon and of the deaneries.

94. PROBATE of the will of Joan late wife of John le Cartere of 'Stubys', Southwark, before the bishop. The administration of the goods granted to the husband, John le Cartere, named as executor in the will.

Southwark, 21 August 1347

95. PROBATE of the will of Thomas Prideux, knight, of the county of Devon, who died at Southwark, 28 August, 1347. Administration granted to Richard Pedegrew and William Trenayn, executors named in the will.

Southwark, 28 August 1347

96. COMMISSION to correct abuses and debts by a visitation, entrusted to M.J' de Wolveleye, rector of Arreton and A' de Wamburgh' rector of Ashbury, on the complaint of the provost and priests of the chapel of St Elizabeth, Winchester. The bishop has heard reports of indebtedness through extravagance, with consequent diminution of divine service and other grave scandal. They are to seek a fitting remedy after an enquiry into the state of the chapel, firmly to correct what needs correction in head and members, so putting an end to what the enquiry has disclosed.

Southwark

97. COMMISSION entrusted to M.J' de W(olveleve). By report the bishop has learned that the priory of Newark is so impoverished and is daily becoming more so; something must be done to prevent its dissolution. He will go the priory and question the prior and the chapter as to the causes and then report to the bishop.

Southwark, 6 August 1347

98. COMMISSION to R' de Fulford' rector of Caerwent and J' de Wolveleye rector of Arreton. The bishop has received the complaint that Matthew rector of the church of Shere has been neglecting the divine sacrifice, dissipating the revenue of the church and continues to live dissolutely. One Walter de Holnhurst irreverently disturbs the divine service and damages the fabric, with other extravagances. Appearing before the bishop they freely consented to an enquiry being held, in spite of its being harvest-time. The afore-named are to go to the church and hold an enquiry, in view of the good of souls in the parish; they are to send a report.

Date as above

293

99. MANDATE TO DENOUNCE AS EXCOMMUNICATE THOSE WHO IMPEDE REC-TORS OR THEIR SERVANTS FROM ENTERING AND LEAVING THEIR LANDS, addressed to the dean of the Isle of Wight, the rector of Gatcombe and the perpetual vicar of Carisbrooke. The bishop has learned that certain supposed Christians have entered the rectory house at Brighstone unauthorized, and carried off goods, disposing of them without the permission of M. John le Yonge, rector, or of those in charge. They have injured the collectors of tithes, preventing them from going in and out of the church and lands to collect the tithes. These malefactors incur the sentence of excommunication as laid down by provincial councils. The clergy of the deanery are to assemble in the church of Brighstone and elsewhere, on Sundays and feastdays, solemnly to pronounce the sentence. If any are discovered to be guilty, the bishop is to be informed by a certificatory letter of their names.

Southwark, 6 August 1347

100. MANDATE TO DENOUNCE THOSE WHO PREVENT THE EXECUTION OF THE PROVISIONS OF A WILL, addressed to the dean of the Isle of Wight. The bishop has received the complaint of the executors of the will of M. John le Boys, late rector of Brighstone, who died after Maundy Thursday last, while the autumn crops of the church were still growing. According to the statutes of the diocesan synods these crops belong to the deceased, once the sum at which the church is assessed for the tenth has been paid. Certain evil men without authority have seized and hidden part of the remainder and scheme to seize more of the goods which the deceased was free to bequeath, and did so in his will, to which the bishop has granted probate. Such malefactors for impeding the execution of a will incur the sentence of excommunication, according to the provincial council of London of J' archbishop of Canterbury. The sentence is to be pronounced as in the preceding entry and the names sent to the bishop.

Date as above

101. MANDATE TO SEQUESTRATE the autumn crops of the church of Brighstone on account of armed resistance, addressed to J' de Ware, sequestrator-general and the dean of the Isle of Wight. The bishop has learned how wicked men are planning to collect the autumn crops of the church of Brighstone, which is of the bishop's collation, and by armed force to deprive the executors of the will of M. John le Boys—fruits due to the bishop as of the first year of his election. The bishop orders all these autumn crops to be sequestrated, to be harvested and put in safe keeping, awaiting the bishop's will. The names of any who violate the sequestration are to be sent to the bishop.

Same date

294

102. PROBATE of the will of Richard Dansey of Wiltshire, who died at Southwark. Since the executors named in the will did not appear, the bishop entrusted the administration of the goods to John, son of the deceased, reserving the right to entrust the administration to the executors should they come, which John accepted.

Marwell, 28 September 1347

103. PROBATE of the will of Henry Whisser, who died at Southwark. The bishop entrusted the administration of his goods in the diocese to Katherine his widow as named in the will, reserving to himself the power to entrust the same to the co-executors, John Blundel and Geoffrey de Lammedon', if they accept, or to nominate others.

Southwark, 1 October 1347

104. COMMISSION OF OFFICIALITY granted to M. Roger de Fulford' rector of Caerwent, doctor of law, to have cognizance of all causes in the city and diocese raised by the parties, to hear and to terminate them, as well as to enquire into and correct offences and all excesses, as official of the diocese.

Marwell, 28 September 1347

105. RECEIPT for 20s. from the prior and convent of Leeds for the emoluments due because of the vacancy of the parish church of Leatherhead, being the sustomary payment arising from the appropriation of the church to the priory, due at Michaelmas at Wolvesey.

Southwark, 28 September 1347

106. EXECUTION OF THE ARCHBISHOP'S MANDATE FOR A PROVINCIAL COUNCIL addressed to M. Adam de Wambergh' rector of Ashbury and John de Wolveleye rector of Arreton. The bishop has received letters from Ralph, bishop of London, that J' archbishop of Canterbury, desiring to remedy excesses which have arisen for the church and clergy since the last provincial council, proposes to call another council of his suffragans. The bishop is ordered to summon the different ecclesiastical persons or their procurators to appear at the church of St Paul, London, the first law-day after the feast of St Jerome [30 September], to treat of reform. The bishops are to invite all to set down in writing what evils and excesses should be considered.

295

Lambeth, 30 July 1347

By this authority the bishop orders that they shall summon to be present at the place and date indicated, there to stay until the council ends, the cathedral prior and the other abbots and priors—each convent or college being represented by one procurator—the clergy by two—except for the mendicants of any order. They will set down in writing the matters recommended for discussion and forward to the bishop.

Stepney, 4 August 1347

The details and list of names to be sent before the feast of St Matthew [September 21].

Southwark, 21 August 1347

107. MANDATE TO THE PRIOR AND CHAPTER OF THE CATHEDRAL summoning them.

No date

108. ACKNOWLEDGEMENT by the bishop that he has received the archbishop's mandate concerning the provincial council, 15 August last, and has acted as requested, sending the lists.

Farnham, 30 September 1347

296 **109.** ADMISSION of John de Bereford' as apparitor for the archdeaconry of Surrey, just as for W' Jolyf above.

Southwark, 16 October 1347

110. DISPENSATION granted to M. Roger Bryan, clerk, that, having resigned the office of registrar of the Winchester consistory, he may freely resume the office of procurator in the same court, which he had been holding without the licence of the official or the commissary. He may hold the same place in the consistory, constitution, custom or oath notwithstanding.

Wolvesey, 25 September 1347

111. MANDATE to J' Ware to go to Bighton and by interviewing the rector, discover if he is incapable of holding his office, as the bishop is informed; then to appoint a suitable assistant. The bishop is to be informed before St Nicholas [6 December].

No date

112. LICENCE for an oratory granted to Joan of Kent, countess of Salisbury, in her manor of Woking, to be used when her health or the weather prevents her going to church.

Southwark, 18 October, 1347

113. LICENCE granted to John de Pembrok', rector of the church of Thruxton, to be for one year at the service of Margaret, countess of Kent.

Southwark, 5 November 1347

114. COMMISSION to absolve an excommunication for assault, entrusted to Walter de Peveseye, rector of Pewsey and William de Mere, rector of Sutton; to absolve Margaret Poyns, nun of Romsey, from her major excommunication for laying violent hands on Nicholas, perpetual vicar of the parish church of Romsey, sacriligeously in that church. If she is penitent, then to impose a salutary penance for the enormity of her offence.

Southwark, 8 November 1347

115. SIMILAR COMMISSION addressed to M. John de Godalmynge, professor of Holy Writ, to absolve Hugh Stovyle, priest, from his sentence of major excommunication for an assault on William Jolyf, clerk; to see whether the gravity of the case is within the bishop's power to absolve.

Southwark, 3 December 1347

116. GRANT of a private oratory to John Wace of the parish of Stratfieldsaye within his house.

Southwark, 31 october 1347

117. COMMISSION to the crier of the official to admit for compurgation Gilbert de Asshele, clerk, and then for his release from prison.

Same date

118. LICENCE granted to M. John de Stok', rector of the church of Abbotsworthy, to be at the service of M.J' de Lech', official of the court of Canterbury.

Southwark, 18 October 1347

297 **119.** LICENCE for an oratory granted to Robert de Hoo and Lucy, his wife, in their house at Meonstoke.

Southwark, 10 November 1347

120. SIMILAR LICENCE to Gilbert de Esteneye, valetudinarian, to hear mass for one year in his house in Portsea. Letter to the vicar of Portsea.

Southwark, 11 November 1347

121. SIMILAR LICENCE to Reginald Forester for his house in Beddington for one year; also to choose his own confessor. Letter to the rector of the parochial chapel of Beddington.

Southwark, 14 November 1347

122. SIMILAR LICENCE to Margaret de Gatewyk', an old frail woman, for her house in Chipstead, for one year.

Southwark, 5 December 1347

123. SIMILAR LICENCE to Margery widow of William de Weston', for their home in West Clandon, for 2 years.

Southwark, 5 December 1347

124. COMMISSION to the official of Winchester for the compurgation of Richard Cokay, clerk, imprisoned. His release to be announced by the crier.

Southwark, 13 December 1347

125. COMMISSION to the prior of Merton to absolve fr. John Paynel, clerk, for assault on the prior's servant, imposing a salutary penance.

Southwark, 14 December 1347

126. LICENCE for an oratory granted to Thomas de Thornecumbe for his house in Compton, near Winchester, for one year.

Southwark, 19 December 1347

127. SIMILAR LICENCE to Laurence de Pageham, knight, for oratories in his houses at Drayton, Bere and Pury; and to M. Roger Bryan, in his house at Merston Pagham, whenever he visits sir Laurence. Licence for one year.

Southwark, 19 Janaury 1348

128. SIMILAR LICENCE to Robert Martyn for his house in 'Barnseye' with his wife and family, without prejudice to the parish church of Romsey, for one year. Letter to the vicar of Romsey.

Southwark, 26 January 1348

129. SIMILAR LICENCE to Philip de Drokenesford for his houses in Bedenham and Droxford, for one year.

Southwark, 29 January 1348

298 **130.** SIMILAR LICENCE to Margery de Sutton' for her house in the parish of St Olave, Southwark, until Easter next. Letter to the rector of St Olave.

Southwark, 4 February 1348

131. SIMILAR LICENCE to Matilda Gatelyn for her house in Middleton, in the parish of Egham, for one year. Letter to the vicar of Egham.

Southwark, 11 February 1348

132. ADMONITION FOR NON-RESIDENCE, addressed to Walter atte Brugg', sequestrator-general for the archdeaconry of Surrey and to the dean of Ewell. On the complaint of John Lovekyn, pàtron of the chapel of St Mary Magdalen at Kingston and of others, the bishop has learned that Walter Douk of Fenny Stratford, chaplain of the said chapel, has been absent in remote parts for some time without licence or reasonable cause. Nor has he appointed anyone to take charge of the chapel, which is not being served, the buildings not cared for. They are to admonish the said Walter to return within a fortnight.

Southwark, 26 February 1348

133. LETTER to the official and clergy of the diocese. John Faber of Woodmasterne, diocese of Winchester, is under sentence of major excommunication for laying violent hands on William lately chaplain of the parochial chapel of Banstead. And since for legitimate reasons he has been unable to go to the Roman curia to seek absolution as the canons direct, the bishop directs the official to announce the absolution publicly.

Southwark, 2 March 1348

134. APPOINTMENT OF A COADJUTOR. Since John de Schaftesbury, canon of the conventual church of Wherwell and prebendary of Goodworth, is blind and cannot fulfil the obligations of his office; lest there be any diminution of divine service, the bishop appoints Philip Payn, priest, at the request of John, to be his coadjutor.

Southwark, 9 March 1348

135. RECEIPT for 4 marks due from the church of Kingsclere, from John de Boxgrove its perpetual vicar, for the term beginning Ladyday, 1348; being due through the church being appropriated to the priory of Bisham, as laid down in the ordination of the vicarage.

Southwark, 6 April 1348

299   **136.** MANDATE CONCERNING AN INDUCTION addressed to the archdeacon of Surrey. The bishop has recently seen documents which clearly show that John de Colonia was not inducted to the church of Lambeth by the archdeacon of Surrey of that date, nor by his authority, but by a special commission from Adam, the bishop's predecessor. Legal experts have begun to question the validity of this induction. On learning of this doubt as to his induction, John has humbly sought that this defect should not be imputed to him; further, he has spent considerable sums from the church revenue on necessary repairs. The bishop clears John of all blame, declares him to have been canonically instituted and orders the archdeacon to induct him. Then he is to report to the bishop.

Southwark, 10 April 1348

137. MANDATE to the deans of Winchester, Alresford and Alton. The bishop has learned that some unknown persons with no reverence for the clerical state laid violent hands on Walter, priest and Edmund de Merlawe, clerk, prior of the hospital of St John of Jerusalem in England, knowing them to be such, at the priory manor of Sotherington, diocese of Winchester, striking them violently with inhumanity, thus incurring the sentence of major excommunication. To be pronounced in the customary manner, with enquiry as to names.

Southwark, 11 April 1348

138. MANDATE to the official of the archdeacon of Surrey and to the dean of Ewell. The bishop has received the complaint that Hubert Husee of Mickleham, on the first Sunday in Lent, after the offertory of the principal mass, stood up during the prayers, shouting aloud that Thomas de Brayles, the parish priest, had revealed secrets of the confessional, that no one should go to him for confession or make offerings, thus disturbing the service. They are to go to the church and make diligent enquiry; then on Palm Sunday to order no one to pay attention to what was said, or to cease from making offerings, since the priest had been carrying out directions. The bishop is to be informed by Maundy Thursday next.

Same date

139. LICENCE for a private oratory granted to Margery de Sutton' with physical infirmities, in her house in the parish of St Olave, Southwark, for the duration of her malady.

Southwark, 12 April 1348

140. LICENCE granted to Margery de Grymstede, who is sick and is transferred from place to place and so cannot easily hear mass, to do so in her house for one year.

Southwark, 14 April 1348

141. LICENCE to John de Brommore of Fordingbridge to hear mass in his house for one year.

Southwark, 8 April 1348

142. MANDATE to the dean of Southwark and to the perpetual vicar of Camberwell. Matilda in the Lane, legitimate wife of Thomas le Clerk of that parish has sought a separation from him, as he threatens her and she has pleaded before the jurisdictional president of the archdeaconry of Surrey. William in the Lane, her brother, gave false witness to secure the separation. Since William and Matilda, before the bishop in the presence of Thomas, openly admitted everything, William and his sister are to appear on three consecutive Sundays when there is the largest congregation, to declare aloud to all that knowingly and wickedly they had spoken falsely; then to seek mercy and the discipline of the rod, seeking absolution. The bishop is to be informed for Pentecost.

Southwark, 25 April 1348.

143. MANDATE TO THE SAME, to warn and induce Thomas le Clerk and Matilda in the Lane with an exhortation on matrimony. As they have freely confessed, they should now live together and keep the marriage bond. The bishop is to be informed of what both the clergy and the couple have done.

Southwark, 25 April 1348

300

301 **144.** ANOTHER MANDATE FOR A MATRIMONIAL CASE, addressed to the vicar of East Meon. Report has informed the bishop that John de Meone, 'cornmangere' and Alice Damie, who are solemnly married in the eyes of the Church, have separated, both living dissolute lives. Since they are both under the vicar's jurisdiction, their way of life could be imputed to his negligence; he must exhort them to amend their ways and to resume married life.

No date

145. MANDATE TO CITE the coadjutor of the rector of Sherborne to give an acount of his administration, addressed to the archdeacon of Winchester. The rector, Robert Jarom has complained that he was granted as assistant because of his age and infirmity Robert de Lanyngton', rector of Nately Scures. Though he was not to take the place of the rector, he took the fruits and revenue of the rectory for his own purposes, not allowing Robert Jarom the clothing and food befitting his station, and not paying the dues of the church. The archdeacon is to look into the matter, to take a statement on oath. Robert de Lanyngton' is to appear in the church of St Magdalen at Kingston on the first law-day after Low Sunday to account for his administration.

Southwark, 16 April 1348

146. COMMISSION to proceed against the chaplain of the chapel of St Mary Magdalen at Kingston, addressed to the official. Walter Douk' of Fenny Stratford perpetual chaplain has without licence or reasonable cause for some time left the chapel without a minister to conduct the services. He has been admonished frequently to return or appoint a man in charge. The official is to proceed against Walter; he must reside or be replaced.

Southwark, 5 May 1348

147. COMMISSION TO THE BISHOP from John, archbishop of Canterbury. He has received the petition of Alianora Giffard', who desires to take vows of chastity and to receive the mantle and ring. The archbishop requests the bishop to carry out the ceremony.

Maidstone, 5 May 1348

302 Authorized by this commission, the bishop received her vows during pontifical mass in the manor chapel of Southwark (formula given, in French: 'formerly the wife of John Gyfferd').

Sunday 18 May 1348

148. COMMISSION to M. Walter atte Brugg' of Wamberg' clerk, to be sequestrator for the archdeaconry of Surrey, with power to sequestrate on half of the revenue of vacant benefices held by secular clerks; to have custody during vacancy of the bishop's share; to collect and have the custody of the goods of those dying intestate within the archdeaconry.

Southwark, 28 May 1348

149. COMMISSION FOR THE CUSTODY OF SEQUESTRATED TITHES, addressed to the official, to the sequestrator-general M. John de Ware and to the dean of Basingstoke. The bishop's predecessor Adam (de Orleton) had granted all the greater tithes of Foxcote in Kingsclere (known as the portion of 'la Heth', lying between Lutlebrugg' and Exenford) of the tenants of the priory of Bisham by appropriation of the church. With the consent of the perpetual vicar, for reasons accepted by both parties, these tithes had been sequestrated and their custody entrusted to William de Brokhurst', who, being busied with outer matters, cannot deal with them. The bishop orders that these greater tithes of Foxcote be sequestrated and guarded until further notice. The commissioners will enquire into the estimated value of the tithes collected by William under the authority of the bishop's predecessor. They are to summon the prior and the vicar to appear at St Margaret, Southwark, should it seem expedient, on the first law-day after the feast of SS. Processus and Martinianus (2 July).

Same date

150. CITATION for the reform of St Thomas Hospital, Southwark, to the brothers and sisters. The bishop has heard of certain irregularities in their church and community, liable to cause scandal. To remedy such, on the next law-day after the Nativity of S. John Baptist, an enquiry will be held before the bishop or his official in the chapter-houe of the hospital; those now absent are to be recalled.

Southwark, 18 June 1348

303

151. COMMISSION to enquire into the discord between the prior and convent of Selborne, addressed to M. John de Wolveley, rector of Arreton. The bishop orders him to go to the priory and make an enquiry before prior and convent in their chapter-house, to correct and impose penalties, then informing the bishop.

Southwark, 26 June 1348

152. LICENCE FOR AN ORATORY granted to Thomas de Thorncombe of Compton near Winchester, for one year.

Esher, 15 June 1348

153. COMMISSION CONCERNING THE DOMINICANS, addressed to M. Griffin ap Rees, archdeacon of Brecon, in the diocese of St. David and to John de Ewe and Thomas de Staunton, canons of the cathedral of Hereford. From the prior and brethren of the dominican convent of Bangor, constituted outside the kingdom of France, the bishop has received the complaint that a certain William du Kenwricus Koua and others of the town and district of Caernarvon in the diocese of Bangor, have assaulted fr. Gervase de Aber, prior and Howell de Penros, priests and many others brothers, clerics and professed of the Order, knowing them to be such, in criminal malice. They have incurred major excommunication according to the constitutions of Oxford. The brethren ask that the bishop seek a remedy, but, being busy with other matters, he entrusts the enquiry to the commissioners.

Southwark, 8 July 1348

154. COMMISSION to enquire into and correct abuses in the priory of Holy Cross, Reigate, addressed to M. John de Usk', chancellor and M. John de Wolveleye, rector of Arreton. Held on the first law-day after the Translation of St Swithum.

Southwark, 15 July 1348

155. LICENCE FOR AN ORATORY, informing the rector of Bedhampton, granted to Thomas Huscarl, knight, and Lucy his wife for their manor in that parish, for one year; they will go the the parish church on Sundays and major feasts.

Southwark, 4 July 1348

156. COMMISSION TO ADMINISTER THE GOODS OF AN INTESTATE, addressed to William de Farlee, canon and prebendary of All Cannings in the conventual church of Nunnaminster. Robert de Preston' of the diocese died directing that William should deal with his goods. The bishop entrusts this to him.

Southwark, 5 July 1348

304 **157.** COMMISSION TO COLLECT SYNODALS, addressed to the archdeacon of Winchester, from rectors, vicars and other holders of ecclesiastical benefices, even exempt, as by custom.

Southwark, 5 July 1348

158. LICENCE FOR AN ORATORY granted to John de Harewell' clerk, for one year, at his manor of Merdon, diocese of Winchester.

Southwark, 26 July 1348

159. GRANT OF PROBATE for the will of Robert Bynde, commissary, as shown before the bishop by John Wygge and John Dyne executors.

Southwark, 2 August 1348

160. LICENCE FOR AN ORATORY granted to Guy Bryan, knight, for his manor at Bertegrave in the parish of Epsom.

Southwark, 8 August 1348

161. SIMILAR GRANT to Roger de Engulfeld' of the parish of Meonstoke, for his manor of Flexland.

Same date

162. COMMISSION directed to fr. Richard de Merwelle, monk of St Swithun's, to be confessor of the nuns of Romsey, as they freely wish, until Easter next.

Highclere, 19 September 1348.

163. RECEIPT FOR THE PENSION due from the priory of Leeds, diocese of Canterbury, for the church of Leatherhead, appropriated to them; 20s. received at the castle of Wolvesey for the year ending Michaelmas.

Southwark, 19 September 1348

164. LICENCE FOR AN ORATORY granted to Robert Dool of the parish of St Nicholas, Guildford, for his house at Loseley, for one year.

Southwark, 10 October 1348

165. GRANT OF A COADJUTOR to Robert, rector of Sherborne St John, addressed to R' de Burton, archdeacon of Winchester. He is old and frail and cannot fully exercise his ministry; he is to retain his due share of the revenue.

Southwark, 10 October 1348

305   **166.** MANDATE FOR PRAYERS TO AVERT THE PESTILENCE, addressed to the prior and chapter of the cathedral. Lamentation at the distress. The clergy are to appeal to the faithful for acts of penance; for the recitation of the seven penitential psalms and the fifteen gradual psalms on Sundays; for processions through the city, reciting the litany.

Southwark, 24 October 1348

167. SIMILAR MANDATE to the archdeacon of Winchester or his official, to appeal to all grades of clergy and religious, that on Sundays and Wednesdays and Fridays they meet in the churches for the same penitential exercises.

Same date

168. SIMILAR MANDATE to the archdeacon of Surrey and his official.

169. PROBATE OF WILL of Roger de Oklee, priest, before the bishop. Administration granted to John de Calverton' priest and William Chamis of Southwark, executors.

Southwark, 21 October 1348

306   **170.** LICENCE FOR AN ORATORY granted to Margaret de Borhunte in her manor of Boarhunt in the parish of Southwick; she will go to the parish church on major feasts.

Southwark, 28 October 1348

171. PROBATE OF THE WILL of Henry Herman, late rector of Stoke next Guildford, before the bishop. Administration granted to M. John de Rokeslee, rector of Chelsfield, diocese of Rochester, and Peter atte Burchette, chaplain in the diocese of Winchester, executors named in the will. They are to render their account at the second consistory after the feast of St Michael.

Southwark, 4 November 1348

172. COMMISSION CONCERNING A WILL addressed to M. J' de Ware sequestrator-general and to John de Ludeseye, clerk. Joan, daughter of the late Margaret de Norton', has petitioned that when Margaret was executrix of the will of her husband James de Norton', Margaret was granted the administration. The goods came into the hands of Margaret, from which 50 marks were due to be paid to Joan. Edmund de Kendale, knight, took the goods of Margaret at the time of her death and disposed of them at his free will. Joan has received nothing as yet. The commissioners are to summon the parties and others, so that the goods of the intestate may be at the disposal of the bishop of the diocese, leaving the 50 marks claimed by Joan.

Southwark, 6 November 1348

173. PROVISION FOR HEARING CONFESSIONS in reserved cases, addressed to the archdeacon of Winchester, on account of the pestilence, to be granted to all rectors, vicars and chaplains, who should encourage recourse to the sacrament of penance on account of unexpectd death.

Southwark, 17 November 1348

307   **174.** SIMILAR PROVISION for the prior and chapter of the cathedral.

175. SIMILAR PROVISION for confessors for the abbot and prior of Hyde and all priors within the diocese.

176. SIMILAR FACULTIES to be granted to the two or three priests chosen by the abbess of Nunnaminster, for reserved cases, lasting until Easter.

177. SIMILAR FACULTIES for all nuns of the diocese.

178. LICENCE FOR AN ORATORY granted to Robert le Dóol of the parish of St Nicholas, Guildford (Double of 164, but dated 21 November).

179. MEMORANDUM THAT THE BISHOP, AT THE ORDER OF THE KING set out from Southwark for Calais, 24 November 1348

180. COMMISSION to the prior of Winchester, M. John de Usk', chancellor, rector of Cheriton, and M. John de Wolveleye, rector of Arreton, to act as vicars-general during the absence of the bishop, in all matters of his jurisdiction.

Southwark, 24 November 1348

308   **181.** COMMISSION from the said vicars-general to the vicar of the parish church of Kingston, with mandate to inquire into the goods of John le Bakeres, who died in that parish intestate; to make a true inventory, sequester the goods and report before the feast of St Andrew Nov. 30. Sealed with the bishop's seal.

Southwark, 25 November 1348

182. INSTITUTION on Henry de Blytheworth' of Nottingham, clerk, as rector of the parish church of Gatton, vacant, at the presentation of the prior and convent of St Pancras, Lewes. Letter to the archdeacon of Surrey for the induction.

Southwark, 29 November 1348

183. INSTITUTION of John Bolt of Southampton, clerk, as rector of the parish church of St Michael, Fleshmonger Street, Winchester, at the presentation of the prior and convent of St Denys, Southampton. Letter to the archdeacon of Winchester for the induction.

Southwark, 1 December 1348

184. LETTERS DIMISSORIAL for fr. William de Boklonde for minor orders, Geoffrey Kyngot, John Ride, William de Walcombe, William de Caresbrok', John de Cosham acolytes for the subdiaconate, Richard Balaam for the diaconate and John de Stone for the priesthood—monks of Quarr.

Southwark, 2 December 1348

185. SIMILAR LETTERS for Henry de Blytheworth' of Nottingham, rector of Gatton, acolyte, for all orders.

Same date

186. MANDATE from M. John de Usk' to the dean of Southwark to summon Symon Stokwelle of Wandsworth to appear in the conventual church of St Mary, Southwark. From the vicarage house and buildings of Wandsworth he has removed beasts without permission of their guardians; also he has laid violent hands on John, the vicar, priest.

Southwark, 2 December 1348

187. PROBATE of the will of Hugh de Mursele, lately rector of Peper Harow, before John de Usk'. Administration granted to Thomas, rector of Wisley, and John, rector of Puttenham, as named in the will.

Southwark, 3 December 1348

188. MANDATE to the archdeacon of Surrey at the petition of Robert, rector of Dunsfold. William Chervere, when commissary of the archdeacon of Surrey, pronounced major excommunication on the said Robert, without warning or reasonable cause, at the instance of the prior and convent of the hospital of St Mary, Bishopsgate, London. The archdeacon is to enquire into the matter within 10 days, to summon the prior to appear at St Mary's, Southwark, to explain why Robert should not be absolved.

Southwark, 4 December 1348

309 **189.** PROBATE of the will of Nicholas de Stokebysshop', lately vicar of Egham, before John de Usk'. Administration granted to William Goudman, chaplain, Thomas de Busham and William Wodelond', executors named in the will, with reservation to admit John Brideport', executor named, should he come to claim his right.

Southwark, 9 December 1348

190. DIMISSORIAL LETTERS granted by M. John de Usk', vicar, to fr. William de Rammesbury, Baldwin de Brynkeleye and Robert de Sancto Mamueo, William de Lond', Robert de Wyndlesore and John de Schapeya, acolytes, canons of Merton, for the subdiaconate.

Southwark, 9 December 1348

191. INSTITUTION of Thomas de Colyngborne, priest, to the church of St Mary above Northgate, Winchester, vacant by the resignation of John Blanchmal, at the presentation of the abbot and convent of Hyde. Letter for the induction to the archdeacon of Winchester.

Southwark, 12 December 1348

192. CESSATION OF THE VICARIATE. The bishop returned from Calais, 12 December 1348

193. APPOINTMENT AS SEQUESTRATOR-GENERAL for the archdeaconry of Surrey of M. Robert de Pernicote, rector of the church of Mickleham— duties set out as to vacant benefices, testaments, sequestration.

Southwark, 16 December 1348

194. LICENCE FOR AN ORATORY granted to Philip de Drokenesford' of the parish of Alverstoke, for one year, at his house at Bedenham in that parish.

Southwark, 18 December 1348

195. SIMILAR LICENCE to Eleanor Baynard of Silchester for her house there. Letter to the rector.

Southwark, 23 December 1348

196. BLESSING of fr. John, as abbot of Netley, cistercian, in the manor chapel of Southwark at pontifical mass. Text of oath given.

Sunday, 21 December 1348

197. FACULTY TO RECONCILE the cemetery of St Swithun, Kingsclere, after bloodshed, by any catholic bishop.

Farnham, 7 January 1349

198. LICENCE for an oratory granted to Nicholas Wodelok' and his wife at their home in Twyford.

Farnham, 11 January 1349

310   **199.** MANDATE to the official to publish the indulgences granted by the pope to all orders of the clergy for confessors in view of the general mortality. Until Easter.

Esher, 19 January 1349

200. SIMILAR MANDATE to the prior and chapter of the cathedral.

201. MANDATE to the cathedral prior, the abbot of Hyde and the official. The bodies of the dead lie in consecrated ground awaiting the resurrection. Nevertheless, the bishop has learned how wicked men have entered the cemetery at Winchester, assaulted fr. Ralph de Staunton when officiating
311   at a funeral, and for their own profit removing the body to a place for animal refuse. And this at a time of great mortality, when cemeteries need to be enlarged. The faithful are to be instructed in this article

of the faith; those who assaulted fr. Ralph are to be denounced as excommunicated. The bishop expects a reply before Sexagesima.

Esher, 22 January 1349

202. LICENCE for an oratory granted to Ela, widow of Elias de Godele, for her house in Funckton in Christchurch Twynham. Valid for 1 year.

Esher, 26 January 1349

203. MEMORANDUM that by order of the bishop the chancellor M. John de Usk' has handed over to prior William of St Thomas' hospital, Southwark, and to Walter de Merlawe a *confrater*, in gold and silver and jewels, previously owned by fr. Robert de Lambeth', *confrater* now deceased, to the value of £15 19s. 4d., with other of his goods to the total sum entered in the Register.

Southwark, 31 December 1348

204. LICENCE for an oratory granted to John atte Berugh' for his house in the parish of Crondall, for one year.

Esher, 27 January 1349

205. NOTIFICATION to the clergy that the bishop has nominated John de Oxtede as apparitor-general.

Esher, 2 February 1349

206. MANDATE to the dean of the Isle of Wight, the rectors of Newchurch, Gatcombe and the chapel of Standen, to warn a priest that he is to keep to the agreement made with a vicar of Arreton, about serving the church and parish after the death of the said vicar. It is decreed that such a convention must be observed for a year. The late vicar R' had made an agreement with Robert de T' priest that he should administer the church for one year from Michaelmas. The service was maintained until the death of the vicar, when Robert went back on the agreement, neglecting the parish. Since the custody of a vicarage during a vacancy belongs to the bishop, he orders that the agreement be upheld under threat of canonical censures.

312

Esher, 2 February 1349

207. COMMISSION addressed to the dean of the Isle of Wight to sequestrate the goods of Roger le Boys, lately the exector of the will of M. John le Boys, late rector of Brighstone. To render account with an inventory before the first Sunday in Lent.

Esher, 29 January 1349

208. LICENCE for an oratory granted to William de Tudenham for his house, called Daperons, in the parish of Bletchingley. For 1 year.

Southwark, 16 March 1349

209. SIMILAR LICENCE to Henry de Strete for his house in Mitcham.

Same date

210. SIMILAR LICENCE to Thomas Grene, rector of Fawley, to celebrate in his house. For 1 year.

Farnham, 13 April 1349

211. PROBATE of the will of Thomas de Babynton', late vicar of Basingstoke, before the bishop at the castle of Farnham. Administration of the goods in the diocese granted to John Piperwhit', Ralph vicar of Monk Sherborne and William Maresch', as named in the will. Inventory to be presented before the Ascension.

Farnham, 13 April 1349

212. RECEIPT FOR THE ANNUAL PENSION of 20 marks from M. Richard Vacham, archdeacon of Surrey, through Thomas atte Putte. Pension due annually at Easter for synodals of the archdeaconry, for Peter's pence, for the farthings of St Swithun.

Winchester, Monday in Easter week, 13 April 1349

213. RECEIPT for the pension of £20 from Robert de Burton', archdeacon of Winchester, for the Easter term.

Southwark, 19 May 1349

214. BLESSING OF THE ABBESS Joan Gervays of Romsey by the bishop at his manor of Esher, elected and solemnly confirmed, according to the Rule of St Benedict.

Esher, Ascension Day, 21 May 1349

313 **215.** BLESSING OF ABBOTS, fr. John for Waverley and fr. Robert for Quarr, cistercians, at the manor chapel of Esher during pontifical mass. Formula given.

Esher, Sunday, 24 May 1349

216. TESTIMONIAL LETTER from Stephen, bishop of St Pons de Thomières, papal chamberlain, that the bishop of Winchester has made his triennial visit to the papal curia in the person of Holyas Peligrini, dean of the church of Le Vigan, diocese of Cahors, his procurator.

Avignon, 2 May 1348

217. EXTENSION OF THE PLENARY INDULGENCE granted to all the clergy and religious of the city and diocese of Winchester by pope Clement VI, from Stephen, archbishop of Arles, papal chamberlain. Extension from Easter until Michaelmas, at the request of M. Reginald de Bugwell', canon of Exeter.

Avignon, 28 April 1349

218. EXECUTION OF THE ABOVE extension of the indulgence. Letter from the bishop to the official, who is to announce this clearly and speedily.

Esher, 25 May 1349

219. MANDATE addressed to the official to order all ecclesiastical persons, even if exempt from the archdeaconry of Winchester, to pay the customary synodals and Peter's pence due from all benefices.

Southwark, 17 June 1394

220. LICENCE FOR AN ORATORY granted to Christina atte Ok' of Woodhay.
Highclere, 22 July 1349

314 **221.** COMMISSION CONCERNING THE MOLESTATION OF A FRIAR, from the bishop as conservator of the privileges of the Friars Minor, with the bishops of London and Worcester, addressed to M. Robert Hereward, archdeacon of Taunton, and Thomas le Yonge, advocate of the court of Canerbury. To enquire into the violence done by David Kelyng', priest of the diocese of Bath and Wells, against the brethren of the convent of Bridgewater, and to proceed according to the privileges of the order.
Hursley, 10 August 1349

222. LICENCE FOR AN ORATORY granted to Peter de Perschute for his house in Mottisfont.
Hursley, 10 August 1349

223. RECONCILIATION OF THE CEMETERY of the church of Hursly by the bishop after bloodshed.
Hursley, 11 August 1349

224. PROBATE of the will of John de Grey, knight, by the bishop. Administration of the goods within the diocese granted to William Banastre, as named in the will.
Southwark, 14 October 1349

225. RECEIPT for the pension of 20s. due annually at Michaelmas from the prior and convent of Leeds, augustinian, for the appropriation of the church of Leatherhead.
Southwark, 1 October 1349

226. APPEAL TO AUGMENT A VICARAGE from Adam Seyncler, perpetual vicar of Selborne, with the chapels of Oakhanger and Blackmoor, appropriated to the prior and convent of Selborne. He pleads that many of the emoluments from various sources have been unjustly usurped by the priory and begs for a remedy. The official is ordered to make an enquiry.
Southwark, 21 November 1349

227. COMMISSION to the official concerning the witholding of tithes and dues. Although the rectors of the church of St Peter, Colebrook Street, Winchester, had been accustomed to use the nave of the conventual church of the nuns of Nunnaminster, before the altar of St Anne, and to minister to the parishioners of St Peter for the services and sacraments on Sundays and feastdays and the baptism of infants from time immemorial; yet John Fode and Thomas le Palude, now deceased, parishioners of St Peter's, wronged the rector of the said church by witholding tithes
315 and other dues, doing grevious harm to the rector, contrary to ancient custom, obliging him to perform the said ministry in the church of

St Peter and to erect a font there. The official will hold an enquiry with statements on oath from reliable people.

Southwark, 14 November 1349

228. COMMISSION addressed to M. John de Wolveleye, canon of Salisbury, and chancellor to the bishop, to enquire into and correct abuses in the priory of St Mary, Merton, which if not speedily corrected will cause grave scandal. He is to go there on Tuesday and hold an enquiry in the chapter-house, punishing the offenders.

Southwark, 18 January 1350

229. COMMISSION of Richard de Hayhuge, rector of the church of Colmer, to be penitentiary, to hear confessions in cases (listed) reserved to the bishop.

Southwark, 5 February 1350

230. SIMILAR COMMISSION to the abbot of Chertsey, William de Langeleye, rector of Ringwood, Hugh de Patryngton', rector of Woodhay, and Hugh de Brekelesworth, rector of St Olave's, Southwark.

Southwark, 22 February 1350

231. COMMISSION to John, prior of the cathedral church of Winchester, to be present in the cathedral as penitentiary on Ash Wednesday, as also on Maundy Thursday.

Southwark, 5 February 1350

232. COMMISSION from the bishop as conservator of the privileges of the Friars Preachers, to M. John de Oo, canon of Hereford, and J' Thurstayn, canon of London, to deal with the case between the prior and brethren of Chelmsford, diocese of London, and M. John de Hyntona, rector of the church of Rayleigh, diocese of London, on the subject of injury done to the dominicans concerning their faculties to **316** hear confessions.

Southwark, 2 March 1350

233. GENERAL ADMONITION addressed to the official against non-residence. Through absence the ministry is neglected and the church buildings fall into disrepair. He will enquire into such absences and admonish the offenders. Report to be sent before the feast of St John Baptist (June 24).

Southwark, 9 April 1350

234. RECEIPT for the pension due from M. Richard Vaghan, archdeacon of Surrey, paid by William Chevere, for 20 marks, his annual pension due at Easter for synodals and emoluments such as Peter's Pence and St Swithun's farthings. Witnesses John Payn, Walter de Meone, William de Mertone and John de Beautre.

Southwark, 13 April 1350

235. SIMILAR RECEIPT from Robert de Burton', archdeacon of Winchester for £20 for the same term.

Southwark, 7 May 1350

236. ADMONITION concerning non-residence addressed to J' de Ware, sequestrator-general and the dean of Basingstoke. William Elyot, rector of Farleigh Wallop, near Basingstoke, neglects the cure of souls and is absent without permission in unknown parts, spending the revenue of the church. They are to admonish him, to get his friends to make him return within a month to resume his ministry and repair the buildings. They are to ensure that the divine service is maintained by some suitable
317   chaplain, supported from the revenue of the church. To report before the Translation of St Thomas the Martyr (7 July).

Southwark, 10 June 1350

237. APPEAL to the abbot and convent of St Vigor of Cerisy, diocese of Bayeux. Their dependent priory of Monk Sherborne, at its foundation well endowed with lands and buildings, through the negligence of superiors and of farmers or guardians during the wars with France, has reached such desolation and spiritual decline, with sterility of its lands, that the place is now destitute. To remedy the situation, with the consent of John de Sancto Philiberto, knight, the bishop proposes to reduce the brethren to eight persons with the prior; and to transfer four brothers,
318   William Taillepie, John de Porta, Ralph le Rouz and Giles Engeranni to Cerisy for the time being. In view of the restoration of the priory the bishop has felt obliged to take these necessary measures.

Southwark, 8 June 1350

238. MANDATE to the prior of Monk Sherborne to order four of his monks to return to Cerisy, because of the state of the priory, as above. Four are to be sent back to the mother-house, leaving three monks John Bense, John de Sancto Melano and Ralph Mauricius with the prior. The others are to leave by the bishop's authority, not to return for the duration of the war.

Southwark, 8 June 1350

239. MANDATE, as from the archbishop of Canterbury, addressed to the two archdeacons, to compel parish priests to maintain the cure of souls. The clergy surviving the pestilence are not sufficient to permit any negligence. They are not to seek or demand excessive fees. They are not to retain chaplains unnecessarily, who are to be suitably paid. Report to be sent before the feast of the Assumption (August 15).

Southwark, 10 July 1350

240. RECEIPT for the annual pension of 20s. from the prior of Leeds for the church of Leatherhead.

Southwark, 2 October 1350

319   **241.** LICENCE FOR AN ORATORY granted to Gilbert de Ledrede for his house of Gosestrode, in the parish of Wotton.

Southwark, 24 March 1351

242. SIMILAR LICENCE for William de Retherwyk' at his house in the parish of Egham, for one year.

Southwark, 24 March 1350

243. COMMISSION to be penitentiary for the deanery of Ford and the New Forest, to fr. John de Hayles, subprior of Beaulieu abbey, in the bishop's pleasure; to deal with reserved cases.

Southwark, 29 May 1351

244. SIMILAR COMMISSION for M. John Chaumpaign' of Dunham, rector of Worting, for the deanery of Basingstoke; in the bishop's pleasure.

Southwark, 2 June 1351

245. COMPLAINT ABOUT REPAIRS TO THE CHANCEL of the chapel of St Peter, Hayling. The parishioners declare that the roof repairs were never legally their responsibility, as the official claims. In times past this was the burden of the prior and the vicar, as can be seen from the records of John de Pontissara, alternately. Because of the difficulties of the times, the parishioners could not meet these repairs even if this were their legal responsibility. The bishop orders that, without creating any precedent for the future, the repairs should be paid for by those who have been hitherto responsible, but for this once sharing the expense.

Southwark, 15 June 1351

246. RECEIPT from Robert de Burton', archdeacon of Winchester of £20 for the term ending Easter 1351.

Southwark, 18 June 1351

247. COMMISSION for the administration of the goods of Hubert Husee, deceased, intestate, addressed to the sequestrator-general of Surrey. The widow, Margaret, has requested the bishop to grant her the adminis-tration. The bishop asks the sequestrator to expedite the matter and to report to him before Michaelmas.

Esher, 21 August 1351

248. FACULTY TO RECONCILE the church of St Michael, Southampton, after the shedding of blood, granted to Peter de Malmeshull', rector of that church, who may request this from any bishop of the Canterbury province, or the archbishop of Nazareth.

Southwark, 27 November 1351

320 **249.** MANDATE against burial at the 'new place' of the Austin Friars at Winchester, addressed to all religious superiors. The friars have recently acquired new land and buildings in the *suburbio* of the city, within its walls, a tenement or dwelling called 'Hoyvile', not without great presump-tion on their part. Many of the faithful who follow their offices and value their prayers have chosen to be buried there. The friars do not hesitate to say mass in an unconsecrated building, which is illicit and causes damage and scandal. The clergy are to forbid burial at this place under pain of excommunication. This is to be proclaimed in the vulgar tongue at masses on Sundays and feast-days. Report to be sent before Christmas.

Southwark, 23 November 1351

250. LICENCE FOR ABSENCE granted to William Peyto, rector of the church of Buckland, for one year.

Southwark, 5 July 1352

251. GRANT OF A COADJUTOR for Henry de Forde, rector of the church of Freshwater, now broken down in health. The bishop deputed as coadjutors John de Beautre, rector of Burghclere and William de Bradeweye, priest.

Esher, 28 December 1351

321 **252.** MANDATE TO PROHIBIT FRIARS FROM HEARING THE CONFESSIONS OF NUNS, addressed to Thomas de Enham', rector of Froyle. The endowments of nuns have suffered greatly with the times, yet mendicant friars frequent nunneries excessively and receive help from the nuns more than is expedient. Order to prohibit religious, especially friars, from hearing the confessions of nuns. Instead two or three priests are to be nominated by the nuns' superiors, then to be confirmed by the bishop's authority.

Southwark, 23 November 1351

253. FACULTY TO RECONCILE A CEMETERY granted for St Margaret, Southwark, to fr. Richard, archbishop of Nazareth.

Southwark, 20 January 1352

254. TESTIMONIAL LETTER from Stephen, archbishop of Toulouse, papal chamberlain, that the bishop of Winchester has made his visit to the Holy See in the person of Reginald de Bugwell', his procurator.

Avignon, 21 April 1351

255. LICENCE FOR AN ORATORY granted to James de Boreford', knight, for his house at 'Stokwell' in the parish of Lambeth, for one year only.

Southwark, 8 February 1352

256. COMMISSION TO MAKE A VISITATION of the priory of St Mary, Southwark, addressed to M. R' de Fulford' and J' de Wolveleye, after the bishop has heard that certain reforms are needed to avoid scandal.

Southwark, 23 August 1349

322 **257.** RECEPTION OF THE MANDATE OF THE ARCHBISHOP, forwarded by Ralph, bishop of London. To restrain chaplains who are excessive in their demands of salary. Their avarice is insatiable when ministering or serving oratories; they refuse to be content with the salary laid down by the archbishop. The bishops are to act strenuously, if necessary suspending; they should act with a common policy, informing the archbishop before St John Baptist.

Mayfield, 6 March 1352
Southminster, 2 April 1352

The bishop will carry out the archbishop's directions.

Southwark, 18 June 1352

258. MANDATE CONCERNING IMPRISONED CLERKS from the archbishop. Recently in parliament, complaints were raised that judges were inclined to outstrip their powers with clerical offenders, not fearing the death penalty. To which it was replied that under pretext of clerical privilege, the clergy were audacious in committing crimes. They should be handed over to representatives of the Church, to be more favourably treated, according to the law of the kingdom. They need not punishment, but consolation to help them back to their former life. It was decided in parliament that the bishops would so arrange for their custody that they will not return and become a scandal. Their food should be: Wednesday, Friday, Saturday, bread and water once a day; other days bread and small beer; Sundays, bread, beer and vegeables. Before their purgation, there should be an enquiry. Report back before St John Baptist.

323

Lambeth, 1 March 1352

The bishop will observe all this.

Southwark, 18 June 1352

259. LICENCE to be at the service of Mary, countess of Pembroke, granted to Everard de Pratellis, rector of St George, Southwark.

Southwark, 30 June 1352

260. RECEIPT for the pension of 20s. paid by the prior and convent of Leeds, for the appropriation of the church of Leatherhead, for the Michaelmas term.

Southwark, 1 October 1352

261. RECEIPT for the annual pension of 20 marks from John de Edyndon', archdeacon of Surrey, through [Robert de] Pernycote, clerk.

Farnham, 11 April 1352

262. LICENCE FOR AN ORATORY granted to John Amiger, citizen of Southampton, in the parish of St Michael, for one year only.

Farnham, 21 October 1351

324 **263.** MANDATE FROM THE ARCHBISHOP concerning the liberties conceded to the Church by the King, forwarded by Ralph, bishop of London. (The articles in French). The King recitès the petitions presented at the parliament at Westminster, St Hilary (Jan.13) 1351 by the archbishop concerning certain grievances. All earlier privileges are to be maintained and the king will abide by the ruling of his parliament in the 14th year (1340), especially as regards presentations to benefices. As for the trial

325 of clerks before secular judges, criminal clerks are to be handed over on demand to the bishops; the bishops promise to punish these offenders; for contempt the fine shall always be reasonable. Benefices still void after six months devolve to the ordinary through lapse of time—this is not

326 the concern of secular judges.

The king is burdened with business; other points are left in suspense. If in the meantime any clerk is found guilty of counterfeiting coin, he will not be executed, but imprisoned, and not delivered to the bishop except by special order.

Westminster, 20 February 1352

Bishops must certify that this has been published by Michaelmas.

Mayfield, 12 July 1352
Stepney, 31 July 1352

264. MANDATE TO THE PRIOR OF ST SWITHUN'S to declare the state of his monastery. The bishop has heard that the temporalities of the cathedral priory have been not a little diminished both by the deaths of tenants, causing a loss in rents and services, as also by accumulated debts. Desiring a return to the former prosperity, the bishop is sending some of his own staff to enquire into the state of the priory and the conduct of the obedientiaries, as he himself is busy with national affairs. The bishop is concerned at the decline of divine worship, at the maintenance of the estates, of hospitality. The officers will arrive 21 January, for both a common and an individual visitation, and will draw up a full statement.

327   Esher, 31 December 1352

265. COMMISSION OF ENQUIRY into the state of St Swithun's, its goods and delapidated buildings, addressed to J' de Wolvel', W' de Farlee, canon of Salisbury and M. T' de Enham, rector of Froyle. To enquire into the general decline in observance, due to penury of resources, as also into the repairs of buildings. They are to look into all the offices of the priory, and see how much of the indebtedness has been paid off in the present year. To examine all the obedientiaries.

Same date

266. SIMILAR COMMISSION to enquire into the state of Christchurch priory, addresed to R' de Fulford' and J' de Wolvel', chancellor, on the report that the resources of the priory are so diminished that the situation will rapidly be a public scandal. They are to enquire into the state of the priory, its discipline and its income, its indebtedness—to enquire how this has come about and to send a statement.

Southwark, 14 January 1353

267. ANOTHER COMMISSION INTO THE CONSISTORY, addressed to J' de Wolvel' and T' de Enham. Complaints are made against the consistory at Winchester. They are to enquire into the conduct of the president, as also of the registrar, advocates, examiners, procurators and other ministers—what business they effect, what justice they meet out, what are the possibilities of corruption. To report with a statement.

328

Southwark, 30 December 1352

268. COMMISSION to the abbot of Chertsey to be the penitentiary for the archdeaconry of Surrey: to be at the door of the parish church of

Chertsey on Ash Wednesday, even dealing with reserved cases. He will receive back penitents the day before Maunday Thursday.

Southwark, 4 February 1353

269. MANDATE CONCERNING SANCTUARY addressed to the prior of the cathedral and to the official. Although anyone extracting a person, be he guilty of bloodshed, who has taken sanctuary in a church, cemetery or cloister, incurs major excommunication, yet the bishop has heard that certain perverse men have violently taken away Robert de Totteford from his refuge in the church of St Andrew, Winchester. The excommunication is to be pronounced in the cathedral and the city churches within the next six days; Robert is to be restored to the liberty of the Church. The culprits are to appear at the conventual church of St Mary, Southwark.

Southwark, 8 February 1353

329

270. DISPENSATION FROM THE LENTEN FAST on the vigil of Lady Day addressed to the archdeacon of Winchester, for all parishioners.

Southwark, 27 February 1353

271. SIMILAR DISPENSATION addressed to the archdeacon of Surrey.

272. MEMORANDUM that M. Roger Bryan, late registrar of the consistory was relieved of his office at Southwark, 20 May 1353, and M. John de Stok' was substituted, taking the oath.

273. RECEIPT for the annual pension of 20 marks from the archdeacon of Surrey, through M. Thomas de Enham, for the Easter term.

Southwark, 20 May 1353

374. COMMISSION TO ENQUIRE INTO AN INTRUSION INTO A BENEFICE, addressed to J' de Ware, sequestrator. The bishop has learned that John Camyn, chaplain, dispensed from dubious birth, obtaining a certain vicarage, abandoned it and secured the office of perpetual chaplain in the chapel of St Elizabeth, suppressing his defect without canonical dispensation. He simply resigned the one and intruded himself into the other. He is to hold an enquiry and remove John if required.

Southwark, 26 July 1353

275. LICENCE FOR CONSECRATION AS BISHOP granted to fr. Thomas, monk of Merevale, elect of Magnesia. To be received from any bishop in communion with the Holy See, with two or three assistant bishops at the conventual church at Southwark.

Southwark, 26 July 1353

276. SIMILAR LICENCE granted for Thomas Waleys, o.p., elect of Lycostromium, for consecration in the same church or elsewhere in the diocese.

[Bishops] Waltham, 16 August 1353

277. APPOINTMENT of Bartholomew Sperner, chaplain, to be coadjutor to Thomas Crie, vicar of Farnham, now broken down in health. To have charge of the vicarage of St Thomas, sharing its income in the customary manner.

[Bishops] Waltham, 28 August 1353

278. LICENCE for an oratory granted to Eva de Sancto Johanne for her manor at Empshot, valid for one year.

[Bishops] Waltham, 22 August 1353

330

279. DECREE OF NO IMPEDIMENT OF IRREGULARITY granted to John de Fulford, priest, by letters from Giles, cardinal priest of St Clement. John had gone to visit a friend and then bade him farewell, when an ill-disposed person came upon him with insulting words, to which John made no reply. On his way home the man rushed up to him saying *"Defende te"* and struck him with a big stick. John shouted: "Do not kill me" and received a second blow. Seeing that he could not flee or avoid death, John struck the man with his sword. Though at first the assailant recovered, he eventually died. In the face of gossip against himself, John sought a remedy from the Holy See, freeing his conscience.

Avignon, 24 May 1353

The bishop declares him free from any irregularity, he was not culpable.

Southwark, 2 October 1353

280. DISPENSATION by letter from Giles, cardinal priest, for Richard Bernard, priest, addressed to the bishop. Richard Bernard, the bearer, has shown his petition. When a simple clerk, he was in a war in which there was much homicide, in which he and his companions could not avoid taking part in self-defence. Ignorant of the law, he later advanced to all the orders, taking part in the ministry and holding a benefice, which he freely resigned. He requested the Holy See to allow him, as in minor orders, to hold a benefice, without cure of souls. He was granted his dispensation.

Avignon, 6 July 1353
Southwark, 5 October 1353

281. LICENCE FOR AN ORATORY granted to Walter de Skidernor for his manor at Wells, valid for one year.

Southwark, 17 October 1353

282. RECEIPT of the annual pension from the prior and convent of Leeds for the church of Leatherhead.

Southwark, 8 October 1353

283. LICENCE FOR AN ORATORY granted to Walter Helyon for his house in the parish of Allington, valid for one year.

Southwark, 4 November 1353

331 **284.** SIMILAR LICENCE granted to Henry de la Pevyle, knight, for his house in Codeford, in the parish of Northgate, valid for one year.

Southwark, 11 October 1353

285. ACQUITTANCE FOR THE ADMINISTRATION OF A WILL. Approving the account for the administration of the goods of John Gabriel, late citizen of Winchester, by Robert de Certeseye and W' Forst of Southampton, the executors. Any other goods still to come to be distributed according to the will.

Esher, 18 January 1354

286. RECEIPT for the pension of 20 marks from the archdeacon of Surrey, through John de Rennelour, clerk, for the Easter term.

Southwark, 30 April 1354

287. MANDATE from Simon, archbishop of Canterbury. John, earl of Kent, died leaving property in various dioceses of the province. The administration of his will belongs by right and custom to the archbishop and to no inferior. Certain persons are handling his funds, e.g. to pay debts. The bishop is to sequestrate and keep safe any of his goods awaiting instructions, sending a statement before Ladyday.

Otford, 31 January 1354

The bishop informed his two archdeacons to deal with the matter and report.

Southwark, 21 March 1354

288. ABSOLUTION from major excommunication granted to Jordan de Newenham; it had been imposed by Roger de Lysewy and John Seles with episcopal authority.

Southwark, 7 May 1353

332 **289.** CERTIFICATORY LETTER from Stephen, archbishop of Toulouse, papal chamberlain, declaring the bishop to have made his visitation to the Holy See in the person of M. Philip de Codeford', doctor at law.

Avignon, 17 April 1354

290. COMMISSION TO THE BISHOP AS CONSERVATOR OF THE FRIARS MINOR (with the bishops of London and Worcester) and to the officials of York and Durham. The complaint has reached the Holy See from from the friars at Newcastle that on Friday in the first week of Lent, some armed men noisily entered and attacked a member of the order, with swords drawn, seeking to carry him off. The archbishop of Toulouse, being much occupied with other business, requests the addressees to deal with this sacrilegeous act.

Farnham, 19 April 1354

291. MANDATE to the official. Formerly during a vacancy at Winchester Walter, archbishop of Canterbury, ordered the rectors of the church of Fordingbridge to say mass in the chapel of Bighton three times a week,

Sunday, Monday and Friday. This was later reduced to once a week in the absence of the lord of Bighton. The present rector, Edmund Morteyn, has also been dilatory in the matter. The official is to order the celebration to be resumed.

[no date]

292. FACULTY granted to the abbess of Romsey to have two confessors chosen by the nuns, with the faculties renewed until Michaelmas next for reserved cases.

Southwark, 6 March 1354

293. SIMILAR FACULTY granted to William de Fyfhide, valid for two years.

Same date

333 **294.** FACULTY TO RECONCILE A CEMETERY granted by the bishop to Caesarius, bishop of St Mary *de Rosis* for the cemeteries of Guildford, Merrow and St Martha, polluted by bloodshed.

Southwark, 26 September 1354

295. LICENCE for an oratory granted to William de Tudenham for his house called Daperons in the parish of Bletchingley, valid for one year.

Hambledon, 2 September 1354

296. COMMISSION OF OFFICIALTY addressed to John de Wolveleye, rector of Alverstoke, to hold a consistory, to hear causes etc. and to reach settlements; to annul or to arrange for the administration of testaments; to deal with delinquencies.

Southwark, 27 September 1354

297. LICENCE for an oratory granted to Richard Trenchard for his house at Hordle in the parish of Milford, valid for one year.

Southwark, 19 October 1354

298. MANDATE addressed to the official of the archdeacon of Surrey to order Matthew rector of the church of Shere to find a chaplain at his own expense to minister at the Lady altar, which had been endowed at its foundation with lands and a wood. Matthew has admitted his negligence.

Southwark (no date)

299. RECEIPT for the pension of 20s. from the priory of Leeds for the church of Leatherhead, for the Michaelmas term.

Southwark, 24 October 1354

300. LICENCE for an oratory granted to Walter Heywode for his house at [Kings] Somborne, valid for one year.

Southwark, 7 November 1354

301. LICENCE granted to John, archbishop of York, to hold a tribunal at St Mary, Southwark, or elsewhere at his choice, to hear the case of the prior and convent of Ellerton, diocese of York, order of Sempringham, concerning the church of Acton, same diocese, appropriated to the priory.

Southwark, 15 October 1354

334 **302.** ANNUAL PENSION agreed to be paid to the bishop by the abbess and convent of Romsey for the appropriation of the prebend called the portion of St Laurence, in the church of Romsey, to meet the expenses of the abbey. The nuns agree to a pension of 6s. 8d. at Ladyday to the treasury of Wolvesey, with the right to sequestrate in case of non-payment.

Romsey, the chapter-house, 10 July 1351

303. ANNUAL PENSION agreed to be paid by Margaret, abbess of Nunnaminster for the appropriation of the church of Froyle. As indemnity they will pay to the treasury at Wolvesey 6s. 8d. at Ladyday.

Nunnaminster, chapter-house, 6 February 1354

304. LICENCE for an oratory granted to William Croyser by letters of the king's marshal, for the rectory-house of the church of Albury, valid for one year.

Esher, 28 March 1355

305. SIMILAR LICENCE granted to Philip le Wayte for his house at Denmead.

[Bishops] Waltham, 1 January 1355

306. LICENCE to choose a confessor even for reserved cases granted to Richard Sweye of Southampton, valid for one year.

Farnham, 9 January 1355

335 **307.** INDENTURE granting to Luke de Manyfeld, for services rendered, 1 messuage, 1 carrucate of land and 1 acre of meadow in Freefolk, which had been held by James de Bourghcote, land which the bishop had recovered from James in court as of the right of the church of Winchester. To have and to hold by Luke and his heirs, rendering 10s. annually at the bishop's court at Overton in four payments. At his death the customary heriot will be paid; if he dies without heir, the property will revert to the bishop.

Witnesses: William de Overton', John Fauconer , Hugh atte Hok', John de Bradweye, William Sparwe *et al.*

Southwark, Vigil of SS.Simon and Jude, [27 October] 1354

308. INDENTURE granting to Stephen Carre 3 messuages, 5 shops, 2 stables in the market-place and 1 toft in Taunton, Somerset, with 18 acres of land at Holway, lately held by Richard Polruel senior, and at his death reverted to the bishop. To have and to hold by Stephen and his heirs, rendering annually 17s. 10d. in four payments, paying suit at the borough-court of Taunton, as Richard did. If Stephen has no heir, all will revert to the bishop.

Witnesses: Matthew de Clyvedon', John de Roches, constable of Taunton, Stephen Lanndi (?), John Houndesmor, Henry de Badyngton, John Roges *et al*.

Taunton, Tuesday after St Bartholmew, [24 August] 1354

309. LICENCE TO LEASE AT FARM granted to Robert, prior and the convent of Reigate, the fruits and income of the chapel of Dorking, appropriated to the priory, as they claim it will be more profitable if leased to Walter, perpetual vicar of Dorking. Valid for 4 years.

Southwark, 27 April 1355

310. RECEIPT from the archdeacon of Surrey through M.William Chiure, his official, for the annual pension of 20 marks, for the Easter term.

Southwark, 20 May 1355

336 **311.** MANDATE FOR PRAYERS on behalf of the king and his army, addressed to the archdeacon of Winchester, by letters received from the king. After the concord signed at Calais, peace is still in danger.

Westminster, 1 June 1356

All ecclesiastical superiors to order prayers at mass, processions and sermons for the safety of the country.

312. SIMILAR MANDATE addressed to the cathedral prior.

313. LICENCE granted to John Payn, precentor of the church of St Mary, Southampton, because of his illness, to choose any confessor.

Southwark, 3 May 1355

Pages 337–342 carefully cut out

343 **314.** [ANNOUNCEMENT BY THE KING] that scholars of the diocese may return fearless and secure to the said university under royal protection; the king guarantees them quiet and indemnity.

Westminster, 20 May 1355

315. INHIBITION against the prior of the hospital of St Thomas the Martyr, Southwark, admitting recruits for profession, since the penury of the resources of the hospital hardly suffice for the present members.

Farnham, 23 August 1356

316. RECEIPT for the pension of 20s. due from the prior of Leeds for the church of Leatherhead, for the Michaelmas term.

Southwark, 5 October 1355

317. SEQUESTRATION BECAUSE OF ARMED STRIFE addressed to the rector of Albury. John de Sancto Neoto rector of Shere and Roger de Kerselawe rector of Ewhurst are in dispute over the tithes of wheat and hay, arising from the demesne lands of Gomshall, called Eastcourt, Westcourt, Edgarscroft and la Hole with a water-mill in Eastcourt. Such is the dissension that they are prepared to fight with weapons. To prevent such danger and scandal the bishop orders these tithes to be sequestered and safeguarded by the rector of Albury, awaiting further instructions.

Southwark, 26 July 1356

318. LICENCE for an oratory granted to the prior of Hayling, to celebrate mass in the rectory-house of Warblington, valid for one year.

Southwark, 13 October 1356

319. EXECUTION OF ROYAL LETTERS entrusted to the archdeacon of Winchester, ordering thanksgiving services for the victory of the prince of Wales over the French army near Poitiers, 19 September, when king **344** John de Valois was taken prisoner with many of the nobility.

Westminster, 10 October 1356

Orders to the clergy to arrange these celebrations.

320. MANDATE to the cathedral prior to carry out the king's request, with services on Sundays and Fridays.

321. RECEIPT of the annual pension of 20s. from Leeds priory for the church of Leatherhead.

Southwark, 2 October 1356

322. LICENCE for an oratory granted to John Adryan of Brockham for his house in the parish of Betchworth, except for greater feasts.

Southwark, 17 December 1356

323. RECEIPT for the pension of 20 marks from the archdeacon of Surrey for the Easter term, by the hand of M. John de Totteford.

Southwark, 2 June 1356

345 **324.** MANDATE to the prior and chapter of the cathedral to consider the request of queen Philippa that the Dominican sisters of Dartford, diocese of Rochester, founded by the king and queen, should appropriate the church of Witley, diocese of Winchester. M. T'de Enham will represent the bishop.

325. COMMISSION OF ENQUIRY into the decline of the priory of Selborne, which through negligence is urgently in need of correction. The chancellor is to conduct the enquiry in the chapter-house and administer correction.

326. COMMISSION addressed to the abbot of Chertsey to act as penitentiary from Ash Wednesday, acting in his own monastery for any penitents of the archdeaconry of Surrey.

327. COMMISSION to act as penitentiary addressed to John Bernard, rector of St Olave, Southwark, for the same archdeaconry, with certain reservations.

Last day of February, year as above

328. RECEIPT FOR PROCURATIONS by Robert, rector of St Gregory, London, from Simon de Sudbury and fr. Thomas de Ryngstede, collectors for the bishop of Elne and the abbot of Cluny, on a peace mission to England from the Holy See, being procurations authorized by the Simon, archbishop of Canterbury, and levied on the city and diocese of Winchester, together with certificatory letters, by the hand of John Beautre: three procurations levied on benefices:
procurations of the bishop and abbot £5 15s. 9¾d (on the pound)
    of Simon 62s. 1d. (on the 40s.)
    of fr. Thomas 30s 5¾d. (on the 60s.).
Sealed by Simon de Sudbury with the seal used for procurations.

London, 15 April 1357

329. LICENCE for an oratory granted to Peter atte Wode for his house at Wood in Coulsdon, valid for one year.

Southwark, 2 May 1357

330. SIMILAR LICENCE for John de Ingepenne for his houses of Wolveston in the parish of St Mary, Southampton and at Gauclacre in the parish of Middleton, valid for one year.

Southwark, 5 July 1357

331. SIMILAR LICENCE for Philip le Wayte for his house at Denmead, in the parish of Hambledon.

Same date

346   **332.** RECEIPT for the pension from the priory of Leeds for the church of Leatherhead, for the Michaelmas term.

Southwark, 20 October 1357

333. LICENCE for an oratory granted to Eleanor countess of Dormund for her house of la Vacherie, valid for one year.

Southwark, 12 December 1357

334. SIMILAR GRANT to Guy Bryan, knight, for his house at Ashley, at the bishop's pleasure.

Southwark, 16 December 1357

335. RECEIPT FOR PROCURATIONS for the first year from Pontius de Veryreris, rector of Walpole, diocese of Norwich, as procurator for cardinal Tallerand, bishop of Albano. He has received from the bishop of Winchester, as collector for the archdeaconry, by the hand of Hugh de Provan' £103 8s., viz:
from the portion touching the bishop from benefices and ecclesiastical goods: £37 4s. 5½d.
in part payment of procurations due for the first year of the nunciature: £66 3s. 6½d.

London, 13 August 1357

336. SIMILAR RECEIPT from Luke de Tholomeis of Sienna, receiver for Nicholas, cardinal-priest of St Vitale, apostolic nuncio, by the hand of Hugh de Provan', being payment made by the bishop.

337. RECEIPT for the cardinal's procurations for the second year. Pontius de Veireris has received from the bishop of Winchester, as collector for the archdeaconry of Winchester £37 4s. 5½d., in part payment from the bishop and £50 3s. from the benefices and ecclesiastical goods in part payment for the second year of the nunciature and £4 8s. 9¾d. in part payment of arrears for the first.

London, 20 December 1357

338. ANOTHER RECEIPT for similar sums from Luke de Thelomeis received for the said cardinal of St Vitale for the sums mentioned above.

339. GRANT by Walter, abbot of Hyde with the consent of the chapter, in consideration of the generosity to the abbey of John de Hampton. His son Thomas is informed that his father's name will be inscribed in the martyrology and that on his anniversary a full office will be celebrated i.e. on 4 August: *placebo*, *dirige* and the next day commendation and mass sung (*cum nota*); also a daily remembrance at the altar of St Judocus.

Hyde, the chapter-house, 14 February 1357

347

340. LICENCE for an oratory granted to Richard de Farnhull' for his house at Twynham, at the bishop's pleasure.

Southwark, 24 January 1358

341. SMLIAR LICENCE for William de Sancto Omero for his house Berkeleye, in West Horsley, valid for one year.

Southwark, 8 February 1358

342. COMMISSION to act as penitentiary addressed to Peter de Davyntree rector of Streatham, to hear the confessions of those of the diocese who come to him, with certain cases reserved to the bishop.

Southwark, 7 March 1358

343. LICENCE granted to Reginald de Cobham, knight, and Joan his wife for mass to be celebrated in any suitable place in the county and diocese at the bishop's discretion; also for a marriage to be celebrated between their daughter Joan and Henry son of John de Gray at the castle of Sterburgh, diocese of Winchester.

Southwark, 13 April 1358

344. LICENCE for an oratory granted to John Mayn the king's armourer in his house in Bletchingley, valid for one year.

Southwark, 20 May 1358

345. SIMILAR LICENCE for Richard Trenchard' in the parish of Hordle, valid for one year.

Southwark, 4 October 1358

346. SIMILAR LICENCE for John Frommond at Sparsholt, at the bishop's pleasure.

347. RECEIPT FOR PROCURATIONS for the cardinals for the second year. Luke de Thelomeis, canon of Siena, commisary of N' cardinal priest of St Vitale, together with T' bishop and the cardinal-abbot of Cluny, has received from the bishop of Winchester by the hands of the prior of Merton, sub-collector of the procurations of the two cardinals for the archdeaconry of Surrey: £28 11s. 9½d. in part payment of procurations due to cardinal N' for benefices and ecclesiastical goods in that archdeaconry out of the total procurations due to the cardinals for the second year.

London, 22 December 1357

348. ANOTHER RECEIPT from Pontius de Vereriis, rector of Walpole, as procurator for T' cardinal of Albano, as also for N' cardinal of St Vitale. From the bishop of Winchester he has received from the hand of the prior of Merton, procurator for the cardinals and collector for the archdeaconry of Surrey £28 11s. 9½d. in part payment for the procurations due for the second year.

London, 22 December 1357

349. ANOTHER RECEIPT from Luke de Tholemeis, commissary of cardinal Nicholas, by the hand of Thomas de Enham, from the bishop of Winchester £13, in part payment of arrears in the procurations for the second year of his nunciature from the clergy of the county and diocese.

London, 29 April 1358

350. DECLARATION from John Dagworth', canon of Lincoln, procurator for T' cardinal of Albano that he has examined the accounts of Pontius de Veireriis, lately receiver of procurations for the first and second years of the nunciature of England. On the last day of April Pontius received by the hand of Thomas de Enham in part payment of what was due for the second year for the archdeaconry of Winchester £13. Signed by Hugh Pelegrini, treasurer of Lichfield.

London, 17 October 1358

351. RECEIPT for the cardinals' procurations, third year, from John Dagworth', procurator for cardinals Tallerand and Nicholas, by the hand of the prior of Winchester, as deputy for the bishop £14 10s., in part payment for the procurations due from the archdeaconry for the third year of their nunciature, being only the portion of the cardinal of Albano.

London, 2 October 1358

352. SIMILAR RECEIPT from Luke de Tholemeis of Siena, receiver for cardinal Nicholas for £54 10s. by the hand of the prior of Winchester, collected from the clergy of the archdeaconry of Winchester.

Date as above

353. RECEIPT from John de Dagworth' as procurator for T' and N', cardinals, for £30 19½d. from the bishop of Winchester through the prior of Merton, sub-collector for Surrey, as part payment for the third year, only the portion of the cardinal of Albano.

London, 2 October 1358

354. SIMILAR RECEIPT from Luke de Tholomeis for £30 10s. from the clergy of the archdeaconry of Surrey, by the hand of the prior of Merton.

Same date

355. ANOTHER RECEIPT by John de Dagworth', procurator for the two cardinals for the portion of the cardinal of Albano, for the goods of the bishop of Winchester in England: £37 4s. 5d.

London, 4 September 1358

356. ANOTHER RECEIPT for the third year of procurations by Luke de Tholomeis, canon of Siena, commissary for cardinal Nicholas from the bishop by the hand of John Beautre, canon of Exeter his chaplain, £37 4s. 5d. owed by the bishop for his own goods. The bishop is absolved from the penalties involved by non-payment in the first and second years in the person of the said John.

London, 4 October 1358

357. LETTER from the bishop to the abbess and convent of Nunnaminster: by the right of his church, he requests them to receive as a nun Joan, daughter of Thomas de Coleshull', formerly his 'valet'.

Southwark, All Souls Day 1358

358. LICENCE granted to Alan de Suton' of the parish of Shirley to hear mass in his house, valid for one year.

Southwark, 2 November 1358

359. SIMILAR LICENCE for Richard de Houlond, knight, for his manor at Tolworth, parish of Malden.

same date

360. SIMILAR LICENCE for Robert de Ledrede, royal armourer, for his house in the parish of Fetcham.

same date

349 **361.** LICENCE TO CELEBRATE MATRIMONY between Hamon de Modham and Catherine de Taleworth in the royal chapel of Sheen, parish of Kingston, granted to any fitting chaplain.

Southwark, 29 November 1358

362. RECEIPT FOR PROCURATIONS by John de Dagworth' as procurator for T' cardinal bishop of Albano and N' cardinal of St Vitale. For the third year, for the cardinal of Albano only, from the prior of Winchester in part payment from the clergy of the diocese £30.

London, 24 November 1358

363. ANOTHER RECEIPT by Luke de Tholomeis for N' cardinal of St Vitale from the bishop, by the hand of Peter de Oxon', monk of Winchester, £30 in part payment of arrears in procurations from the clergy of the city and diocese.

London, 24 November 1358

364. MEMORANDUM that the prior of Ogbourne has paid to the procurator of T' cardinal of Albano £10 11s. 11½d. and to the procurator of N' cardinal of St Vitale £12 5s. 5½d. for the first and second years of the nunciature.

365. RECEIPT showing that the rector of Nether Wallop has paid 66s. 8d. in procurations for the first and second years as from the rector and his church.

366. RECEIPT from the prior of Leeds, 20s. for the appropriation of the church of Leatherhead for the Michaelmas term.

Southwark, 19 February 1359

367. RECEIPT FOR PROCURATIONS by John de Dagworth' as procurator for the cardinals from the bishop in part payment to the cardinal of Albano for the third year £4 2s. 11½d.

London, 16 March 1359

368. SIMILAR RECEIPT by Richard de Kylmynton' dean of St Paul's, as procurator for cardinals N' and T', from the bishop in part payment from the diocese to cardinal N' for the third year £4 2s. 11½d.

London, 16 March 1359

369. RECEIPT by John de Dagworth' from the bishop 71s., as procurations for the third year, in part payment from the clergy, being the portion of the cardinal of Albano.

London, 11 May 1359

370. RECEIPT by Richard de Kylmyngton' for the cardinal of St Vitale from the bishop 71s. in part payment for the procurations for his spiritualities and temporalities.

London, 11 May 1359

371. RECEIPT by the hand of John de Totteford', official of the archdeacon of Surrey, 20 marks pension due for the Easter term 1357.

Southwark, 22 July 1359

350   **372.** COMMISSION to proceed against the prior of Selborne addressed to the official. Edmund the prior is reported to have wasted the goods of the priory, is accused of incontinency and other faults. The bishop, wishing to avoid a dangerous situation orders the official to enquire of the brethren, clerics and laymen as to the truth of the accusations; to order him to make no alienations of temporal goods. The priory seal is to be sequestrated.

Southwark, 19 June 1359

373. LICENCE FOR DEMOLITION of certain buildings at Yateley addressed to M. John de Lech', rector of Crondall with the adjacent chapels, of the bishop's patronage. From recent discussion it appears that buildings at the chapel of Yateley, once lavishly constructed, are now a burden, being useless and decayed. Previous rectors had neglected repairs to the roofs, so that now the buildings can only be repaired at great expense. The bishop permits demolition of what is useless, except for a hall, chamber, kitchen, barns and stable.

Southwark, 16 July 1359

374. NOTE FOR THE NUNS at Wherwell. Christina la Wayte, A' de L' and J' de B', nuns made their solemn profession before the bishop, who veiled them as nuns. In his address he told them to venerate the feast of the Nativity of Blessed Mary every year as their profession anniversary.

375. MANDATE to the sub-prior and convent of Selborne. Because of his excesses prior Edmund is deprived of all right to alienate the goods of the priory.

Southwark, 16 August 1359

351 **376.** MANDATE from Simon, archbishop of Canterbury, through Michael, bishop of London, concerning the proper observance of Sunday and prayers for the success of the expedition of the king and the prince of Wales with their army. Sunday should be observed from vespers to vespers, with no markets or fairs. For the king there should be processions twice a week.

Otford, 14 August 1359
London, 26 August 1359

352 **377.** EXECUTION of the mandate asking prayers for the king and his army, with almsgiving, processions and 40 days indulgence.

Southwark, 24 September 1359

378. ANOTHER MANDATE for the above addressed to the archdeacon of Winchester to make known the appeal for Sunday observance and for prayers for the army.

same date

379. RECEIPT for the pension from the prior of Leeds for the appropriated church of Leatherhead, for the Michaelmas term, 20s.

Southwark, 13 October 1359

380. LICENCE FOR SOLEMNIZING MATRIMONY granted at the request of William earl of Northampton and Richard earl of Arundel, between Humphrey, eldest son of the said William and Joan, daughter of the said Richard; also between Richard, son of the same Richard, and

Elizabeth, daughter of the same William. To be celebrated in any church by the prior of Lewes, or any other priest.

Southwark, 17 October 1359

381. RECEIPT from Robert de Burton', archdeacon of Winchester, for £20, for the Easter term 1360.

Southwark, 2 June 1359

382. SIMILAR RECEIPT, by the hand of his official John de Totteford', from the archdeacon of Surrey, 20 marks, for the Easter term 1358.

Southwark, 3 June 1360

353

383. FOUNDATION OF A CHANTRY by John, abbot of Chertsey, for the soul of Robert de Ledrede, king's armourer. He left to the abbey lands, tenements and other goods when he died at Leatherhead. In gratitude the monastery ordains a daily mass at the Holy Cross altar in perpetuity; his name to be inscribed in the a martyrology among their benefactors.

Chapter-house, Chertsey, 9 January 1360

384. SETTLEMENT OF THE DEBTS of the said Robert de Ledrede accepted by the abbey.

Chertsey, 9 January 1360

385. LICENCE granted to the priory of Reigate to lease at farm the fruits and tithes of the chapel of Dorking to Roger de Brecham, for his life at an annual sum of money.

Southwark, 28 January 1360

386. PROBATE of the will of Robert de Stangrave, knight, deceased. Administration granted to hs his widow, as named in the will, and to Thomas Austyn, instead of John de Stratford', co-executor.

Southwark, 29 February 1360

354

387. COMMISSION TO ADMINISTER THE GOODS OF INTESTATES granted to Walter de Bockstede, of the parish of St Mary, Southwark. Since the administration of such goods pertains to the bishop, he entrusts this to Walter in the case of William de Overesfle.

Southwark, 28 June 1360

388. LICENCE granted to M. John de Lech', rector of Crondall, for mass to be celebrated in the rectory house, at the bishop's pleasure.

Southwark, 23 July 1360

389. ABSOLUTION FROM SUSPENSION FOR IRREGULARITY granted by the bishop to Adam Hermer. He had been suspended for blessing the second marriage of Nicholas Kyng' at mass, in ignorance of the law, and of taking part in divine service during his suspension.

Southwark, 28 July 1360

390. LICENCE for an oratory granted to John Mayn, king's armourer, for one year, for his house in Bletchingley.

Southwark, 30 July 1360

391. DISPENSATION granted to the *prepositus* of St Elizabeth's chapel, Winchester, John de Nubblegh', from residence and the daily celebration in the chapel, on account of his work as administrator of the chapel, with permission to wear clothing of a more simple colour.

Marwell, 7 August 1360

392. TESTIMONIAL LETTER for the bishop's triennial *ad limina* visit to the Holy See, granted by Stephen, archbishop of Toulouse, as having been made by M. Noion, his procurator.

Avignon, 1 July 1360

393. DISPENSATION from attendance at the consistory at Winchester, as laid down by Henry, late bishop, granted to John Say, rector of Sutton for two years.

Southwark, 20 January 1361

394. PROBATE of the oral testament of Thomas Seint Leger, knight, before M. Thomas de Enham, chancellor. Administration granted to Nicholas de Lysh', according to the will.

355　**395.** COMMISSION TO ACT AS PENITENTIARY for the Isle of Wight, addressed to James atte Oki, rector of the chapel of Wootton.

Southwark, 8 February 1361

396. PROBATE of the will of John le Sadelere of Southwark, layman, before M. Thomas de Enham. Administration granted to Margery his widow and to Alan Vyel, clerk.

Southwark, [ ] March 1361

397. PROBATE of the will of John de Grantham, clerk, formerly master of the king's stables, before the same M. Thomas. Administration of his goods in the diocese granted to Edmund de Lenham and John de Mockyng' of Southwark.

Southwark, 16 March 1361

398. RECEIPT from the priory of Leeds of the pension of 20s. for the church of Leatherhead, for the Michaelmas term.

Southwark, 16 November 1360

399. LICENCE FOR A PILGRIMAGE to St James, granted to Edmund, rector of the church of Oakley, to be absent in fulfilment of his vow, until Michaelmas next.

no date

400. RECEIPT of the pension of 20 marks from M. Edmund de Eston', official of the archdeacon of Surrey, for the Easter term 1359.

Southwark, 4 May 1361

401. COMMISSION entrusting the hospital of St Thomas to fr. Richard de Stokes, canon of St Mary, Southwark, because of its pitiful state. He will make an inventory of the goods of the hospital in the presence of fr. John Bonenfaunt and sister Agnes.

Esher, 13 May 1361

402. RECEIPT for £20 from the executors of Robert de Burton', deceased, late archdeacon of Winchester, for the Easter term, 1361.

Esher, 4 July 1361

403. COMMISSION to M. John de Ware, rector of the church of Cranleigh, following the death of M. John de Wolvele, late official Since the bishop wishes the consistory to settle urgent business and to check abuses, he appoints him to stand in as official for this purpose.

356

Edington, 23 July 1361

404. COMMISSION to exercise the jurisdiction of the archdeacon of Winchester, vacant—jurisdiction which reverts to the bishop—until the vacancy is determined, addressed to M. John de Ware, rector of Cranleigh.

Edington, 23 July 1361

405. COMMISSION to confer vacant benefices in the city of Winchester, addressed to M. J' de Ware, commissary-general of the bishop, during the vacancy of the officiality through death.

Highclere, 7 August 1361

406. COMMISSION to act as confessors to the nuns of Nunnaminster, addressed to Walter Brok', rector of St Pancras, Winchester and to Richard Lewelyn, chaplain, valid until All Saints day next.

Highclere, 7 August 1361

407. PROBATE of the will of Roger Husee, knight, before the bishop. Administration granted to John atte Hurst; the other executors not appearing, the bishop nominated John Husee, brother of the deceased.

Wargrave, 23 September 1361

408. PROBATE of the will of Reginald de Cobeham, knight, before the bishop. Administration granted to Amand de Fytlyng' and to a certain J', named in the will.

Southwark, 7 October 1361

409. RECEIPT for the pension of 20s. from the priory of Leeds for the church of Leatherhead, for the Michaelmas term, 1361.

Southwark, 1 November 1361

410. PROCURATION for his *ad limina* visit granted by the bishop to M. John de Wormenhale, John Blaunchard' and John Corf'.

[Bishops] Waltham, 22 February 1362

411. COMMISSION to act as official in the archdeaconry of Surrey, addressed to fr. John Wibon', prior of Chertsey, for the duration of the vacancy.

Southwark, 8 March 1362

357　**412.** MANDATE to the archdeacon of Winchester to summon the beneficed clergy of all ranks of the city and archdeaconry of Winchester within the bishop's jurisdiction, to appear in the cathedral on Saturday after the feast of St Dunstan (19 May) to hear the mandate from Simon, archbishop of Canterbury.

Southwark, 8 May 1362

413. SIMILAR CITATION directed to the archdeacon of Surrey.

414. COMMISSION to publish the mandate of the archbishop, received 1 May, through Michael, bishop of London. Lately the bishops considered the subsidy requested by pope Innocent VI from the English clergy. They entrusted certain friends with the task of explaining that the sum was excessive, while recognising the situation of the Holy See through rebellions and invasions. The sum was the equivalent of a tenth, payable between St John Baptist and the Purification in two equal portions, payable to the receiver, Robert, rector of St Gregory, London.

Mayfield, 14 April 1361

358　Edmonton, 3 May 1362

To be published in the cathedral, Saturday after St Dunstan before the clergy. The first portion to be paid at the date stated, at the customary assessment; in the archdeaconry of Winchester to the prior of Winchester, in that of Surrey to the abbot of Chertsey as receivers.

Southwark, 11 May 1362

415. POWERS granted to the prior to be collector for the archdeaconry.

same date

416. SIMILAR POWERS to the abbot of Chertsey for the archdeaconry of Surrey.

417. MANDATE to the abbess and convent of Nunnaminster to receive on the occasion of her abbatial election, Alice, daughter of John Waleys, knight, in the convent as a nun (in French).

Southwark, 1 June 1362

418. RECEIPT for the pension from the archdeacon of Surrey, through M. John de Totteford', 20 marks for the Easter term.

Southwark, 1 June 1362

419. LICENCE granted at the request of the countess of Dormund to celebrate the marriage between Walter Fitz Wat' and Eleanor de Dagworth', her daughter, in the chapel of the countess at la Vacherie, in the parish of Cranleigh.

Southwark, 23 June 1362

359 **420.** TESTIMONIAL LETTER for the bishop's *ad limina* visit, in the person of M. John de Wormenhale as procurator, granted by Arnald, archbishop of Auxio, papal chamberlain.

Avignon, 22 February 1362

421. ACKNOWLEDGEMENT addressed to the archbishop that the mandate has been received and the bishop has ordered its contents to be made known to the clergy, as also who are the receivers in the two archdeaconries and to whom the money is to be sent.

Southwark, 20 June 1362

422. EXECUTION OF THE ARCHBISHOP'S MANDATE for collecting the tenth. The bishop admits that there has been murmuring and hesitation concerning this imposition, hence to remove all ambiguity the archbishop has sent another mandate.

The archbishop and the bishop of Ely have received the bull of Innocent VI. Text of the bull: because of the urgent needs of the Church, the English bishops have offered a subsidy of 100,000 florins. In view of the difficulty and danger of transferring such a sum, this is the plan: King John of France is due to pay a ransom to King Edward, who is willing
360 to deduct the 100,000 florins from the larger sum due to him from King John. Ecclesiastical censures for non-payment.

Avignon, 1 April 1362

All the bishops, including the archbishop of York, have accepted the bull; the archbishop of Canterbury orders the contents of the bull to be made known and the money to be sent to the collectors at the times fixed.

Lambeth, 21 May 1362
361 Southwark, 26 May 1362

423. CERTIFICATE of the archbishop's mandate concerning the tenth, addressed to Robert, rector of St Gregory, London, the receiver, and of the bishop's intention to implement it.

Southwark, 20 June 1362

424. LICENCE to be absent for one year for study at a university, granted to Ralph Caperon, rector of Titsey.

Southwark, 15 July 1362

425. FACULTY granted to any catholic bishop to receive the profession of Joan de Borhunte, nun of Romsey, in the customary manner.

Farnham, 17 September 1362

426. LICENCE TO SOLEMNIZE MATRIMONY between John Kayli and Matilda atte Boure of the diocese of Canterbury, granted to M. Richard de Wodelond', rector of Lambeth.

Southwark, 26 October 1362

427. FACULTY granted to R' bishop of Salisbury to receive the profession of Joan Borhunte, Sibyl Holte, Isabella de Chertseye and Tamasin Blount, nuns of Romsey.

Southwark, 5 November 1362

428. COMMISSION TO GRANT ABSOLUTION FROM SUSPENSION. The bishop, as sole executor of a favour granted by the Holy See to John de Swynleye, of the collegiate church of St John, Chester, addresses a commission to M. John Smyth' doctor at law and Robert de Greodon, rector of St Peter, Chester. Since the absolution of all who have incurred sentence under the bishop concerning the favour granted is reserved to the bishop or his superior, all those who sought to prevent the said John from securing the canonry in the said collegiate church and the prebend which M. Walter de Chilterne held during his life-time, were in a legal process suspended and excommunicated by the bishop. The commissioners are to lift the suspension by apostolic authority.

Farnham, 28 December 1362

362   **429.** PARDON for the £10 due to the bishop by apostolic authority, the portion due from the priory for the subsidy, granted to the priory of Selborne out of charity on account of their distress.

Farnham, 4 January 1363

430. MANDATE to the abbess of Wherwell to receive into her community Margaret Cokerel, being recommended by the bishop.

Farnham, 4 January 1363

431. RECEIPT for £20 from M. Robert de Weykford' archdeacon of Winchester for the Easter term.

Southwark, 16 November 1362

432. RECEIPT from the prior of Leeds 20s. being the pension for the church of Leatherhead, for the Michaelmas term 1362.

Southwark, 20 February 1363

433. COMMISSION from the bishop as sole executor, to provide a benefice for Thomas Grys, poor priest of the diocese of Chichester at the presentation of the prior of Bermondsey, cluniac, as deputed by the Holy See, addressed to Robert de Weykford, archdeacon of Winchester, and John Blaunchard doctor at law, rector of Elingdon, diocese of Salisbury. To enquire into the character of the said Thomas in view of the provision.

Esher, 18 March 1363

434. SIMILAR COMMISSION to provide a benefice for John Craft poor clerk of the diocese pf Salisbury, at the presentation of the abbess of Nunnaminster, to enquire into his manner of life.

Esher, 28 April 1363

435. SIMILAR COMMISSION for Walter Levenac' poor priest of the diocese of Exeter at the presentation of the abbess of Romsey, to enquire into his life.

Southwark, 20 April 1363

363 **436.** SIMILAR COMMISSION for Thomas Isaac poor priest of the diocese of Bath, at the presentation of the prior and chapter of Winchester, for an enquiry, addressed to the prior of St Mary, Southwark and the archdeacon of Winchester.

Esher, 2 May 1363

437. SIMILAR COMMISSION for James Fehew poor priest of the diocese of Dublin, at the presentation of the priory of Merton, for a similar enquiry addressed to the official and the dean of the court of Canterbury.

Esher, 9 May 1363

438. SIMILAR PROVISION for Adam Hermere of Sigglesthorne, poor clerk of the diocese of York, at the presentation of the abbot of Hyde, addressed to the official of Winchester.

Highclere, 29 May 1363

439. LICENCE AND FACULTY TO CONSTRUCT AND DEDICATE A CHAPEL and the surrounding burial ground, granted at the request of the parishioners of the hamlet of Haslemere within the parish of Chiddingfold, at the petition of Thomas Quarreour rector; licence to consecrate granted to any English bishop, or the bishop of Ossory, Ireland, or the bishop of 'Lamburgen'.

Wolvesey, 3 June 1363

440. MANDATE to request prayers for the expedition of the prince of Wales to Aquitaine.

Highclere, 29 May 1363

441. GRANT OF FACULTY to transfer the body of John de Wynkefeld, knight, from the church of Byfleet to that of Winchfield, his place of origin, where a perpetual chantry for him and his parents has been endowed. Addressed to Eleanor, his widow.

Farnham, 28 July 1363

364 **442.** COMMISSION TO PROVIDE A BENEFICE for John Robyn, poor priest of the London diocese, at the presentation of the priory of St Denys, Southampton. The official is to enquire into his life.

[Bishops] Waltham, 27 August 1363

443. PROBATE of the will of John Bardolf, knight, before the bishop. Administration of his goods granted to Simon, rector of Castre.

Southwark, 21 October 1363

444. CONCESSION granted by the bishop to the rector of Wolverton, at the petition of E' de Sancto Johanne, knight, that because of the ruinous condition of the buildings of the rectory house, he may keep the autumn crops, due to the bishop, for repairs.

Southwark, 23 November 1363

445. LICENCE FOR AN ORATORY granted to the abbot of Westminster and his monks for their use in their manor of Pyrford, for one year.

Newark, 18 December 1363

446. SIMILAR LICENCE to Matilda, countess of Salisbury, for her manor of la More, near Bermondsey. Valid for one year.

Esher, 18 December 1363

447. COMMISSION TO SEQUESTRATE the fruits and revenue of the arch-deaconry of Winchester, which reverts to the bishop during the vacancy, entrusted to Walter Gourda, rector of Stoneham. He is to enquire into the goods of the intestate and of deceased ecclesiastics, acting as sequestrator-general.

Highclere, 3 January 1364

365

448. SIMILAR COMMISSION for the archdeaconry of Surrey, entrusted to Robert, rector of Puttenham.

Southwark, 16 January 1364

449. MANDATE addressed to the abbess and convent of Nunnaminster, reminding them that they are not to receive more sisters than they can afford to maintain, not to accept corrodians or seculars beyond what are necessary as servants, nor ladies for longer than one month. All this is to be corrected within 15 days, with a certificate sent before the Ascension.

[Bishops] Waltham, 10 March 1364

450. SIMILAR MANDATES to the abbesses of Romsey, Wherwell and the prioress of Wintney.

451. LIFTING OF THE SEQUESTRATION addressed to the dean of Alton. Thomas Warin had pledged himself in a certain sum of money to remedy defects in the chancel, in books, vestments and buildings, of the rectory of Newton Valance, according to an estimate reached by an enquiry. For this the autumn corn and fruits within the rectory buildings were sequestrated. This is now lifted and Thomas may dispose of the crops.

[Bishops] Waltham, 4 April 1364

452. LICENCE TO LEASE AT FARM the church of Mickleham granted to the priory of Reigate for 2 years. There must be no loss in divine service, or in the cure of souls.

Southwark, 16 April 1364

366

453. RECEIPT for the £20 due annually from M. Robert de Wykford, archdeacon of Winchester, by the hands of John Broun, his registrar and receiver; for the Easter term.

Wolvesey, 6 May 1364

454. COMMISSION TO ABSOLVE AN EXCOMMUNICATE, William de Notton, knight, justiciar of the king, entrusted by the bishop to M. Thomas de

Bokton' official of York, after letters received from Androynus, cardinal-priest of St Marcellus. Following process in the court of Rome, instituted by Thomas, bishop of Ely, William de Notton and others were publicly excommunicated. Since then pope Innocent VI in letters to the abbot of Cluny, nuncio to France and England, has lifted the sentence. The executors of the bishop (of Ely) are satisfied that William at his death was penitent. Urban V, at the request of the executors and heirs of William, orders the absolution to be declared publicly and the body of William given ecclesiastical burial.

Avignon, 18 June 1363
Southwark, 8 February 1364

455. CERTIFICATE OF THE LIBERATION of William de Ayete, knight and clerk. The bishop had written to M. John de Ware sequestrator-general for the archdeaconry concerning William de Ayet, accused of having taken from a certain vicar in Portsmouth 1 horse, 1 portable breviary and 1 bag, valued at £10, through men from the hundred of Fawley. He was imprisoned and convicted before a secular judge, then as a clerk imprisoned at Wolvesey. William seeks canonical purgation. Mandate to enquire of worthy men who know sir William, whether he is guilty. If 367   innocent, this to be publicly proclaimed in the churches and markets of the city and district of Winchester. Any objectors are to appear in the cathedral on Tuesday after Trinity Sunday. He was liberated.

Winchester, Tuesday [6 June] 1363

456. MANDATE FORM THE ARCHBISHOP against clergy receiving excessive stipends. From Simon, archbishop of Canterbury to the bishop, forwarded to the archdeacon of Surrey. The cupidity of present-day clergy often leads to insufficient care of souls, to the scandal of lay-folk. Suspension for 20 days should be imposed. No priest is to transfer to another diocese without a certificate from the first diocesan. A report on what has been done to be sent before the Purification (2 February).

Lambeth, 13 November 1362

Order to publish the mandate and to report before St Hilary (13 January).

Southwark, 16 November 1362

457. SIMILAR MANDATE to the archdeacon of Winchester.

368   **458.** MANDATE from the archbishop against secular judges intruding upon ecclesiastical jurisdiction. From Ralph bishop of London, forwarding the letter of Simon the archbishop. Recently in parliament the matter was raised of secular judges exceeding their powers, trespassing on ecclesiastical liberties. Treats of how guilty clerks should be treated by ecclesiastical judges, and when in prison with fasting.

Lambeth, 29 February 1361

To report before St John (24 June).

Stepney, 14 March 1361

459. MANDATE on the observance of feast-days from Simon, archbishop of Canterbury, addressed to Simon, bishop of London. To remind the faithful to abstain from work on Sundays and ecclesiastical feasts, avoiding business and taverns, eating and drinking, which cause scandal. List of days to be observed: Sunday from Saturday vespers, feasts of the church's year, saints' days, feasts of the locality. Clergy to remind the people of their obligation to their parish church.

369

Mayfield, 17 July 1362

Order to carry out the mandate.

Stepney, 31 July 1362

Execution of the mandate entrusted to the bishop's official, who is to bring it to the notice of clergy and people.

Southwark, 2 November 1362

370

460. MANDATE TO ANNOUNCE THE LIFTING OF A SENTENCE OF EXCOMMUNI-CATION, addressed to the dean. John Bullok' and his brother Robert were excommunicated for laying violent hands on William, rector of St Laurence, Winchester, when in the exercise of his duties. On the Sunday after St Augustine (28 August) the two will walk, barefoot and bare-headed, from the place at Hyde Abbey, where the rector was maltreated, carrying a candle weighing 3 lb., to the cathedral to offer it at the high altar, there to receive absolution. A report to be sent before St Barnabas (11 June).

Wargrave, 22 May 1364

461. MANDATE TO RECALL A RECTOR TO RESIDENCE, addressed to the archdeacon of Surrey, concerning Robert, acting as a rector of half the church of Abinger Jarponvile, neglecting the priestly office and the cure of souls, leaving the church destitute. He is at some distant place, squandering the resources of his church. He is to be ordered to return within a month, to reside personally, to care for the rectory house and to appear before the bishop on the 20th law-day after the expiry of the month, since many doubt if he is in holy orders.

Wargrave, 6 May 1364

462. REMISSION OF A DEBT. At the request of the duke of Lancaster, the bishop remits the debt owing to the bishop by the prior and convent of Mottisfont, under the name of "charitable subsidy" granted by the clergy.

Southwark, 7 February 1360

463. RECEIPT from John de Edyndon', archdeacon of Surrey, by the hands of M. John de Totteford, 20 marks owing for the Easter term 1361, for the annual pension.

Esher, 12 July 1364

464. RECEIPT from the prior of Leeds, for the Michaelmas term 1363, 20s., the pension for the church of Leatherhead.

Southwark, 30 November 1363

371   **465.** PROCURATION for the *ad limina* visit, the bishop being busy with urgent business, granted to Roger de Freton, doctor-at-law and John de Uphull, rector of Havant.

Southwark, 6 July 1364

466. MANDATE addressed to M. Walter Gourda, sequestrator-general for the archdeaconry of Winchester. King Edward has presented to the bishop by letters patent M. William Othyn for the church of Bighton, which is, as he asserts, of his patronage. Hence there must be an enquiry concerning the presentation, since the incumbent is now William Dymayn. As the bishop desires to be just to both parties, he needs to know whether William Dymayn is within his jurisdiction and to summon him to appear in the cathedral the next law-day after the Exaltation of the Cross (14 September) to show why the king's presentee should not be admitted, instituted and inducted as rector, to do and receive what is right and reasonable. And as regards dilapidations and consumption or removal of corn, fodder and crops, even of this autumn, belonging to the church, which according to reliable men are in danger of being wasted, the crops and fodder are to be sequestrated and kept safe awaiting further instructions. And as regards the cure of souls and divine service, this is to be served by some suitable chaplain. And of what has been done towards the said William Dymayn and the sequestration, the bishop asks for a certificate 6 days before the aforesaid law-day.

Coleshill, 4 August 1364

467. TESTIMONIAL concerning penance imposed by papal authority on a certain layman for killing a clerk. Letter received by the bishop from fr. Thomas de Brynton', papal penitentiary, concerning Helias Rardeele, a layman, the bearer of the letter, who as he will relate, by the inspiration of the devil, murdered a certain clerk. Under sentence of excommunication on that account, we are sending him back to you for absolution, and among other things consequent on the oath he has taken, that at all the main churches where so great a crime was committed, let him proceed bare body and feet, with arms bound, carrying a lash in his hands and a thong around his neck; and at the church doors let him be whipped by the priests for the space of a penitential psalm. Let this be done before

372   a crowd of people, as he publicly confesses his guilt. The bishop is to judge that the penance is salutary and a warning to others. Should he refuse to undergo this penance, he at once relapses under the sentence of excommunication.

Avignon, 30 August 1364

The bishop has considered the fault and finds the penance laid down to be salutary.

Farnham, 29 November 1364

468. ABSOLUTION of John Harm, layman, for laying violent hands on the rector of Lasham. The bishop recalls that absolution for attacking clerks, wounding or mutilating them, is reserved to the Holy See. John Harm incurred sentence of major excommunication for attacking Richard, rector of Lasham, priest, damaging the index finger of his left hand. Having made satisfaction by an oath to go personally to the Holy See before 20 January in accordance with the law, the bishop meantime grants him the benefit of absolution.

Farnham, 29 November 1364

469. COMMISSION addressed to M. Walter Gourda, rector of North Stoneham, jurist, to act at the consistory in the absence of the official, settling cases put forward, correcting and punishing offenders.

Farnham, 3 January 1365

470. LICENCE granted to John atte Feld of Romsey to postpone his journey to the Holy See imposed on him for having attacked Thomas de Lench', priest, until three weeks after Easter next.

Southwark, 15 February 1365

471. COMMISSION to exercise the office of penitentiary entrusted to the abbot of Chertsey, for the archdeaconry of Surrey from Ash Wednesday until Maundy Thursday, at the doors of his monastery, valid for one year.

Southwark, 20 February 1365

472. Duplicate of 470.

473. COMMISSION addressed to M. John de Wormenhale, doctor-at-law, to preside at the consistory (cf. 469), settling cases presented.

373

[Bishops] Waltham, 30 March 1365

474. LICENCE granted to John Harm, layman, to postpone his journey to the Holy See (cf. 468) until three weeks after Easter next, so that in the meantime he may receive the sacraments of the Church from some suitable chaplain, whom the bishop authorizes.

[Bishops] Waltham, 31 March 1365

475. TESTIMONIAL LETTER from Arnald, archbishop of Auxio, papal chamberlain, for the triennial visit *ad limina* in the person of John de Uphull', rector of Havant as his procurator. This procurator made no offering on the occasion.

Avignon, 19 February 1365

476. MANDATE addressed to the dean of the Isle of Wight. There is a complaint from certain parishioners of the church of Gatcombe that Thomas, the rector, in sheer cupidity, is striving to impose on them a new kind of tithe, hitherto unused, on animals and other things, spurning the authority of the bishop in such matters. And what is worse, when they come for Lenten confession, he refuses absolution unless they take an oath to pay the required tithe. The dean is to admonish the rector not to refuse the sacraments; to allow the parishioners for this occasion to choose any confessor they wish. If the rector will not obey, he is to appear at the next consistory before the official at the cathedral, i.e. on the second day. The dean will report.

No date

374 477. RECEIPT FOR THE TENTH GRANTED TO THE POPE. The bishop has received from the prior of the cathedral church, as collectors of the tenth from the English clergy, from the archdeaconry of Winchester £745 11s. 4¾d;

by the hand of John Bleobury .... £587 2s. 4¾d.
             M.W' de Sevenham
             treasurer of Wolvesey .... £106 1s. 8½d.
             the cathedral prior .... £34 11s. 8d.
             the abbot of Hyde .... £17 15s. 7½d.
less £297 15s. 7d. the tenth by concession of the bishop
      £1 10s. 8d. the tenth of the church of Sutton in the bishop's hands
      £6 13s. 4d. by allowance to fr. Peter de Exon' for his work and
            expenses.

Bishops Waltham, 18 April 1365

478. LICENCE for an oratory granted to William Wyke of the parish of Silchester for his house there, valid for one year.

Farnham, 25 April 1365

479. COMMISSION to enquire into the discipline of the house or priory of Barton, Isle of Wight, entrusted to the official. For some time much complaint has been heard of the lack of discipline, the tepidity of divine worship and the extravagant living, so that the house is becoming an object of shameful neglect. Wishing to avoid such a situation, an enquiry must be made into the truth of the accusations from members and reliable clerks and laymen. Correction to be administered where necessary and regulations laid down for the future. A certificate to be sent.

Southwark, 5 June [1365]

480. LICENCE for an oratory granted to Margery Brayboeuf in her house in the parish of West Horsley. Valid for one year.

Southwark, 14 June 1365

481. SIMILAR LICENCE to William de Cusynton', knight, for his house in Camberwell, valid until Michaelmas.

Southwark, 18 June 1365

482. RECEIPT from M. John de Edyngdon', archdeacon of Surrey, for 20 marks by the hand of M. John de Totteford his official, owing for the Easter term 1362.

Esher, 22 June 1365

483. MANDATE to the official. The bishop has learned from reliable sources that Henry Mannyon, rector of the parish church of South Tidworth, blinded by avarice and for sordid gain, has recently erected a certain hut like a sheep-fold in his parish for a chapel with a statue, to be called St Catherine's Mount, where he holds services and receives offerings, neglecting his parish—without any licence from the bishop. The bishop orders the hut to be demolished and the statue to be taken to the parish

375 church. The rector is to receive canonical punishment.

Witney, 12 July 1365

484. RECEIPT from M. Robert de Wykford', archdeacon of Winchester, by the hand of John de Wytchebury, perpetual vicar of Kingsclere, registrar and receiver of the archdeacon, £20 for this Easter term past, part of the annual pension.

Hursley, 18 August 1365

485. LETTER to the official of the bishop of London. The discord between Adam de Brabazon and Margery his wife, who is being deprived of her alimony and necessary expenses by her husband, was settled in the presence of the bishop by mutual friends. The two accepted this by oath, but Adam by his stubbornness risks breaking the concord by perjury. If this be true, the bishop asks that now that Adam is living under the jurisdiction of London, he be cited to appear in the church of Farnham the next law-day after St Clement (23 November). A certificate to be sent before the said feast.

Southwark, 28 October 1365

486. COMMISSION to depute to coadjutor for the rector of Freshwater, Isle of Wight, entrusted to the official. John Mot, the rector, is so afflicted bodily and mentally that he can no longer exercise his duties. The official will make an enquiry and then entrust the custody of the church and its goods to the rector of Calbourne and J' de S', securing some sign from John the he consents to the appointment.

Dat'

487. MANDATE TO INHIBIT FROM SOLEMNIZING A MARRIAGE addressed to the archdeacon, his official and the dean of Droxford. In a certain matrimonial and divorce case between William Serle and Edith his alleged wife, of the parish of Meonstoke, recently introduced in the consistorial court, it was argued as a case of nullity, because of a previous contract of Edith to marry John Ropple of Farnham. Until the definitive sentence is promulgated and the said marriage is declared null and void, there must be no question of matrimony. The clergy of the archdeaconry are

376 strictly inhibited from allowing any marriage between the said William and any other woman to be solemnized in church, until the process has been duly examined and the bishop has pronounced.

[Bishops] Waltham, 14 September 1365

488. COMMISSION for hearing the confessions of the nuns of Wintney, including specially reserved cases (detailed), entrusted to John, rector of the church of Elvetham.

Highclere, 26 December 1365

489. COMMISSION to the abbot of Chertsey to hold the office of penitentiary on Ash Wednesday for the archdeaconry of Surrey, and for conducting public penance on Maundy Thursday.

Highclere, 10 February 1366

490. PROBATE of the will of M. Edmund Morteyn, late rector of Fordingbridge before the bishop. The administration of his goods in the diocese granted to William Marchal, rector of Merton, the executor named in the will. Since the deceased possessed no landed property, the administration of his goods was entrusted to Edmund Avenal, knight, lord of Crux Easton.

Highclere, 10 Febraury 1366

491. LICENCE TO RECONCILE A CEMETERY after bloodshed granted to Richard de Haungre, John de Dupedene and John de Polane, patrons and parishioners of the church of Dibden, who may request this of Thomas, bishop of Lycostomium, or any other bishop of the Holy See.

Wolvesey, 20 February 1366

492. LICENCE for an oratory, sent to the rector of the church of Bedhampton, for Elizabeth countess of Kent, for her manor there, valid until Michaelmas next.

Wolvesey, 20 February 1366

493. SIMILAR LICENCE granted to William de Melbury for his house in Sopley, valid for one year.

Same date

494. SIMILAR LICENCE to Geoffrey Roche, for his houses at Roche and Denmead, for one year.

Same date

377	**495.** FACULTY granted to Peter de Brugg' to have an altar, which he has newly set up on the north side of church of Andover in honour of the Annunciation, consecrated by any catholic bishop.

Hursley, 30 March 1366

496. FACULTY to hear confessions even in reserved cases granted to Robert vicar of Andover until the octave of Easter next.

Hursley, 30 March 1366

497. COMMISSION for the administration of the goods of John Mot, late rector of Freshwater, Isle of Wight, intestate, granted to John Mot his relative, for which he took the oath and will render an account.

Esher, 20 May 1366

498. LICENCE TO DEMOLISH A BUILDING for a vicar's house at Kingston-on-Thames. The bishop remembers the request of the perpetual vicar. When John Lovekyn, citizen and 'stokfyssmongere' of London, out of devotion and for the salvation of his soul, having obtained a certain messuage with appurtenances in Kingston, with buildings newly erected, Nicholas de Irthyngburgh', the preceeding vicar, secured by charter from the king that this property be a dwelling-house for the vicars, to possess it in perpetuity. From that time the vicars have held it peaceably as owners, it being suitably near the church, in the ground (*placea*) near the river and the highway, to the east of the church (this by the authority of the prior of Merton and confirmed by the bishop). The building is now delapidated, would be costly to repair even on a temporary basis; the bishop allows a demolition to replace old buildings for the vicarage.

Southwark, 6 May 1366

499. RECEIPT for the annual pension of 20 marks due from the archdeacon of Surrey, M. John de Edyndon', by the hands of M. John de Totteford', his official, for the Easter term 1363.

Esher, 1 June 1366

500. LICENCE for an oratory granted to Philippa de Mortuo Mari, countess of March, for her 'hospicium' at Southwark, or in some suitable place. Valid for one year.

Esher, 4 May 1366

378

501. RELEASE from the suspension and interdict on the chapel of Yateley, following on the attack on Simon, its chaplain, who was abducted by certain of his parishioners, wounding him and causing bloodshed.

Esher, 6 June 1366

502. MANDATE TO SEQUESTRATE the fruits of the priories of the abbey of Tiron, France. The bishop has learned that the parish churches of Hamble, Andwell and St Cross, Isle of Wight, which had been maintained and endowed by benefactors, had been leased at farm, without the bishop's consent, to a layman, Richard Wynnegod, who has neglected divine service and hospitality, turning the revenue to his own purposes, neglecting the buildings, which have become uninhabitable. The bishop orders M. Walter Gourda, the sequestrator-general, to examine the situation and then to sequester to goods so as to meet the obligations of the priories and effect repairs. To report before St John Baptist (June 24).

Esher (no date)

503. COMMISSION to the dean of Guildford and rector of Worplesdon and vicar of Shalfleet, to demand from the king's justices the delivery from Guildford gaol and elsewhere in Surrey all clerics whatever their offences and to conduct them safely to the bishop's prison at Wolvesey.

Esher, 15 May 1366

504. MANDATE TO SEQUESTRATE the goods of an intestate, addressed to M. Walter Gourda. William Schawe of the New Forest with property in various places around Southampton and the New Forest, died in distant parts, intestate. The goods are being wasted or removed. Order to sequestrate the goods in the archdeaconry of Winchester, to be dealt with according to the will, if discovered, or otherwise; meantime they are to be evaluated. Report before St Peter's Chains (August 1).

Wargrave, 14 July 1366

379 **505.** RECEIPT from M. Robert de Wycford, archdeacon of Winchester, by the hands of John de Whithebury, perpetual vicar of Kingsclere, registrar and collector of the archdeaconry, £20 for the Easter term last, being the annual pension.

Hishclere, 5 August 1366

380 Blank.

381 FIRST QUIRE OF BULLS AND OTHER APOSTOLIC LETTERS, SUITS AND THE EXECUTION THEREOF

506. BULL FOR THE CONSECRATION OF THE ELECT OF WINCHESTER. Clement [VI] to William, the elect of Winchester, approving his consecration by any catholic bishop, with two or three assistant bishops. The consecrating bishop will receive the oath of fidelity to the apostolic see and of submission to his metropolitan, the archbishop of Canterbury.

Avignon, 1 February 1346

507. THE OATH taken by the bishop (text in full): fidelity to the pope and his legates, with *ad limina* visits; to keep the estates of the cathedral intact.

508. TESTIMONIAL OF THE CONSECRATION AND THE OATH. John, archbishop of Canterbury, testifies that on Sunday, 14 May 1346, in the manor chapel of Otford, assisted by the bishops Ralph of London and Robert of Chichester, during solemn mass, consecrated the new bishop and after the rite received from him the oath prescribed, recited word by word.

Otford, 14 May 1346

382 **509.** COMMISSION TO PROVIDE A BENEFICE for Ralph de Iwerne, poor clerk of the diocese of Salisbury, at the presentation of the prior and convent of Merton, addressed to the archdeacons of Winchester, Surrey, London and Salisbury, and the deans of Andover and Southwart, with the rectors of St Maurice, Winchester, Abbotsworthy and Crawley. The bishop, who is the sole executor of the papal provision, entrusts this task to the above. He is using the seal of before his consecration.

Southwark, 25 May 1346

510. SIMILAR COMMISSION to provide a benefice for John Portmon, poor clerk of the diocese of Salisbury, at the presentation of the priory of St Denys, Southampton, addressed to the archdeacon of Salisbury and M. John de Sarum, canon of Salisbury. To enquire into the life of the said John.

Southwark, 7 December 1346

511. SIMILAR COMMISSION to provide a benefice for Peter, *natus Johannis ad Fontem* of Farthinghoe, poor clerk of the diocese of Lincoln, at the presentation of the priory of Merton, entrusted to M. John de Usk', rector of Burghclere. This will be at the presentation of Roger son of Hugh de Dennes, priest, to the vicarage of Cuddington for the said Peter, by order of king Edward, by reason that the priory of Merton is in the king's hands. The said Peter is to be admitted to the vicarage and inducted.

Southwark, 31 October 1346

512. FACULTY to grant dispensation from defect of birth granted to the bishop by apostolic letter from Clement [VI,] concerning John Coneys of Wokingham, diocese of Salisbury, holding the first clerical tonsure. Since many poor clerks in England with defect of birth are unable to cross the sea and journey to the apostolic see for dispensation, the pope grants the bishop authority to dispense twelve persons suitable for advancement to major orders and cure of souls.

383

Avignon, 2 January 1347

The bishop dispenses John, who may proceed to ordination.

Southwark, 23 May 1347

513. SIMILAR DISPENSATION granted to John de Anne, tonsured clerk.

Southwark, 23 May 1347

514. SIMILAR DISPENSATION granted to William Lucas of Farnham, tonsured clerk, for the defect of his birth which he had not revealed, but has been pardoned according to the letters of Gaucelinus, bishop of Albano, papal penitentiary, addressed to the bishop concerning the said William.

Avignon, 17 April 1343

William is to keep this letter to prove his dispensation.

Southwark, 23 May 1347

515. BULL OF CLEMENT VI addressed to the bishop, William de Edyndon, as master of the hospital of St Cross. Before his death Clement V reserved to the apostolic see all benefices held by papal chaplains, when vacant by death. The late bishop Adam had ordained that the mastership of St Cross should be a benefice for the secular clergy. At the death of Peter de Galicianis, late master, pope John XXII had conferred the mastership on William de Edyndon', which he had held for eight years, restoring the buildings at great expense. The said Peter at the time of his death was a papal chaplain; this being so, only the said pope John or Benedict XII should have the collation to the hospital. The revenue which the bishop has received, the pope remits, but the papal provision must remain.

384

Avignon, 25 April 1344

516. DISPENSATION from defect of birth granted to Thomas Wygon of Romsey, tonsured clerk; he may proceed to major orders. This is the third case mentioned in the preceeding folio.

Southwark, 1 February 1348

517. SIMILAR DISPENSATION for John Bryan of Winchester, tonsured clerk. This is the fourth case.

Southwark, 28 April 1348

518. RECEIPT FOR THE CARDINALS' PROCURATIONS. Bindus de Pillis, canon of Arras, and fr. Barnabas Maffei of Florence, as procurators for Anibaldus, bishop of Tusculum and Stephen of SS. John and Paul, receiving procurations due from the kingdom of England for the said cardinals for the 2 years as nuncios from the holy see for business in France and England. They have received from the bishop of Winchester in part payment of the procurations due from the bishopric £575 2s. 4d., i.e. from the revenue of the episcopal *mensa* and £148 17s. 8½d., being the residue of the sum collected from the clergy of the city and diocese. The procurators acknowledge that they have received these sums, in payment of the aforesaid procurations, sealing with their common seal. As this seal is not well known, they add the seal of Reymond Pelegrini, papal nuncio in England.

London, 20 October 1348

519. DISPENSATION FROM DEFECT OF BIRTH granted to John Waker', diocese of Chichester, tonsured clerk, who may now proceed to major orders.

Southwark, 26 April 1349

385

520. ADMISSION TO THE OFFICE OF NOTARY granted to Thomas de Calyngburne, not in holy orders, diocese of Salisbury. The bishop informs Thomas of the bull of Clement VI and confers the office by handing over the inkwell and charter by M. Peter de Hakenesse, public notary.
Witnesses: M. John de Usk' chancellor, John de Wolveleye, jurist and Nicholas de Kyngeston' priest. Peter de Hakenesse, clerk, diocese of York, witnesses to the integrity of the bull, which was read out and put into effect in his presence.

Southwark, 24 November 1348

521. ABSOLUTION FROM SUSPENSION for Thomas Whitecroft, priest, received from Stephen, papal penitentiary, cardinal-priest of SS. John and Paul. Thomas the bearer of the dispensation had owed a certain sum of money to a certain creditor and was under sentence of excommunication by a certain ecclesiastical judge, being bound by oath to repay this money: this he did not do, thereby incurring the sentence, through simplicity and ignorance of the law, and taking holy orders. He had sought a remedy from the apostolic see. The bishop is instructed to absolve him and to lift the suspension from the exercise of his orders and his irregularity.

Avignon, 15 July 1349

Since Thomas has satisfied his creditor and has been freed from his suspension and the transgression of his oath, the bishop confirms the dispensation.

Southwark. 12 October 1349

522. BULL OF CLEMENT VI addressed to the bishops of London and Winchester. Simon, archbishop elect of Canterbury has requested the pallium from the pope through M. Roger de Dorkyng', canon of Chichester; the pope appoints the aforementioned bishops to confer the pallium and to receive the oath of fidelity to the Roman see and then to declare this in writing to the pope.

386

Avignon, 29 January 1350

By this authority the pallium was conferred on Simon, with the oath (text in full),

Esher, Maundy Thursday, 25 March 1350

523. TESTIMONIAL LETTER from the bishop to Clement [VI] that on Sunday, St Valentine, 14 February, at the conventual church of St Mary, Southwark, assisted by the bishops John of Worcester and fr. Caesarius of St Maria de Rosis, by faculty of the apostolic see, he consecrated John, archbishop of Dublin; they received his oath of fidelity to the apostolic see, in the form of the preceeding entry.

Southwark, 6 June 1350

524. DISPENSATION FROM DEFECT OF BIRTH granted to Robert le Despenser, diocese of Worcester, priest, on receipt of letters from Clement VI, permitting him to proceed to further orders and hold a benefice.

Southwark, 10 October 1350

525. CONSECRATION of John, bishop elect of Rochester, by the bishop assisted by John, bishop of St Asaph, and fr. Caesarius, bishop of St Maria de Rosis, by commission of the apostolic see, at the conventual church of St Mary, Southwark, receiving his oath according to the formula sent by Innocent VI.

Southwark, Passion Sunday, 10 March 1353

387 **524.** PALLIUM CONFERRED on the archbishop of York, John de Thoresby, by apostolic authority, with the formula prescribed.

Esher, the manor chapel, Friday in Easter week, 29 March 1353

527. CERTIFICATE from the archbishop of York to Innocent [VI] that the bishop of Winchester conferred on him the pallium as directed by the bull sent to the bishops of Winchester and London. John had been elevated to York by Clement VI; M. Gilbert de Welton', canon of York, had requested the pallium before the death of the pope. The pope directs Gilbert to ask the aforesaid bishops to confer the pallium and to receive the oath.

Avignon, 4 January 1353

The pallium was conferred and the oath received, according to formula sent for the archbishop of Canterbury, as above, in the manor chapel.

Esher, 29 March 1353
London, 6 April 1353

528. DISPENSATION FROM DEFECT OF BIRTH granted to John Benmond of Titchfield, clerk, by Giles, cardinal priest of St Clement, papal peniten- tiary. His concealment of the fact on entering the clerical state is pardoned.

Southwark, 7 November 1353

529. SIMILAR DISPENSATION granted to Henry Coyne of Wormingham and Gilbert Trussel of Stone, diocese of Coventry and Lichfield, tonsured clerks. Henry is the sixth and Gilbert the seventh to benefit by the bull.

Farnham, 30 December 1353

388   **530.** SIMILAR DISPENSATION granted to Geoffrey de Byketon', according to the bull. This is the eighth.

[Bishops] Waltham, 28 December 1354

531. SIMILAR DISPENSATION granted to Bartholomew Ponchardon', diocese of Winchester, son of a priest.

[Bishops] Waltham, 11 July 1354

532. CONSECRATION of the bishops of London and Whithorn (Candida Casa) by the bishop, assisted by Caesarius, bishop of St Maria de Rosis: Michael, the elect of London and Michael Mackenlagh' of the cathedral church of Whithorn, of the province of York, by commission of his archbishop, in the conventual church of St Mary, Southwark, during solemn mass at the high altar. They took the oath of fidelity to pope Innocent VI.

Sunday, 12 July 1355

533. COMMISSION from John, archbishop of York, for the consecration of Michael Mackenlagh' as bishop of Whithorn, by any catholic bishop with assistants; from his manor near Westminster.

8 July 1355

534. BLESSING OF THE ABBOT OF NETLEY, fr. William of the monastery of St Edward of 'Lettele', cistercian, followed by submission and obedience promised to the bishop (text in full), according to the holy fathers and the Rule of St Benedict.

Farnham, 30 August 1355

535. CONSECRATION of Thomas, bishop of Norwich, in the monastery church of Waverley, by the bishop, assisted by bishops Robert of Salisbury and Robert of Chichester. He took the oath using the formula sent by Innocent VI.

Sunday, 3 January 1356

536. DISPENSATION FROM DEFECT OF BIRTH granted to Thomas de Upham', authorized by letters from Guy, bishop of Porto, addressed to the bishop,
389   authorized by pope Innocent VI and dated:

monastery of Andres, diocese of Thérouanne, 29 November 1353
Marwell, 11 September 1356

537. SIMILAR DISPENSATION granted to John Codhyne of Tinhead, diocese of Salisbury, tonsured clerk. He may advance to higher orders and hold a benefice, according to the bull; this is the ninth.

Southwark, 24 April 1357

538. SIMILAR DISPENSATION for Henry Luterel, diocese of Bath and Wells, tonsured clerk. This is the tenth according to the bull.

Southwark, 21 October 1357

539. OFFICE OF NOTARY conferred on William de Leveryngton', diocese of Norwich, clerk, unmarried, not in holy orders, according to the formula set out above; this is by authority of the apostolic see, for which he took the oath.

Witnesses: M. Thomas de Enham, Robert de Burton', archdeacon of Winchester, Thomas de Durlegh', Richard de Lyntesford' and John Beautre, apostolic notary.

Southwark, 21 December 1357

540. SIMILAR GRANT of the office of notary conferred on John de Lond', priest of the diocese of Winchester.

Witnesses: M. William Lenn', Robert de Burton, archdeacon of Winchester, Thomas de Enham, chancellor, and John Beautre, notary apostolic, in the manor chapel,

Southwark, 26 November 1357

541. DISPENSATION from defect of birth granted to William de Welles, scholar of the diocese. By letters from Francis, cardinal priest of St Mark, papal penitentiary, which William has brought back from the holy see, where he sought a remedy from his defect of being the son of a priest. The holy see granted this, leaving the bishop to examine his suitability for advance.

Avignon, 1 December 1360

The bishop confirmed the dispensation.

Farnham, 4 January 1361

390   **542.** SIMILAR DISPENSATION by apostolic authority from the earlier bull for John Crabbe, clerk of Oxford.

Wargrave, 18 September 1361

543. SIMILAR DISPENSATION for Robert de Muskham *literatus,* diocese of London, son of a priest.

Esher, 23 September 1361

544. CONSECRATION of the bishop of St Davids by the bishop with fr. Richard, archbishop of Nazareth, and Thomas, bishop of Lycostomium, assisting, M. Adam de Houton, consecrated by apostolic authority, took the oath of fiedlity to the holy see.

Witnesses to the oath: M. Robert de Wykford, archdeacon of Winchester, John Beautre, John Corf' and John Essex' of Harlow, public notaries,

Thomas de Durlee, Richard de Hampton' and others, in the manor chapel.

Southwark, Sunday 2 January 1362

545. CONSECRATION of the bishops of Ely and Worcester at St Paul's cathedral, London, the bishop, assisted by bishops Robert of Salisbury and Adam of St Davids. Simon, abbot of Westminster, to Ely and John Barnet to Worcester, received consecration and took the oath of fidelity to pope Innocent. Were present among the notabilities M. Robert de Wykford archdeacon of Winchester, William de Leveryngton', John Essex' of Harlow, John Beautre, public notaries.

Third Sunday in Lent, 2 March 1362

546. DISPENSATION from defect of birth granted to John Umfrai, diocese of Winchester, *literatus,* by authority of letters from Francis, cardinal priest of St Mark, papal penitentiary, letters which John will preserve.

Southwark, 15 May 1362

547. SIMILAR DISPENSATION for Walter de Stoke, scholar, diocese of Winchester, granted by the aforesaid cardinal, by letters transferred to Walter.

Witney, 18 August 1362

548. SIMILAR DISPENSATION for John Penkeston', clerk, diocese of Salisbury, by letters from William, cardinal deacon of St George *ad velum aureum,* papal penitentiary.

Avignon, 13 April 1362

After due examination the bishop grants the dispensation, pardoning the fact that John had not revealed his defect.

Southwark, 4 January 1363

549. SIMILAR DISPENSATION for Robert de Fremantel *literatus,* by authority of William, cardinal priest of St Laurence *in lucina,* papal penitentiary.

Esher, 11 March 1363

550. CONSECRATION of the bishop of Lincoln in the parish church of Wargrave, diocese of Salisbury, by the bishop assisted by Robert, bishop of Salisbury, and fr. John, bishop of Ossory. John de Bukyngham, the elect of Lincoln as confirmed by apostolic letters, was consecrated and took the oath in the form contained in the letters of Urban V.
Present as witnesses: Philip Engelfeld' and Gilbert Elsefeld', knights, M. John de Houlond', John de Edyndon', archdeacon of Surrey, N' de Kaerwent, John de Bleobury, John Corf' and John Beautre.

Sunday, 25 June 1363

551. EXECUTION OF LETTERS from the papal penitentiary, fr. Thomas de Brynton', concerning John Smalseme, a layman, who had killed a priest and so lay under sentence of excommunication. He now seeks by public penance, going through the streets by the church where the deed was

391

done, barefoot, bearing a lash and a strap around his neck, to be lashed before the church doors, while the priests recite the penitential psalm. This is to take place when there will be a crowd of people to see his act of reparation. He will lose any rights of patronage he might have, and any sons of his the right to hold a benefice without dispensation. Should he refuse, then he has relapsed.

Avignon, 10 November 1364

The bishop entrusts the execution of these letters to his official.

Wargrave, 8 June 1364

392 552. MANDATE to enquire into the proposed foundation of a chapel at Hook. Pope Urban V has received a petition from the inhabitants to erect a church on account of the distance (2 miles) and of the flooding of the pond between the said *opidum* and the church of Titchfield. In bad weather many cannot get to the church; at times many cannot receive the sacraments when sick and children die without baptism. The pope orders the bishop to consult the rector of the parish and to enquire into the endowment for a chaplain to serve the church, preserving the rights of the parish church.

Avignon, 15 March 1364

Mandate to enquire from laymen and clerics and to report to the bishop.

[Bishops] Waltham, 14 September 1365

553. RENUNCIATION by the provincial prior, and the prior and brethren of the Austin Friars of their rights to a manse and other buildings within the city of Winchester. The friars had secured a licence from Clement VI to transfer from the *suburbio* outside the South Gate to a more convenient site within the city, which had been granted to them by Oliver de Bohun, knight, and his wife Margaret. Without episcopal licence they made the transfer, leaving the church in which citizens had sought burial.
393 The new buildings were consecrated secretly by night by an "alleged" bishop. The provincial prior, viewing all the circumstances and seeking to avoid scandal, renounces their rights to the buildings and the licence granted by the pope, with all the brethren, freely and absolutely.

Winchester, 12 March 1351

554. DISPENSATION from defect of birth granted to John Passelewe, scholar, by letters from William, cardinal priest of St Laurence *in lucina,* papal penitentiary. John, the son of a priest, may now proceed to orders (full text of the letter).

Avignon, 19 May 1364

The bishop grants his assent.

Highclere, 4 January 1366

555. GRANT OF OFFICE OF NOTARY to William Gardiner, married clerk of the diocese of Chichester, by letters from Urban V. The bishop is to
394 examine him and receive his oath (text in full).

Avignon, 21 August 1365

The bishop has examined him and authorizes him, handing him the ink-pot and charter.

Highclere, 6 February 1366

395   **556.** FIRST QUIRE OF LETTERS AND BRIEFS CONCERNING TEMPORALITIES AND OTHER ROYAL LETTERS WITH THEIR EXECUTION

557. COMMISSION to Thomas de Pentelowe to be constable of Farnham and bailiff of the manor of Wargrave, to guard the lands and franchises, to hold courts and to maintain the rights and franchises, at the bishop's pleasure.

Southwark, 25 May 1346

558. COMMISSION to R' de Hungerford', knight, and John de Inkepenn' to deal with all pleas of the crown concerning debts, transgressions and contracts of any kind at St Giles' Fair, and to deal with all other business there.

[Bishops] Waltham, 28 August 1346

559. RECEIPT from John, bishop of Hereford, as executor of the will of Adam, the late bishop, for £79 13s. 11d. in part payment of the sum of £159 7s. due to the bishop.

London, 3 October 1346

560. COMMISSION addressed to Robert de Hungerford', knight, John Payn rector of Bishops Waltham and Adam de Kynefare rector of North Waltham and William de Overton to audit the accounts of the reeves and other ministers who are due to render account to the bishop, to make the allowances, to levy arrears and if necessary to distrain; if expedient, to remove from their office and to appoint suitable men.

Southwark, 6 October 1346

561. COMMISSION to act as bailiff of the manor of Waltham in lands and franchises, entrusted to John Payn parson of Bishops Waltham, to maintain all the manorial rights.

Southwark, 10 April 1347

562. COMMISSION to act as constable of the castle of Farnham entrusted to R' de S', to maintain its rights and franchises.

Date as above

396   **563.** INDENTURE to lease at farm to Robert de Lymere and John Welewe the mills of the bishop's manor of Witney, i.e. 2 corn-mills at 'Wodeford-mulle' and 1 corn-mill at 'Waleysmulle' with 1 fulling-mill there also, for the life-time of the bishop, rendering him annually £14 13s. 4d. at the 4 quarter-days in equal portions. They will keep the mills in repair and will find the stone required at their own expense, the bishop providing the heavy timber when required. For non-payment the bishop can distrain on their lands and tenements in Witney.

Witney, Monday after Epiphany 8 January 1347

564. APPOINTMENT of an attorney, John Elys of Thame, to receive seisin of all lands and tenements for which John de Newebury, chaplain, was enfeoffed in Witney, Sandford, Cowley, Littlemore and Iffley.

London, 20 April 1347

565. APPOINTMENT as attorney of Henry de Loxele to receive seisin in the manor of West Bedfont, co. Middlesex, with all the goods in the manor, and to appoint reeves and ministers.

Southwark, 1 June 1347

566. QUITCLAIM by John de Bresey to Rigaud, bishop of Winchester and his successors of all right to the advowson or patronage of the church of Steeple Morden, co. Cambridge, diocese of Ely.
Witnesses: John de Scures, John de Ticheborne, James de Norton', knights, Richard le Clerc of Southwark, Robert de Hoe, Henry le Taillour Thomas Coleman', Ralph le Bruere, John Chalon', Robert le Chandeler et al.

Southwark, Wednesday, 29 September 1322

567. COMMISSION to audit the accounts of reeves and ministers, entrusted to Robert de Hungerford', W' de Farle, J' de Nublel', J'Payn and W' de Overton' in the manner as above.

Southwark, 18 October 1347

568. APPOINTMENT of Phelippe Danndely as surveyor and keeper of the episcopal parks, dealing with all concerning his office in the bishops pleasure.

Southwark, 16 January 1347

397   **569.** COMMISSION entrusted to Thomas de Pentelowe to be bailiff of Witney and keeper of the manors of Adderbury, Brightwell, and Harwell, at the bishop's pleasure.
Similar commission to John Elys to be bailiff and keeper of Wargrave, West Wycombe, Merton and Ivinghoe.
A third commissions for Reginald Forest to be constable of the castle of Farnham and keeper of the manors of Esher and Southwark.

Southwark, 17 November 1348

570. RECEIPT of the final account from John de Nubbeleye, treasurer of Wolvesey, for the receipts and expenditure during his time as treasurer up to 30 September, except for silver vases etc. which he received by indenture from the bishop and William de Meone, the wardrobe. So that he will be answerable in the next account for £376 6s. ¼d. in arrears. The bishop is satisfied with this account and acquits the said John and his heirs, save for the £376 6s. ¼d. and the vases.

Farnham, 7 January 1349

571. CONFIRMATION CHARTER from the bishop to John de Saxlingham and Cecilia his wife of all the tenements which Henry, his predecessor, had granted to Matilda, widow of Philip de Horsham, in the manor of

Havant, which came into the bishop's hands by surrender of Thomas de Aspale and John de Saxlingham; tenements which John and Cecilia hold by fine in the bishop's court, for life, rendering annually at the court of Brockhampton 8s. 6d. at the customary times, paying suit of court in the said manor. All to revert to the bishop at their death.

Farnham, 10 January 1349

572. APPOINTMENT of Richard de Wyke as bailiff and keeper of the franchises in the county of Southampton.

Esher, 10 June 1349

573. MEMORANDUM that John de Hanlegh' was appointed bailiff of Downton.

Southwark, 1 November 1350

574. MEMORANDUM: Robert Seint Manifee appointed constable of Farnham.

Esher, 26 December 1350

575. COMMISSION to Symon de Clere to be bailiff for the county of Southampton, to maintain the rights and franchises.

No date

576. MEMORANDUM: Thomas de Passelewe appointed steward.

Farnham, 18 April 1354

and John Pain treasurer of Wolvesey.

28 April

and John des Roches constable of Taunton and Roger Gervais bailiff of Meon.

28 April

398 **577.** APPOINTMENT of William atte Consolde as bailiff of the soke of Winchester, to hold courts, to collect rents and amercements; also in the county of Southampton. To render account for both.

Southwark, 2 November 1356

578. APPOINTMENT of Thomas de Hungerford as bailiff of Downton.

Southwark, 2 November 1356

579. APPOINTMENT of Walter Noht, rector of Michelmersh, to be treasurer and receiver of Wolvesey, to give acquittances and tallies in the bishop's name.

Southwark, 28 April 1358

580. APPOINTMENT of Walter Noht as bailiff of Waltham.

Southwark, 28 April 1358

581. TWO APPOINTMENTS William de Consold' to be constable of the castle of Farnham and John de Alresford to be bailiff of East Meon.

30 June 1358

582. COMMISSION to John de Ingepenne and Thomas de Pentelowe to audit all the crown pleas and dues for transgression at St Giles' Fair.

Southwark, 28 August 1359

583. APPOINTMENT of N' de Kaerwent as *hospicius* and Thomas de Pentelowe as steward of episcopal lands and Philip de Upton' clerk to audit the accounts of ministers and reeves.

Southwark, 3 October 1359

584. APPOINTMENT of William de Consold' as bailiff of Sutton, as also of East Meon; of Thomas le Warn' to be bailiff of the liberty of the bishopric in the county of Southampton and the soke of Winchester.

Sutton, 7 December 1359

585. APPOINTMENT of Walter de Shawe as bailiff of Wintney.

Southwark, 12 January 1360

586. APPOINTMENT of Thomas de Pentelewe as steward of the lands of the bishop and of John de Ingepenn' to audit all the pleas arising at St Giles' Fair.

Farnham, 10 August 1360

587. APPOINTMENT of Richard Herdewik' as bailiff of the manor of Coxwell.

Farnham, 7 January 1361

588. APPOINTMENT of Roger de Manyngford' to be bailiff of Downton.

Southwark, 9 November 1362

589. APPOINTMENT of William de Somerford' to be bailiff of Clere.

6 January 1363

399   **590.** MANDATE FROM KING EDWARD to the bishop to summon to appear before the justices at Westminster in the octave of Trinity, Walter de Kemeseye, late parson of the church of Patney, clerk, to respond to Thomas Hamond' of Faringdon, on the plea that he should render him 11 *robas* which are in arrears from an annual payment of 1 *roba* owing to Thomas. The sheriffs of London have informed the justices at Westminster that he is a clerk and holds no lay fee in their bailliwick.

Westminster, J' de Stonere, 20 May 1346

Walter de Kemeseye, lately parson at Patney, now vicar of Milford, clerk, has been ordered by the bishop to appear.

591. MANDATE to summon the prior of Bisham, parson of the church of Kingsclere to appear before the justices at Westminster in the octave of

Trinity, to respond to the abbot of Hyde on the plea that he should repay him 2,100 lb. of wax, arrears from an annual payment of 100 lb. of wax. The sheriff of Southampton informed the justices at Westminster within the fortnight of Easter that the prior is a clerk, holding no lay fee in his bailiwick.

Westminster, J' de Stonore, 17 May 1346

The bishop has ordered him to appear.

592. MANDATE to the bishop to raise £18 from the ecclesiastical goods of Walter de Kemeseye, vicar of Milford. To have this sum before the justices at Westminster in the fortnight of Michaelmas, to render to Peter de Burton', John de Claverle and Thomas de Kemcseye—sum which the said Walter admitted before the justices at Westminster on the morrow of St Edmund, king (20 November) 1342, that he owed to Peter, John and Thomas. He was due to have repaid half at St Peter's Chains (1 August) next and the second half at the Easter following. This has not been paid. The sheriff of Wilts. has informed the justices that Walter is a clerk with no lay fee from which the money can be raised.

Westminster, J' de Stonore, 16 May 1346

Walter de Kemeseye has no ecclesiastical goods in the said vicarage from which the money, or part of it, could be raised.

593. MANDATE to cite Henry de Lym, parson of Newton (Valence), testamentary executor of Thomas West, clerk, to appear at Westminster in the octave of Trinity, to respond to the prior of Bisham Montagu, executor of the will of William de Monteacuto, late earl of Salisbury, on the plea that he, with Richard de Farnhull' and Ralph de Tangele, coexecutors with Henry for the will of Thomas, should repay him 100 marks which he unjustly retains, as it is alleged. The sheriff of Southampton informed the justices in the Easter fortnight that the said Henry is a clerk, having no lay fee in his bailiwick.

Westminster, J' de Stonore, 9 May 1346

The bishop has cited Henry de Lym, parson of Newton to appear.

594. SIMILAR MANDATE. As Bernard Brocas, *contrarotulator* of Nicholas versus maris and Antony versus maris, is a beneficed clerk in the diocese of Winchester, holding no lay fee wherein he could be distrained, as the sheriffs of Surrey and Sussex informed the exchequer at Easter last, it is now asked whether he has ecclesiastical goods in the diocese. The bishop is to cite him to appear before the barons of the exchequer in the octave of Trinity to hand over to the exchequer the counter-rolls of the said Nicholas and Antony, viz. of Antony for the years 1338, 1339, 1340 1341, and of Nicholas for the year 1342, as well as the books and registers containing the receipts of the customs on wine in the fort (*castro*) of Bordeaux, details which Bernard is said to hold; to do and receive what concerns his office as *contrarotulator*. The exchequer is much surprised that there has been no response to the brief already addressed to the bishop, nor to a second, as requested.

Westminster, R' de Sedyngton', 30 May 1346

Bernard Brocaz, clerk, is beyond the seas in the king's service continually. The bishop has sequestrated his ecclesiastical goods, which should be with the exchequer at the time and place stated.

400 **595.** MANDATE FROM THE KING. The bishop, by reason of his recent elevation to the see, is to grant an annual pension to some clerk of the king's nomination, until the bishop shall have found him some benefice. The king proposes Alan de Kyllum.

Porchester, 26 May 1346

596. MANDATE to cite before the justices at Westminster during the octave of St John Baptist (24 June), William Inge, archdeacon of Surrey, on the plea that he should repay to William, bishop of Winchester, 240 marks which are in arrears from the annual pension of 20 marks. The sheriff of Surrey had informed the justices in the octave of Trinity that William Inge was a clerk holding no lay fee in his bailiwick.

Westminster, R' Hillary, 22 June 1346

597. MANDATE TO THE BISHOP. By inspection of the exchequer rolls it appears that the abbot of Hyde, as collector of the triennial tenth granted by the clergy to the king in 1342, in his account for the archdeaconry of Winchester, was debited with 13s. 4d. for the vicarage of Portsmouth; and for the tenth granted in 1344, the first year of the triennial tenth 13s. 4d. for the same vicarage and 14s. for the vicarage of Milford; and in his account for the second year of the same tenth:

13s. 4d. for the said vicarage of Portsmouth
40s. for the vicarage of Milford
10s. for the church of Morestead
4¾d. for the pension of the church of St Peter Whitebread
1d. for the pension of the church of St Michael in Jewry
10s. for the church of West Dean
10s. 8d. for the vicarage of Micheldever
£4 for the church of Cheriton
16d. for the pension in the church of Yarmouth
13s. 4d. for the church of Farlington
28s. for the church of Dogmersfield
5s. for the vicarage of Porchester
12s. 8d. for the church of Blendworth
3s. 4d. for the pension in the church of Newnham
5s. 4d. for the church of Crux Easton, and
26s. 8d. for the church of Combe

These sums have not yet been paid to the collector. The bishop is to enquire whether these moneys have in the meantime been paid, and if so to send them without delay to the collector. The defaulters are to be ordered to appear at the exchequer in Westminster, the morrow of

Michaelmas, to receive what justice shall demand. What has been done will be clearly set out for the use of the Treasurer and his Barons.

Westminster, R' de Sedyngton', 6 July 1346

Wedged in between the items is a list of the payments received, which is identical with the above, except for the vicarage of Portsmouth, which only pays 2s. and of Milford 24s., which have been paid to the abbot of Hyde. John de Draiton, guardian of the priory of Sherborne for the duration of the war, exempts himself by letters from the king.

598. MANDATE to the bishop to have the £24 10s. raised from the ecclesiastical goods of Walter de Kemeseye, late parson of Patney, before the justices at Westminster in the octave of Michaelmas, to hand the money over to Bartholomew, son of Humphrey de Merden'. In the king's court before the justices, Bartholomew won his case against Walter. Mandate further that from the ecclesiastical goods of the said Walter, to take 10 marks to be paid in the presence of the justices to Bartholomew towards the 12 marks adjudicated to him in damages. The sheriff of Wilts. informed the justices that the said Walter held no lay fee in his bailiwick from which the money could be raised.

Westminster, J' de Stonore, 16 May 1346

There are no ecclesiastical goods of Walter de Kemeseye from which the money or part of it could be raised.

401 **599.** MANDATE TO THE BISHOPS CONCERNING ALIEN RELIGIOUS in England. These had been ordered to attend in person or by attorney the king's council, the morrow of St Laurence (August 10) to contribute to an aid for the war against France, an annual tenth of their spiritual and temporal goods, to be paid at Martinmas. Those who did not accept are to be distrained: the rector of Whippingham. His goods are not to be touched until further orders. He is to appear before the barons of the exchequer, on the morrow of Michaelmas to explain why he should not pay.

Westminster, R' de Sedington, 1346

The bishop has distrained the goods of Michael, rector of Whippingham.

600. EXECUTION OF THE KING'S MANDATE FOR A PARLIAMENT. From the bishop to the prior of St Swithun's of Winchester. The king's council has recommended that parliament should be summoned concerning the war, affairs beyond the sea, the defence of the realm and other matters, on the Monday after the Nativity of the Virgin Mary (Sept.8). He requests the presence of the prior and archdeacon with one representative of the chapter, two procurators for the clergy with full powers to act.

Windsor, Lionel, the king's son, 30 July 1346

601. MANDATE to M. Adam de Wanbergh' in the absence of the official, to publish the summons to parliament to those whom it concerns.

602. MANDATE to cite before the justices at Westminster, in the octave of Michaelmas, M. John de Salisbire, parson of the church of Warnford, clerk, to respond to the prior of Bisham Montagu, executor testamentary of William de Monteacuto, late earl of Salisbury, why he has not rendered an account of the time when he received moneys for the earl. The sheriff of Berks. has informed the justices in the octave of Trinity that the said John is a beneficed clerk in the diocese of Winchester, having no lay fee in his bailiwick.

Westminster, R' Hillary, 1346

John de Salesbur' clerk has been cited to appear.

402 **603.** MANDATE to cite Philip de Redynge to appear before the justices at Westminster in the fortnight of Michaelmas. As parson of Michelmershe he is to respond to Richard of Netherhavene for 60s., the arrears of a rent of 6s. 8d. The sheriff of Southampton has informed the justices that he is a clerk having no lay fee in his bailiwick.

Westminster, R' Hillary, 30 June 1346

Philip de Redynge has been cited to appear.

604. MANDATE to cite before the justices at Westminster in the octave of Michaelmas Nicholas Talemach' parson of the prebendal church of Wherwell, clerk, to respond to John Froylle, chaplain, and John Pavy, clerk, testamentary executors of Hugh Pavy, late parson of Itchen, to pay them £12 unjustly retained. The sheriff of Southampton has informed the justices that Nicholas is a clerk with no lay fee in his bailiwick.

Westminster, R' Hillary, 5 July 1346

Nicholas Talemach' clerk has been cited to appear.

605. MANDATE to cite to appear before the justices at Westminster in the octave of Michaelmas John de Colonia, parson of the church of Lambeth, to respond to William le Clerc, citizen and tapisser (*tapiciarius*) of London, testamentary executor of Richard atte Sterre, late citizen of London, on the plea that he should render him £32 4s. 6d. unjustly withheld. The sheriff of London has informed the justices that John is a clerk, with no lay fee in his bailiwick.

Westminster, J' de Stonore, 26 June 1346

John de Colonia has been ordered to appear.

606. MANDATE to cite before the justices at Westminster within 3 weeks of Michaelmas William de Herlaston, parson of the chapel of Yarmouth, to respond to Walter Waleys, parson of Shalfleet, on the plea that he pay the arrears from an annual rent of 13s. 4d. due to him. The sheriff of Southampton has informed the justices that William is a clerk, holding no lay fee in his bailiwick.

Westminster, R' Hillary, 7 July 1346

He has been ordered to appear.

607. BRIEF FROM THE KING CONCERNING ALIENS entrusted to Adam de Wambergh', commissary, requiring the names of all aliens holding benefices in the diocese; whether they are in residence or not. The information is to be sent before Monday after St Edward, king (5 January), or at the latest on the Monday.
Westminster, Lionel the king's son, guardian of England, 15 September 1346

The commissary is to draw up lists for the archdeaconry of Winchester and send to the bishop by the date set out.
Southwark, 21 September 1346

608. SIMILAR MANDATE addressed to the official of the archdeacon of Surrey.

609. ALIENS HOLDING BENEFICES
Prior of Hayling, rector there, annual value 120 marks.
403 Fr. Blaise Doublel', prior of Carisbrooke, rector, 120 mks and of Godshill, 100 mks.
Fr. William, prior of St Helens, rector, 30 mks.
Fr. Michael, prior of Ellingham, rector, 18 mks.
M. Philip, rector of the church of Chilbolton, 35 mks.
Robert, rector of Abbots Ann, 10 mks.
William, rector of ½ the church of Weyhill, 11 mks.
Prior of Andover, rector, 110 mks, at intervals (*interdum*).
Peter, rector of Silchester, 16 mks.
Michael, rector of Whippingham, 36 mks.
Matthias de Valenciis, rector of Wootton, 20 mks.
John Aundelers, rector of Buckland, 20 mks, by turns (*per vices*).
Almaric de Ponte Lacco, rector of Beddington, 40 mks.
Giles, rector of Nutfield, 18 mks.
—resident in the aforesaid benefices.
M. Reymund Pelegrani, rector of Crondal with chapel annexed, £80; is also *custos* of St Cross, Winchester, £7, to which are appropriated and annexed the churches of Fareham, Whitchurch, Hurstbourne, [St Mary] Bourne and Twyford, which are not assessed.
Prior of Wilmington, rector of ½ the church of Weyhill (as above) 11 mks.
Raymund de Fargis, cardinal, dean of Salisbury, holds the church of Godalming, 55 mks.
M. Bernard Brocaz, on the king's service in Gascony, rector of St Nicholas, Guildford, 25 mks.
Prior of Ogbourne, rector of the church of Combe, 20 mks.
Prior of Monk Sherborne, now in the king's hands, rector, 17 mks; he also has the appropriated churches of Bramley, 35 mks, of Upton [Grey], 13½ mks and of Chineham, 11 mks.
Abbot and convent of Lyre receive pensions and tithes from various parishes in the Isle of Wight, by estimation £54 13s. 4d.

Prior of Hamble, rector, 6½ mks and rector of Hound, 10 mks.

M. Bernard Systre, rector of West Meon, 30 mks.

—non-resident in the aforesaid benefices.

The cardinal treasurer of York receives pensions and portions in various churches and places in the archdeaconry of Winchester, £8 11s. 8d.

Prior of the Hospital of St John of Jerusalem holds the church of Woodcott, 6½ mks.

Prior of Bermondsey holds in the archdeaconry of Surrey the church of Warlingham with the chapel of Chelsham 27 mks and the appropriated church of Camberwell, 24 mks.

Same prior receives annual pensions in the churches of St Mary Magdalen, Bermondsey, 2 mks; in St George, Southwark, 20s.; in the church of Rotherhithe, 20s. and in the church of Beddington, 100s.

Prior of Lewes receives an annual pension in the church of St Olave, Southwark, as much as 6 mks.

Abbot of Bec receives from the church of Streatham a pension of 100s. and in the same church a portion of £4.

Same abbot receives in the church of Woodmansterne a portion assessed at 30s.

Abbot of Grestain receives from the aforesaid church of Streatham 4s.

610. PROHIBITION CONCERNING THE ARCHDEACON OF SURREY CITED BY THE BISHOP. The king to the archbishop of Canterbury. The bishop of Winchester had impleaded William Inge before the justices at Westminster on account of 240 marks, arrears of an annual pension of 20 marks. The king had ordered the sheriff to have the archdeacon appear, but the latter did not appear at the bishop's summons. The king orders the sheriff to distrain the bishop for this non-appearance, in his lands and goods in that bailiwick. The bishop is to make his archdeacon appear to hear the judgement on his default. The sheriff had distrained to bishop to the value of £15; according to custom the bishop had distrained the goods of the archdeacon to the value of £15. It was reported that the archdeacon had schemed to avoid accepting the mandate, seeking to summon the bishop before the court of christianity for sequestrating his revenue and fruits in the archdeaconry, against the laws of England. The king orders the bishop to refrain from acting in any way to retard the execution of the brief *Distringas*.

Windsor, Lionel the king's son, 10 November 1346

404   **611.** SEQUESTRATION OF THE ARCHDEACON'S GOODS as demanded by the brief *Distringas*. The bishop to M. Thomas de Enham and Richard de Hyda, rector of Farnham, diocese of London and the clergy of his own diocese. Recently by his brief to the sheriff of Surrey, the king ordered him to have William Inge appear before the justices at Westminster at a certain date to answer the plea that he should render to the bishop 240 marks, the arrears of his annual pension. The sheriff informed the justices that William was a clerk without any lay fee in his bailiwick, that he was the archdeacon of Surrey. After much altercation it was settled that the bishop should order him to appear. The bishop received the mandate from the king for his appearance in the fortnight of St John Baptist.

Westminster, 22 June 1346

account of the war, and to assemble the clergy of the diocese to underline the gravity of the situation. Then to inform the council in London.

Calais, 28 December 1346

620. SIMILAR LETTER to the bishop or his vicar-general. As regards the subsidy of the biennial tenth granted by the clergy of the Canterbury province at its last convocation, in St Paul's London, since the date of payment is far ahead, and in view of the urgency beyond the seas for the defence of the Church and Kingdom, the king requests the bishop to summon the clergy of his diocese and there to advance the date for the payment of the subsidy.

Eltham, Lionel the king's son, 18 December 1346

407   **621.** SIMILAR LETTER from the archbishop of Canterbury. The king in his armed struggle with Philip de Valois is in urgent need, He requests the bishop to urge the clergy to advance the payment which they have already granted.

Lambeth, 28 January

622. ENQUIRY INTO BASTARDY. addressed to M. Adam de Wambergh'. The bishop has received a brief from the king concerning John Gerberd' junior, who in the king's court before the justices at Westminster, claimed from Thomas de Chisenhale 1 acre of land with appurtenances in Broughton, as his right and inheritance, which Thomas was holding unjustly, as by grant of John Gerberd' senior. This was after the first crossing of king Henry, the present king's great-grandfather, into Gascony, as he says. Thomas came to the court and objected that John Gerberd' junior cannot be the heir because he is a bastard. To which John replied in court that he was legitimate and not bastard. And since the cognizance of such a cause belongs to ecclesiastical jurisdiction, the king asks the bishop to assemble those who have cause to be called and to discover the truth, forwarding the conclusions to Westminster.

Westminster, J' de Stonore, 12 February 1347

Order to set up an enquiry with Thomas and others.

623. RETURN OF THE BRIEF CONCERNING BASTARDY. To the justices, replying to the brief as to whether John Gerberd' junior is legitimate or bastard, Thomas de Chisenhale, named in the brief, and others concerned, met for an enquiry and John Gerberd' is evidently legitimate.

Southwark, 11 April 1347

624. MANDATE from the king to the bishop, who is to levy from the ecclesiastical goods and benefices the following:
from Bernard Brocaz, parson of the church of Guildford, for the pardon of his transgression in acquiring a lay fee for himself and his successors, 40s.
from the rector of the church of Godalming, for the first year of the triennial tenth granted by the clergy in 1337, 73s. 3d.

to have the said moneys at the exchequer by the morrow of Easter.

Westminster, R' de Sadyngton, 28 February 1347

408   **625.** MANDATE to have Nicholas Andele *modicum* parson of Ovington, near Alresford, before the justices at Westminster in the three weeks of Easter, to respond to William de Walton', rector of the scholars of Maidstone, to repay him £30 owing and unjustly witheld. The sheriff of Southampton has informed the justices that Nicholas is a clerk holding no lay fee in his bailiwick.

Westminster, J' de Stonore, 9 February 1348

626. BRIEF CONCERNING THE HOSPITALLERS, to the archdeacon of Winchester. The bishop has received from the king a request to know the true assessment of all ecclesiastical persons. The prior and brethren of the Hospital of St John of Jerusalem hold in England appropriated benefices which belong to the Hospitallers and also others which had belonged to the military order of the Temple; the king requires details of these benefices and also to know what pensions or portions or other revenues they receive in the diocese, by what title, in what way. The bishop is asked to search his registers, and those of his predecessors and send the findings by the octave of Easter.

Lionel, guardian of England, 26 February 1347

The archdeacon is to put together the information required and send it before the feast of St Ambrose (4 April).

Southwark, 12 March 1347

627. MANDATE to order Henry Lym parson of the church of Newton [Valence] clerk, to appear before the justices at Westminster in the three weeks after Easter to as answer the charge that as testamentary executor of Thomas West, he with Richard de Farnhull', Ralph Tangele and Nicholas Wyli co-executors, should repay to Henry Peverel, knight, £20 unjustly retained. The sheriff of Southampton has informed the justices that Henry de Lim is a clerk with no lay fee in his bailiwick.

Westminster, J' de Stonore, 28 November 1346

Henry de Lym has been ordered to appear.

628. MANDATE that no procurations be levied or paid for the cardinals. In the last parliament at Westminster, it was ordained that no payments be paid to the cardinals nuncios in France since their passage from England by way of procurations. The king understands that Anibaldus, bishop of Tusculanus and Stephen, cardinal priest of SS John and Paul, who have passed over to France, still have their procurators in England, armed with bulls and letters sent out to the prejudice and injury of the kingdom. The procurators without licence are acting against parliament

409   and its proclamations by bringing such documents clandestinely, without showing them at the ports. The orders from parliament are to be strictly obeyed: no one under pretext of these bulls is to levy any procurations until further notice.

Reading, Lionel, the king's son, 12 April 1347

629. TESTIMONIAL LETTER that all cases concerning ecclesiastical pensions and dues from churches should be the concern of the king's court. So many of the rights of the king have been assailed and withdrawn from his judgement. To know whether questions concerning annual pensions and rents are to be decided by the king's council with legal experts have been convoked; they agreed that pensions and rents, whether held by prescriptive right, or by special grant, have always been referred by custom and right to the king's court, as the records clearly show.

Reading, Lionel the king's son, 10 April 1347

630. MANDATE from the king to the bishop to levy from the ecclesiastical goods or benefices of Adam de Bridlyngton' clerk, £4 2d. owing from advance payments made to him at the receipt of the exchequer for the years 1333 to 1340, so that the said moneys may reach Westminster on the morrow of Trinity.

Westminster, R' de Sadyngton' 20 April 1347

410

631. MANDATE to the bishop to levy from the ecclesiastical goods of Walter de Kemeseye, lately parson of Patney £24 19s. and to have this sum at Westminster within the octave of Trinity, to restore the sum to Bartholomew son of Humphrey de Merden', as the king's court had ordered to be repaid. Also from the goods of the same Walter to raise 10 marks to lay before the justices at the same date, to pay to Bartholomew out of the 12 marks adjudicated to him in the same court, for damages by reason of witholding the debt. The sheriff of Wiltshire has informed the justices that Walter is a clerk, holding no lay fee in his bailiwick from which the money could be raised.

Westminster, J' de Stonore, 13 February 1347

Walter de Kemeseye has no goods from which the sum or even part of it could be raised, as far as has yet been discovered.

632. MANDATE to levy from the ecclesiastical goods of Walter de Kemeseye, vicar of the church of Milford £18 and to have that sum before the justices at Westminster within the fortnight of Easter, to repay Peter de Burton', John de Claverlee and Thomas de Kemeseye, which Walter had acknowledged he owed them, at Westminster on the morrow of St Edmund (Nov. 20) 1342, when he undertook to repay half at St Peter's Chains and half at Easter, which he has not yet done. The sheriff of Wiltshire has informed the justices that Walter is a clerk with no lay fee from which the money could be raised.

Westminster, J' de Stonore, 13 February 1347

633. DEBTS OWING TO THE EXCHEQUER. Inspection has shown that the abbot of Waverley, formerly collector of the triennial tenth granted by the clergy in 1344, in his account for the third year is debited with:
23s. 4d. for the church of Shere,
8s. for the vicarage of Woking,
13s. 4d. for the church of Walton,
5s. for the vicarage of Reigate,

8s. 8d. for the church of Buckland and

3s. 4d. for the church of Streatham, sums still outstanding. The bishop is asked to raise these sums from ecclesiastical goods and benefices, to be paid to the abbot, having first asked for a settlement. If they cannot show acquittances, they are to appear at the exchequer in Westminster in the fortnight of Trinity.

R' de Sadyngton', 16 May 1347

634. COMMISSION as steward of the episcopal lands. Nomination of Thomas de Hungerford' to be responsible for the temporal affairs of the bishop's lands, during the bishop's pleasure.

Castle of Farnham, 15 November 1365

411

635. MANDATE AS TO CLERICAL TENTHS OUTSTANDING. Inspection of the exchequer rolls has shown that the abbot of Hyde, collector of the clerical tenths granted in 1342 for the archdeaconry of Winchester, is debited with:

13s. 4d. for the vicarage of Portsmouth, and for the triennial tenth last granted 40s. for the same vicarage in the two accounts, in the third year of the triennial tenth:

6s. 8d. for the vicarage of Peniton,

20s. for the vicarage of Milford,

5s. for the church of Morstead,

28s. for the church of Weston,

106s. for the church of St Mary, Southampton with its chapel,

2s. 6d. for the church of Farleigh.

These sums have not been paid. The bishop is to raise the money from ecclesiastical goods and benefices and pay the collector without delay, unless they can produce acquittances. To appear at the exchequer in the octave of St John Baptist (24 June).

Westminster, R' de Sadyngton, 2 June 1347

636. EXECUTION OF THE ROYAL BRIEF CONCERNING THE TENTH, to the abbot of Hyde. The bishop has received a letter from the king concerning the needs of the war, and reminds him that, at the last convocation at St Paul's, London, a tenth was granted for two years, to be paid at the Assumption (15 August) and at St Martin (11 November). The bishop is to nominate a suitable collector for this biennial tenth, informing the barons of the exchequer.

Reading, Lionel, the king's son, 14 May 1347

The bishop nominates the abbot of Hyde.

Southwark, 27 June 1347

637. SIMILAR MANDATE for the abbot of Waverley for the archdeaconry of Surrey.

638. MANDATE to levy from the ecclesiastical goods of Walter de Kemeseye, lately parson of Patney, the sum of £24 10s. and to have the same before the justices at Westminster in the octave of Michaelmas, to pay Bartholomew son of Humphrey de Merden', which sum Bartholomew was awarded by the king's court. Also from the same source to find 10 marks toward the 12 awarded in damages. The sheriff of Wiltshire has informed the justices that Walter is a clerk, with no lay fee from which the sum could be raised.

412   Westminster, J' de Stonore, 25 June 1347

The goods of Walter, now perpetual vicar of Milford, have been sequestrated to the value of 5s.; purchasers have not yet been found; other goods at present have not been discovered.

639. MANDATE CONCERNING SEQUESTRATION OF GOODS. The sheriff of Southampton at the exchequer on the morrow of Michaelmas, declared that the prior of Bisham, clerk, holds no lay fee from which money can be raised. The bishop is to raise from his ecclesiastical goods 200 marks towards a debt of £400, which the prior recognized at the exchequer, 18 February 1345, that he owed to William de la Pole, knight, senior, sum which he was due to repay within a fortnight of Michaelmas next, according to the records, and this has not yet been paid. The bishop is to see that the money is at the exchequer on the morrow of All Souls (November 2) to be paid to William.

Westminster, R' de Sadyngton, 5 October 1347

The bishop has sequestered goods of the prior of Bisham, rector of Highclere, to the value of £20, for which purchasers have not yet been found.

640. MANDATE to cite Nicholas Magor, parson of the church of Dibden, to appear before the justices at Westminster, to answer Richard de Farnhull' and Henry de Lym, testimonary executors of Thomas West, on the plea that he should render to them and to Oliver de Slynton, William de Hastinges, John Wake, William West and Nicholas Lamberd', M. Thomas de Upton, William de Greneuil' and Ralph de Tangele, co-executors with the aforesaid Richard and Henry, of the aforesaid will— to present a reasonable account for the time when he was receiver of the moneys of Thomas West. The sheriff of Southampton informed the justices during the octave of Trinity that Nicholas Magor is a clerk with no lay fee in his bailiwick.

Westminster, J' de Stonore, 20 June 1347

Nicholas Magor has been ordered to appear.

641. MANDATE TO LEVY FOR DEBTS. Since the rector of Crondal and Peter de Hope, parson of the church of Alverstoke, beneficed clerks, have no lay fee from which debts can be repaid, as Thomas de Aspale, sheriff of Southampton, declared at the exchequer, the bishop is to raise the money from their ecclesiastical goods and rectories in the diocese—separately: £8 13s. 4d. from the rector of Crondal, owing from the first year of the clerical tenth granted in 1344, 60s. from Peter, owing for a fine for transgression.

The money is to be paid at the exchequer within the fortnight of St Martin.

Westminster, R' de Sadyngton, 10 October 1347

Goods of Peter de Hop', rector of Alverstoke, have been sequestered to the value of 60s., for which as yet there are no purchasers. The rector of Crondal has settled his debt to the king at the exchequer.

642. BRIEF FOR PARLIAMENT. For urgent business parliament is summoned for the morrow of St Hilary (13 January). Prelates and magnates are to appear; the bishop with the cathedral prior and one representative of the chapter, the archdeacons, two procurators for the clergy. To give counsel for the kingdom. The parliament is not for raising an aid or tallage, but to secure justice for wrongs and injuries suffered.

Westminster, the King, 13 November 1347

413 **643.** MANDATE CONCERNING FALSE MEASURES. Robert, bishop of Chichester, in his return to the exchequer on the morrow of Michaelmas last, stated that Robert de Watford' clerk, beneficed at Dunsfold, diocese of Winchester, holds no lay fee from which £10 can be raised on account of fines for using false measures on divers occasions in Kent and in Huntingdon. The bishop is ordered to raise the sum of £10 from the ecclesiastical goods of the rectory or elsewhere and send it to the exchequer for the morrow of St Hilary (13 January).

Westminster, R' de Sadyngton, 5 October 1347

644. MANDATE several times repeated, to levy from the ecclesiastical goods of Walter de Kemeseye, lately parson of Patney £24 5s., to be at Westminster in the fortnight of St Hilary, to render to Bartholomew, son of Humphrey de Merden', out of the £24 10s. which Bartholomew was awarded by the court. Also, to raise from ecclesiastical goods and to be paid in at the same time, 5s. which the bishop has retained from the goods of Walter. And, repeating earlier mandates, to raise 10 marks to be presented at the same term, towards the 12 marks awarded to Bartholomew as damages. The sheriff of Wiltshire has declared Walter to be a clerk with no lay fee.

Westminster, J' de Stonore, 18 October 1347

The bishop ordered goods to the value of 5s. to be sequestered from Walter, perpetual vicar of Milford. He sends by the bearer 3s. 4d. in gold from the goods for which purchasers have been found.

645. MANDATE CONCERNING BISHAM PRIORY. As the sheriff of Southampton declared at the exchequer on the morrow of Michaelmas last that the prior of Bisham is a clerk with no lay fee from which money could be raised, the bishop is to raise from the goods of the prior £50 towards the £500 out of a debt of £2,400, which Thomas the prior, Edward de Monte Acuto and Simon, bishop of Ely, before the barons of the exchequer, 1 June 1345, recognized they together owed to Berard de la Bret, knight—£500 which the same prior was due to have paid at St

John Baptist (24 June) 1346, as is recorded at the exchequer. This has not yet been paid, as Reginald de Pontibus and Joan his wife, sister of Berard and testimonary executrix of the same Berard, William de Sancii, lord of Pomeriis (*Pommiers*), Gerard de Podio, licenciate in law, Peter de Arbussaco, preceptor of Arberiis (*Arveyres*), Fr Arnald Salmerii, guardian of the Friars Minor of Rimontio (*Rions*), Reymund Bovis, canon of Bartholio (*Vertheuil*) and Peter del Bers, called 'Peyronomii', co-executors of the said Joan of the will of the said Berard, all declare. So that the said £50 may be at the exchequer in the fortnight of the Purification (2 February) to be paid to the executors.

Westminster, R' de Sadyngton, 6 December 1347

No goods of the prior of Bisham have been found from which the sum could be raised, in spite of our diligent efforts.

646. MANDATE CONCERNING BISHAM. Fr Thomas, prior of Bisham Montagu, 22 August 1344 recognized in chancery that he and his convent were in debt to Walter Wyvill', treasurer of Salisbury cathedral, to the sum of 1,000 marks, towards which he would pay
    400 marks in the octave of Michaelmas next
    200 marks in the octave of Easter
    200 marks in the octave of Michaelmas following
    200 marks in the octave of Christmas.
From the rolls it is clear he has not paid. The sheriff of Southampton has been ordered to raise 300 marks from the lands and goods in his bailiwick, to be at the chancery in the octave of St Martin (11 November) to pay to Robert, bishop of Salisbury and M. William de Weston, executors of Walter, now deceased. The same sheriff informed the justices that Thomas is a clerk with a benefice in the diocese of Winchester, but without a lay fee in his bailiwick. The bishop is ordered to raise without delay 300 marks from his ecclesiastical goods, to be at the chancery at the Purification next. Order also to the sheriffs of Berkshire to raise 400 marks and of Buckingham, Somerset and Wiltshire each to raise 100 marks in their bailiwicks, and so complete the sum of 1,000 marks.

414

Westminster, the King, 8 December 1347

647. MANDATE to order Philip de la Wyle, late master of the hospital of St James, Westminster, to appear before the justices in the octave of St Hilary (13 January), to respond to the plea of Nicholas de Oxon' for arrears of £40 from an annual rent of 40s. The sheriff of Middlesex informed the justices that Philip is a clerk with no lay fee in his bailiwick.

Westminster, J' de Stonore, 24 November 1347

Philip de la Wyle is now rector of Michelmersh and has been ordered to appear.

648. MANDATE to raise from the ecclesiastical goods of Peter de Hope, parson of Alverstoke, the sum of 60s., which, at the king's orders, the bishop had sequestered according to his reply to the brief in the octave of St Martin last. Peter owes this as a fine for transgression, which is to be paid on the morrow of St Hilary.

Westminster, R' de Sadyngton, 28 November 1347

By virtue of the king's brief 60s. were raised and paid to the bishop.

649. MANDATE CONCERNING BISHAM. From both the ecclesiastical goods of the prior of Bisham, ordered to be sequestered to the value of £20 and still without purchasers (as declared to the barons of the exchequer the morrow of All Souls Day last) and also from the other goods and benefices in the diocese to raise 200 marks towards a debt of £400, which the prior acknowledged at the exchequer, 18 February 1345, he owed to William de la Pole, knight, senior; this debt he had promised to pay in the octave of Michaelmas, as is clear from the rolls. This has not been paid. The 200 marks are to be at the exchequer to be paid to William on the morrow of St Hilary.

Westminster, R' de Sadyngton, 8 December 1347

The sequestered goods raised 66s. 8d. towards the total of £20; this has been sent in gold. The remainder cannot now be raised because of the short time allowed and the lack of purchasers. Other goods of the said prior cannot be found at present.

650. MANDATE to raise from the ecclesiastical goods of Nicholas Talemache, parson of the prebendal church of Wherwell, clerk, £12 to be presented to the justices at Westminster in the octave of St Hilary (13 January), to be paid to John de Froille, chaplain, and John Pavy' clerk, executors of the will of Hugh Pavy', late parson at Itchen, which John and John had recovered from him in the court before the justices at Westminster. Also, mandate to raise 40s. and to be present at Westminster to pay the executors the damages adjudicated to them through witholding the debt—before John de Stonore, vigil of St James the Apostle (25 July) at Winchester.

Westminster, J' de Stonore, 10 November 1347

Goods to the value of £14 have been sequestrated; no purchasers have as yet been found.

651. BRIEF CONCERNING LIABILITY TO CLERICAL TAXATION. In the past, benefices not exceeding an assessment of 6 marks have not been taxed for clerical tenths, unless the benefices were either annexed to some prebend of dignity, or the clerics held other benefices elsewhere. The complain of John de Thresk', prebendary of the prebend of Itchen in the church of Nunnaminster, Winchester, that it is assessed at only 5 marks, has come to the bishop. Although his prebend is not annexed to another benefice or dignity, nor does he hold another benefice, the collectors demand both the triennial and the biennial tenth. Order to enquire since when John holds the prebend, whether it is annexed to another dignity, and whether he holds another benefice, in order to provide more information to the treasurer and barons.

Westminster, R' de Sadyngton, 25 February 1348

Full information is available. John holds the prebend since the penultimate day of November 1345 and holds it now; the prebend of Itchen is not annexed to any other benefice; John holds no other benefice in the diocese, or elsewhere as far as is known.

652. BRIEF CONCERNING THE ABBOT OF HYDE. Walter, abbot of Hyde, fr John Blaunkchival, fr Robert de Middelton', fr John Draycote, fr Roger Tyboud, fr Dominic de Basyngstok', fr Nicholas Ditton' and fr Peter de Bekford', all monks of Hyde, were summoned to answer the plea of John, prior of the Order of Preachers, London, and of fr Arnald de Lym, his *confrater*, that the monks assaulted fr Arnald at Westminster, struck him and wounded him, and from Monday next after the Epiphany 1344, imprisoned him for three days, against the peace of the realm. To which the abbot and monks declared that on the day of the said transgression, the said Arnald was a monk of Hyde, professed in that house, and they said they could prove this to the court. To which the prior and fr Arnald declared that, on the day of the said transgression, Arnald was a brother of the Order of Preachers, London, and professed in that Order, which they were prepared to prove. Since cognizance of such a case belonged to ecclesiastical jurisdiction, the bishop is to hold an enquiry and report by the fortnight of Easter.

Westminster, W' de Thorp', 15 February 1348

653. EXECUTION OF THE BRIEF entrusted to the bishop's official, who is to hold the enquiry.

Southwark.

416   **654.** RETURN OF THE BRIEF. At the enquiry it was found that fr Arnald Lym, at the date of the said transgression, was a monk of Hyde, professed in the Order of St Benedict.

655. MANDATE CONCERNING BISHAM. The sheriff of Southampton replied to the exchequer the morrow of Michaelmas last that the prior of Bisham is a clerk with no lay fee in his bailiwick. The bishop is again asked to raise from ecclesiastical goods in the diocese £50 to towards the £500 out of the debt of £2,400, in which Thomas, the prior, Edward de Monte Acuto and Simon the bishop of Ely in the king's court, before the barons of the exchequer, 1 June 1345, recognized that they were together indebted to Berard de la Bret, knight, and the said £50 were due from the prior at St John Baptist (24 June) 1346, as is clear from the rolls. This he has not yet paid, as Reginald de Pontibus and Joan his wife, sister of the said Berard and testimonary executrix of the same Berard [with others as named in 645] all declare. In order that the bishop will have the £50 at the exchequer on the morrow of Low Sunday (*clausum Pasche*) to pay to the executors.

Westminster, R' de Sadyngton, 22 February 1348

The prior of Bisham has no ecclesiastical goods in the diocese beyond those sequestrated at the instance of William de la Pole, knight.

656. MANDATE to order Nicholas de Flode, clerk, to appear before the justices at Westminster, to reply to the plea of John de Bradele of Alton, that he is witholding unjustly a certain charter. The sheriff of Southampton has declared Nicholas to be a clerk with no lay fee in his bailiwick.

Westminster, J' de Stonore, 8 February 1348

Nicholas has been ordered to appear.

657. MANDATE CONCERNING BISHAM, several times repeated, to raise from the ecclesiastical goods and benefices of the prior £50 towards the £500 of a debt of £2,400 which Thomas the prior, Edward de Monte Acuto and Simon bishop of Ely in the king's court recognized, 1 June 1345, they owed to Berard de la Bret, knight. These £50 the prior was due to pay at St John Baptist, 1346, according to the rolls. This he has not paid, as Reginald de Pontibus and Joan his wife, sister of Berard and executrix of the same Berard [with others as named in 645] declare. In order that the £50 may be at the exchequer in the octave of Trinity for payment to the executors.

Westminster, R' de Sadyngton, 10 May 1348

Goods to the value of £50 have been sequestrated, for which buyers have not yet been found. Other goods have not been discovered.

658. COMMISSION entrusted to William de la Putton' to be bailiff of Waltham, to guard the franchises, parks and lands of the manor, maintaining all its rights.

Waltham, 28 September 1346

417   **659.** MANDATE CONCERNING BISHAM, to raise both from the ecclesiastical goods of the prior lately sequestrated to the value of £16 13s. 4d., still without purchasers, as declared to the exchequer barons on the morrow of St Hilary last; and also from the goods and benefices in the diocese 195 marks toward the 200 marks in a debt of £400 declared at the exchequer 18 February 1345 as owing to William de la Pole, knight, senior, which had been due for settlement in the octave of Michaelmas, according to the rolls, and not yet paid. To have these 195 marks at the exchequer in the octave of Michaelmas, together with the 66s. 8d. lately raised from goods, for payment to the said William.

Westminster, R' de Sadyngton, 9 July 1348

660. MANDATE CONCERNING BISHAM, several times repeated, to raise both 100s. from the ecclesiastical goods of the prior, declared to the exchequer to have been sequestrated, but without purchasers, in the octave of St John Baptist last; as also £50 towards the £500 of the debt of £2,400 which prior Thomas, Edward de Monte Acuto and Simon bishop of Ely declared at the exchequer, 1 July 1345, to be owing to Berard de la Bret, knight; the prior was due to pay £400 at St John Baptist 1346 and has not yet paid, as Reginald de Pontibus and Joan his wife with others [as named in 645] co-executors with Joan declare. The £50 are to be at the exchequer in the octave of St Michaelmas for payment to the executors.

Westminster, R' de Sadyngton, 3 July 1348

661. MANDATE CONCERNING BISHAM. As Thomas, prior of Bisham Montagu in the chancery, 22 August 1344, admitted a debt to Walter de Wyville, treasurer of Salisbury cathedral, of 1,000 marks, of which he was to pay back 400 marks in the octave of Michaelmas, and 200 marks in the octave of Easter and in the octave of Michaelmas next following 200 marks and in the octave of Christmas 200 marks, according to the exchequer rolls and has not yet paid. Mandate, repeated, to raise 300 out of the 1,000 marks from his goods in the diocese without delay. To have the 300 marks at the exchequer in the octave of Michaelmas next to pay to Robert de Wyville, bishop of Salisbury, and William de Weston', executors of Walter, now deceased. Mandate also that the sheriff of Berkshire have 400 marks, the sheriff of Buckinghamshire and Wiltshire each to raise 100 marks from the lands and goods of the prior in their bailiwicks.

Westminster, the King, 8 July 1348

418 **662**. THE ORDINANCE OF LABOURERS AND BEGGARS. The bishop has received a brief from the king. A great number of people, especially of workmen and servants, have died in the pestilence; some seeing the straits of the masters and the scarcity of workmen, refuse to work except at an excessive wage; others prefer to beg rather than to earn their keep. Considering the grave lack of workers, especially in agriculture, the king with the prelates and nobility have decided that every man and woman in the realm, of whatever condition, in good health, under the age of 60, not engaged in trade or craftsmanship, not having ground of his own to till, nor required for the service of another—shall be bound to work for anyone who seeks to employ him and then receive wages or goods in kind which were customary in the district in 1346, or in the 5 or 6 preceding years, unless the masters prefer to accept them as tenants. Provided that they retain no more workers than is necessary. And if a man or woman refuses when required, if this be proved by two men before the sheriff or the constable of the town where this occurs, immediately he is to be locked up in the nearest gaol, kept in close custody, until it is certain that he will work, as laid down above. No one is to be taken into service at a higher wage than that prescribed, if he has not completed the term of his previous service, under pain of imprisonment. If such cases arise, they are to be dealt with in the king's court. If lords of estates or manors act contrary to these orders, then they are to appear before the wapentake or tithing or other court for a treble fine. If anyone had already taken into service a worker at a higher wage than here prescribed, he is not bound to pay the higher wage. Saddlers, skinners, tawers, shoemakers, tailors, smiths, carpenters, masons, tilers, boatmen, carters, and other traders or workers are not to receive for their work more than was customary in 1346 and the other years in that district. Anyone who receives more wages is to be committed to the nearest gaol. Butchers, fishmongers, innkeepers, brewers, bakers, poulterers and other dealers are to sell their produce at a reasonable price for the locality, so that these dealers will make a moderate profit, according as distance requires. Anyone who sells foodstuffs otherwise and is convicted shall pay twice the amount to the injured party; and the mayor and sheriff of townships, markets or ports are to deal with all who act contrary to these orders. Should the mayor and sheriff fail to carry out the instructions, then before the justices they shall pay three times the value of the goods sold to the injured party. And since many healthy beggars refuse to work as long as they can live on alms, spending their time in idleness and drinking, even in robbery and other misbehaviour, no one under pretext of charity is to give anything to those capable of work, so that they may be compelled to work for their living. The king asks that this ordinance be published in all churches and open places, and that the clergy at the same time encourage their parishioners to work, to keep the above ordinances as the urgency of the times demand. Also, to induce stipendary chaplains to be less exacting, to work for the agreed salary, under pain of suspension or interdict.

The King, Westminster, 18 June 1349

419 The bishop therefore orders the clergy to publish the brief in the archdeaconry of Winchester, on Sundays and feasts when there is the greatest concourse of people, and in the vulgar tongue; urging all rectors to encourage their people to work and keep the ordinances—and to control the avarice of certain chaplains in demanding higher salaries because of the lack of man-power through the plague; to appeal to them to be diligent in their service, to accept the customary stipend, under threat of ecclesiastical censure. The bishop should be informed of any such cases before St Peter's Chains (1 August) next.

Southwark, 25 June 1349

663. BRIEF CONCERNING BASTARDY. Before the justices at Westminster, Edward de Leye junior urged his claim to a messuage, 10 ac. land and 2 ac. meadow in Sparkford, as being his against Thomas de Shirborne. Thomas objected that as Edward was a bastard, he could not be heir, though Edward declared himself legitimate. As this concerns ecclesiastical jurisdiction, the bishop is ordered to ascertain the truth and to report.

Westminster, J' de Stonore, 10 October 1349

664. CERTIFICATE in reply, that after enquiry held in the presence of Thomas, Edward de Leye junior is declared legitimate.

Southwark, 18 February 1351

665. EXECUTION OF THE BRIEF CONCERNING THE BIENNIAL TENTH. The bishop informs the abbot of Hyde that the king has written that, at the last convocation of the clergy of the Canterbury province held at St Paul's in London, in view of the dangers imminent to the Church and the Realm and the expenses of the defence, a biennial tenth was granted, payable at the four terms of St Andrew (30 November), Nativity of St John Baptist for the first year, and the Purification (2 February) and Nativity of St John Baptist for the second year, as an aid, certified by

Simon archbishop of Canterbury. In response, mandate that certain persons shall be named as collectors for the first year in the archdeaconry of Winchester, whose names are to be sent to the chancellery.

The King, Tower of London, 1 September 1351

The bishop entrusts the whole matter to the abbot, reporting to the bishop before the Nativity of B. Mary (8 September).

Southwark, 18 September 1351

666. SIMILAR COMMISSION to the prior of Merton, under the same date, for the archdeaconry of Surrey.

420   **667.** CERTIFICATE with the names of the collectors in response to the brief: the abbot and convent of Hyde for the archdeaconry of Winchester and the prior and convent of Merton for that of Surrey—for the first year of the grant.

20 November

668. EXECUTION OF THE BRIEF ON BASTARDY. Recites no. 663 Mandate to the official to hold an enquiry into the day, the month and the year of the marriage between the father and mother of Edward de Leye junior; if it was solemnized, then by whom and in what place, in the presence of whom and the age of the said Edward, and the circumstances, in order to reach the truth. Also, to state whether the said Thomas de Schirborne was present or contumaciously absent. To report clearly.

Southwark, 21 February 1351

669. RESPONSE TO THE JUSTICES. The enquiry was held in the presence of Edward and Thomas, when it was clear that Edward junior is legitimate and not bastard.

Southwark, 27 January 1352

670. EXECUTION OF THE BRIEF FOR THE COLLECTION of the second year of the biennial tenth. The bishop recites to the prior and chapter of the cathedral the brief received, concerning the tenth granted at the convocation at St Paul's; to be collected at St Andrew and Nativity of St John Baptist for the first year and at Purification and Nativity of St John Baptist next following for the second year, as a special aid. The conditions for the second year, as requested by the clergy, were laid down and accepted at the last parliament by the clergy. The names of those deputed to be collectors should be sent to the treasurer and barons of the exchequer without delay.

Westminster, the King, 20 October 1352

421   Mandate to carry out the terms of the brief as far as it concerns the cathedral priory and to reply to the bishop before SS. Peter and Paul.

Southwark, 1 November 1352

671. SIMILAR MANDATE directed to the prior of Merton for the collection of the tenth in the archdeaconry of Surrey.

672. CERTIFICATE addressed to the treasurer and barons of the exchequer. The bishop has received the king's brief and has entrusted the collection of the second year of the biennial tenth to the prior and chapter of the cathedral for the archdeaconry of Winchester and the prior of St Mary, Merton for that of Surrey.

673. COMMISSION IN A CASE OF BASTARDY, addressed to M. Thomas de Enham, the official of Surrey, on receipt of a royal brief. John Ledrede of West Molesey in the husting court of London, claimed a messuage with appurtenances in London against the prior of Holy Trinity, London; also two messuages in the same town against the abbot of Holy Cross, Waltham. The prior and the abbot came and said that John could not be heir because of his bastardy. As cognizance of such a case concerned ecclesiastical jurisdiction, the bishop is to hold an enquiry and to report to the justices at Westminster.

Westminster, J' de Stonore, 30 May 1351

The bishop orders the official to hold the enquiry summoning the prior and the abbot, etc. as in the case of Edward de Leye, above.

Southwark, 29 September 1353

674. CITATION FOR THE CASE, addressed to the official of R[alph], bishop of London. He is to summon the prior and abbot, who are within his jurisdiction, to appear with others before the bishop of Winchester at the church of St Mary, Southwark, on the next law-day after the feast of St Fidis (6 October), for the enquiry.

675. RESPONSE TO THE BRIEF. Concerning John de Ledrede, whether legitimate or bastard, as against to prior and abbot, the enquiry was held. The abbot did not appear, while the prior had appealed from the bishop's commissary to the court of Canterbury, claiming the inhibition of that court by virtue of the said brief as regards John and the abbot. John de Ledrede was declared legitimate and not bastard.

Southwark, 4 May 1354

676. EXECUTION OF THE BRIEF FOR THE COLLECTION OF THE TENTH. The bishop reminds the prior and chapter of the cathedral of the tenth granted to the king at the convocation at St Paul's, now due at St Andrew (November 30) and at Nativity of St John Baptist for the first term entirely, and for the second under certain conditions laid down in the archbishop's certificate. The prior is to nominate suitable collectors without delay for the money due from the benefices; this should reach the bishop before St Andrew. The names of the collectors chosen are to be sent to the exchequer.

Westminster, the King, 25 September 1356

422

The prior is to deal with the collection for the city and archdeaconry of Winchester, and also make the contribution of the prior and chapter, to reach the bishop before the Conception of B. Mary (8 December).

Southwark, 26 October 1356

677. SIMILAR MANDATE to the prior of St Mary, Merton, for the archdeaconry of Surrey.

678. EXECUTION OF THE ROYAL BRIEF FOR THE ANNUAL TENTH. The bishop informs the prior and the cathedral chapter that he has received the king's brief, reminding him of the grant by the clergy at the convocation at St Paul's, of an annual tenth from all benefices on account of the war—one half due at Nativity of St John Baptist and the other at the Purification (2 February), as laid down in the archbishop's certificate. The prior is to nominate collectors, so that the bishop can pay the money to the exchequer. The names of the collectors are to be sent in before Trinity.

Reading, Lionel the king's son, 22 April 1360

The bishop asks for diligence in view of the dangers and requires a reply before SS. Peter and Paul (29 June).

Southwark, 30 April 1360

679. SIMILAR MANDATE to the abbot of Chertsey for the archdeaconry of Surrey.

680. ANOTHER DIRECTIVE for collecting the second term of the tenth sent to the prior and cathedral chapter for the city and archdeaconry of Winchester; and to the abbot of Chertsey for that of Surrey.

423   **681.** APPEAL TO THE KING ON BEHALF OF POOR BENEFICES. Since certain parishes are depopulated since the pestilence and reduced to penury, so that they can hardly subsist the bishop appeals for reductions:
church of Morestead 10s.
church of Ash 8s. 8d.
church of West Dean 10s.
church of Swarraton 8s. 8d.
church of Yarmouth, Isle of Wight, 16d.
church of Dodington 16s. 8d.
church of St Laurence in Wath', Isle of Wight, 8s. 8d.
vicar of Portsmouth 13s. 4d.
church of Eastrop near Basingstoke 8s. 8d.
church of Standen, Isle of Wight, 4s. 2d.
church of St James, Winchester, in pension 10s.
church of St Faith 10s. 7d.
church of St Mary of the Vale 20s. 2½d.

Southwark, 29 June 1361

682. QUITCLAIM as to the advowson of the hospital of St Cross, Sparkford. To John de Pontissara, bishop of Winchester, William de Tothale, prior of the Hospital of St John of Jerusalem in England with the brethren renounces all rights and claims to the advowson of the hospital of St Cross.

Melchbourne, in chapter, 4 June 1303

683. TRANSCRIPT OF A CHARTER of John de Shipton', *prepositus* of the chapel of St Elizabeth, to which the church of Hursley is appropriated. Grant to William, bishop and to his successors the whole ground with garden adjoining in the town of Hursley with the buildings thereon, between the house of the chapel of St Elizabeth and the vicarage house. As rectors of the church, the chapel was accustomed to use the rectory house. This grant is to compensate for the loss of the revenue which the bishop used to receive when the rectory was vacant. Using the seal of the deanery of Winchester, while the dean uses the seal of his office. *Hiis testibus*.

684. (*French*) MEMORANDUM that Roger Gervays was appointed by the bishop bailiff of East Meon, at the bishop's pleasure.

Marwell, 2 September 1364

685. ORDER TO RAISE CERTAIN SUMS OF MONEY. Since the beneficed clerks listed below hold no lay fee, as Thomas de Hampton', sheriff of Southampton, declared in his account to the exchequer of the morrow of Michaelmas 1364, the bishop is to raise from their ecclesiastical goods the sums outstanding:

from Walter, vicar of the church of Portsmouth 13s. 4d., owing from the first year of the triennial tenth granted in 1337

from W', rector of the church of Whippingham 48s., owing from the same

from W', rector of the church of Ellingham 24s., owing from the same

from W', vicar of Portsmouth 13s. 4d., owing from the first year of the biennial tenth granted in 1348

424 from W', rector of the church of Whippingham £4 16s., owing from both years of the biennial tenth, 1338 and 1340

from Robert Warner, vicar of Carisbrooke 13s. 4d., owing from forfeited revenue.

This money should reach the exchequer on the morrow of St Hilary (13 January) by one of the debtors.

Westminster, W' de Skipwyth', 17 November 1364

686. RETURN OF THE BRIEF: have been raised: 24s. from the ecclesiastical goods of the rector of Ellingham and 13s. 4d. from those of Robert Warner, vicar of Carisbrooke, sent by the bearer. The sums due from the rector of Whippingham could not be raised because the autumn crops were stored this year with the rectory buildings in which the crops were recently destroyed by fire; there were no other goods from which money could be raised. So far, no other money has been collected. The vicarage of Portsmouth has been impoverished by the withdrawal of its parishioners on account of various fires and enemy attacks, so that all its revenue is now insufficient for the meagre maintenance of a single priest. Therefore the sum demanded from the vicar of Portsmouth could not be raised.

687. MEMORANDUM from the exchequer: Southampton, for the bishop of Winchester: the triennial tenth for the year 1337, due from the rector of

Ellingham, as mentioned in the brief and in the return of the morrow of St Hilary, 1364, is still in arrears: *verso* treasurer's remembrancer by one tally: 24s. (*inserted*: the tally in payment of this sum remains with the attorney). From Robert Warrenn', vicar of Carisbrooke, from forfeited revenue as set out in the bishop's return to the brief from the exchequer: 1 mark, by another tally. Both tallies levied 12 February 1365.

688. BRIEF CONCERNING THE VICAR OF PORTSMOUTH. To the bishop, mandate to raise from the ecclesiastical goods of the vicarage 13s. 4d., owing from the first year of the biennial tenth, granted in 1346. To be at exchequer within the octave of the Purification (2 February).

Westminster, W' de Skypwith', 21 January 1357

689. REPLY TO THE BRIEF. The vicarage of Portsmouth, by the reduction of its parishioners through epidemics, various fires, depredations by enemy action, is so diminished and reduced to penury, that its present revenue is insufficient to maintain a single priest. The money could not be raised and the bishop must ask to be excused.

690. MANDATE to the bishop to summon before the barons of the exchequer at Westminster within the octave of the Purification, Bernard Brocas, parson of the church of St Nicholas, Guildford, lately comptroller of William de Farle, lately constable of Bordeaux, to deliver to the court the counter-rolls for the time when he was a comptroller of the said William. And then to testify to the details entered into the said rolls, in order to check with the testamentary executor of the said William de Farle the sums and entries in his account to the exchequer for the moneys received by him at the time when he was constable there. That this may be at the disposal of the court.

Westminster, W' de Skypwyth', 28 January 1366

425 **691.** MANDATE from the bishop to to M. Robert, rector of the church of Puttenham, sequestrator-general for the archdeaconry of Surrey. Since, recently, in the king's court, various sums of money, set out on the occasion of the non-appearance of M. Bernard Brocas, rector of St Nicholas, Guildford, (lately comptroller of M. John de Stretle and subsequently of William de Farlee, constable of Bordeaux, when cited to show his counter-rolls for the time when John and William were constables, before the barons of the exchequer at Westminster), on divers occasions the bishop was mulcted and in the event it is to be feared, seriously mulcted on this account. Wishing there to be compensated in this matter of the non-appearance of M. Bernard Brocas, seeing he was in Gascony for a considerable time at the service of the king and is still there in person, no negligence should be imputed to the bishop. The sequestrator is therefore to see that the sums detailed in the document are raised by sequestration by sales of the ecclesiastical goods, and sent to the bishop by *Quasimodo* Sunday, with the certificates duly sealed.

[Bishops] Waltham, 27 March 1365

692. REVENUES FORFEITED BY THE BISHOP in the king's court, on account of the non-appearance of B' Brocaz: his clerk:

in fines and amercements during the king's 34th year (1360):
40d., 2s., 3s. 4d., 2s.
from the revenue for the same reason, 35th year (1361)
2s., 2s., 3s. 4d., 3s. 4d.,
from the revenue for the same reason, 36th year (1362)
3s. 4d.

693. WRIT CONCERNING BASTARDY. On Saturday All Souls' Day last, before the justices William de Fyncheden' and William de Wychyngham, at the assise court for the county of Surrey at Southwark, John atte Hoo of Hoddesdon entered a claim for dispossession against Alice Hurlebat and others, concerning two messuages and 10 acres of land in Lambeth. Alice came before the justices and replied as holding these tenements, and appealed at the bar of the court as the daughter and heiress of Wymarca, one of the daughters of John Hurlebat. Thereupon John atte Hoo replied that Alice could not inherit because she was bastard; to which Alice declared herself legitimate. And since the cognizance of such matters belongs to the ecclesiastical jurisdiction, the bishop was ordered to set up an enquiry to know the truth of the matter.

Westminster, W' de Fyncheden, 12 November 1364

694. GRANT by the bishop to Thomas le Warrenner', for his faithful services in the past and to come, of the Soke of Winchester in the office of bailiff. To have and to hold for his life, receiving the customary payments (*vadia*) and fees, and dealing with all the concerns of the *balliva*.

Witnesses: John de Isle of the Isle of Wight, Bernard Brocaz, knights. Walter Haywode, Nicholas Wodelok', John Francon', Thomas Hampton, Roger Haywod' and others.

[Bishops] Waltham, 20 September 1366

426   **695.** LICENCE from the king to grant one messuage with curtilage and garden adjoining in South Waltham, which he holds from the king *in capite*, and which Nicholas de Shirebourne held from the bishop, but now lapses into the bishop's hands as escheats, because Nicholas was bastard and died without heirs. Licence to grant the messuage to John Guynes of Hannington. To have and to hold on the same terms and services as before it lapsed. Should John die without heirs, the property reverts to the bishop. Neither John nor the bishop is to be molested by any sheriff or bailiff as escheators.

Westminster, the King, 9 May 1365

696. INDENTURE for the above messuage by the bishop to John de Guynes, as recited above. The measuage stands opposite the garden once of Henry Balistarius and extends southwards towards 'Shorlane'.

[Bishops] Waltham, 13 May 1365

697. INSPEXIMUS AND CONFIRMATION by Hugh, prior, and the chapter of St Swithun's of the grant by the bishop to Thomas Chariect', Emma his wife, and Thomas Squiler:

Thomas and Emma and Thomas hold from the bishop a tenement with appurtenances in Southwark by a rent of 33s. 4d. Now, for his good services, the bishop grants to Thomas Squiler for life the rent of 33s. 4d., to be paid to him by Thomas and Emma.

[Bishops] Waltham, Friday next before St Bartholomew, 1366

The chapter approves the concession.

Winchester, the chapter-house, 29 August 1366

427   **698**. CONFIRMATION by Hugh the prior and the chapter of the grant by the bishop to Robert Gerkyn, chamberlain to the bishop, and Joan his wife, with Thomas Squiler, *servitor* of the bishop:
The bishop grants to Robert and Joan and Thomas the tenement with appurtenances which John Payn used to hold in Lestuves, in the parish of St Margaret. To have and to hold for life at the same rent and services as for John Payn, rendering 33s. 4d. in equal portions at Easter and Michaelmas to the bishop. After the death of Robert and Joan, then for Thomas Squiler as long as he lives, rendering that rent to the bishop, plus 100s. in similar portions at the same two dates. After the death of the last holder, the property will revert to the bishop. A tripartite indenture.

[Bishops] Waltham, Friday next after the Assumption, 1366

The chapter approves.

Winchester, the chapter-house, 29 August 1366

699. CONFIRMATION by Hugh, prior and the chapter of the indenture between the bishop and Thomas Chariect', Emma his wife and Thomas Squiler, for the good services of both, granting them the tenement with appurtenances lately held by Robert Tyghelere in Southwark at Lestuves, parish of St Margaret. To have and to hold for their lives, rendering annually the rents and services as hitherto—for the life of Thomas Squiler 33s. 4d. in equal portions at Easter and Michaelmas.
After the death of Thomas and Emma, the tenement will remain held by Thomas Squiler for his life, rendering the same rent and 100s. in equal portions at the same terms. After the three are dead, the property will revert to the bishop.

[Bishops] Waltham, Friday after the Assumption, 1366

Confirmed by the chapter.

Winchester, the chapter-house, 29 August 1366

700. CONFIRMATION by Hugh, prior and the chapter of the grant to Robert Gerkyn, his wife Joan, and Thomas Squiler.

428   Indenture between the bishop and the said Robert, Joan and Thomas. As the bishop has granted them a tenement in Southwark, rendering 33s. 4d., as set out in earlier indentures, the bishop now grants to Thomas Squiler for his good services those 33s. 4d., to be received from Robert and Joan during the lifetime of Thomas.

[Bishops] Waltham, Sunday before St Bartholomew, 1366

The chapter approves.

Winchester, the chapter-house, 29 August 1366

701. CONFIRMATION by Hugh, prior and the chapter of a grant by the bishop. The bishop grants and confirms to Robert Spark all the lands and tenements, rents and services with appurtenances which John Jardyn held from the bishop in Southampton, Northington, Overton 'Burg' and Overton manor in the county of Southampton—which have lapsed to the bishop as escheats, John dying without heirs. To have and hold the above lands and tenements, rents and services by Robert for life and one year after his decease, rendering annually the same rents and services as hitherto.

Witness: John de Motesfonte, John Fauconer, Richard Wammere, Thomas Gylle, Thomas Devenissh', Walter Grene, William Sparwe and others.

Highclere, 6 August 1366

Confirmed by the chapter.

Winchester, chapter-house, 29 August 1366

429 **702.** FIRST QUIRE OF DIMISSORY LETTERS, ORDINATIONS AND COMMISSIONS TO CONFER ORDERS
20 May 1346 at Southwark: dimissory letters for Robert le Wayte, clerk, of the diocese, for minor orders.
8 May 1346 at Southwark, for John de Bynham, rector of Baughurst, acolyte, for the subdiaconate.
4 June 1346, in St Mary, Southwark, Whitsunday, by the bishop's authority, Benedict, bishop of Sardis, celbrated mass and confered all the minor orders on John Creck', rector of Little Berkhamstead, dioc. of Lincoln, with dimissory letters from his diocesan.

703. ORDERS conferred by the bishop in the conventual church of St Mary, Southwark, Ember Saturday in Whitweek, 10 June 1346.

Acolytes
Winchester diocese: Walter de Depham, rector of Elden
John de Brykevyle
Robert Martyn of Bourne
Peter Redynge of Cobham
Robert le Wayte
John Kene of Chertsey
Richard Herbert of Hayling
Thomas de Lyndewode
Thomas Bechurst
Thomas Lee of Chertsey
Thomas Sayour
Fratres: William Pack', monk of Bermondsey; Richard de Wyke, Friar Minor; John de Kerseye, Edmund de Bunpstede, Richard de Kyngeston', Robert de Aylesham, Carmelite Friars.
William Bretevill', rector of Remenham, diocese of Salisbury

Hugh Tranegate of Temple Guiting, dioc. Bath and Wells
Richard Doubleday of 'Colecote', dioc. Salisbury
Robert son of Richard of Edensor, dioc. Coventry and Lichfield
John Horold of Hadleigh, under immediate jurisdiction of the archbishop
    of Canterbury
John son of John de Burton, dioc. York
William son of Alan of Welton near Hyde, dioc. Lincoln
William son of William of Farford, diocese York
John de Sutton, rector of Elworthy, dioc. Bath and Wells

704. *Subdeacons*
Winchester diocese: John de Tygehale, rector of Blendworth
Thomas de Insula, rector of Steventon
William atte Puynde of East Woodhay, *ad tit.* abbot of Notley
William Monck' of Pennington, *ad tit.* prior and fraternity of St Mary
    Kalendar, Winchester
Richard de Elyng', *ad tit.* prior of St Mary Kalendar—
William Horn of Ham, dioc. Chichester, *ad tit.* prior of Tortington
John Peroc of Stratton St Margaret, dioc, Salisbury, *ad tit.* St John's
    Hospital, Lechlade
430 Richard atte Forde, of Burton, dioc. Lincoln, *ad tit.* abbot of Mendham
Roger Maidegod of Hodnell, dioc. Coventry and Lichfield, *ad tit.* prioress
    of Nuneaton
Robert Arundel, dioc. Salisbury, *ad tit.* prior of Snelshall
John Facy, dioc. Bath and Wells, *ad tit.* prior of St. Mary's Hospital
    Cripplegate
Thomas Queynbel of Yeovil, dioc. Bath and Wells, *ad tit.* of his own
    patrimony
Robert Altoftes, dioc. York, *ad tit.*, abbot of Lesnes
William de Boycote, dioc. Lincoln, *ad tit.* prior of St Mary Kalendar,
    Winchester
John Crek', rector of Little Berkhamstead, dioc. Lincoln
John de Dorkyng, rector of Tillington, dioc. Chichester
William called Jerdelegh' of Tanworth, dioc. Worcester, *ad tit.* prior of
    Newark, of the chantry of Ashford
Simon Saltwell' of Preston, dioc. Canterbury, *ad tit.* prior of Leeds
William Wilegh', dioc. Chichester, *ad tit.* prior of Calke
John Testard' of Anmering, dioc. Chichester, *at tit.* prior of Tortington.
Thomas Michel of Wycombe, dioc. Lincoln, *ad tit.* abbot of Medmenham
Roger Baron of Rissington, dioc. Lincoln, *ad tit.* prior of Bushmead
John Kyng' of Eaton, dioc. Lincoln, *ad tit.* prior of Snelshall
Henry Bruton' of Eaton, dioc. Lincoln, *ad tit.* prior of Snelshall
Thomas son of William Westiby of Thwing, dioc. York, *ad tit.* prior of
    Hospital of St John of Jerusalem in England
Fratres: John de Kersyngham', John de Vinetrea, monks of Westminster
John Feryng', Peter Marini, Carmelite Friars
John Clerici', John Dendevers, Dominican Friars
Clement de Sellynge, Carmelite Friar

705. *Deacons*

Winchester Diocese: William son of Andrew le Couk of Micheldever. *ad tit.* prior of St Denys, Southampton

M. Thomas Sadoch, rector of South Warnborough

John Forest of Cheriton, *ad tit.* prior of St Mary Kalendar, Winchester

Walter Selot of Guildford, *ad tit.* prior of Sandown

Richard atte Welle of Somborne, *ad tit.* prior of St Mary Kalendar, Winchester

William de Daumawe, *ad tit.* prior of Newark for the chantry of Ashstead

M. William Joce, rector of Crawley

John Pyket, *ad tit.* prior of St Mary Kalendar, Winchester—

John son of William Carpentarius of [Newton in the] Wold, dioc. Lincoln, *ad tit.* abbot of Sulby

John son of Roger of Great Kimble, dioc. Lincoln, *ad tit.* abbot of Missenden

William Faucons of Rissington, dioc. Lincoln, *ad tit.* prior of Bushmead

Richard son of Thomas Hersout of Edwardstone, dioc. Norwich, *ad tit.* 5 marks from the manor of Nicholas Torney, lord of Cadeby in Cabourne

David son of Adof Duy of Ab de Coneto Arllechwed Uchaph', dioc. Bangor, *ad tit.* 3 marks sterling from the patrimony of David Seys ap Granow his relative, which is entered in the registry of the bishop of Bangor

Robert Chapman of Dean, dioc. Lincoln, *ad tit.* prior of Bushmead

Ralph son of Richard of Winwick, dioc. Lincoln, *ad tit.* prior and canons of Stonely

Adam Banastre, rector of half the church of Fressingfield, dioc. Norwich

431 John Rose of [Newton in the] Wold, dioc. Lincoln, *ad tit.* prioress of Elstow

William de Flamstede of St Albans, exempt from the jurisdiction of the abbot of the place, *ad tit.* prioress of Sopwell

John Jowet of Shelton, dioc. Lincoln, *ad tit.* prior of Stonely

Robert le Couk, dioc. Chichester, *ad tit.* prior of Harnham

Richard son of William atte Cote of Tendring, under the immediate jurisdiction of the archbishop of Canterbury, *ad tit.* prior of Shulbrede

Ralph Tone of Ravenstone, dioc. Lincoln, *ad tit.* prior of St. Mary, Southwark

James de Fynnere, dioc. York, *ad tit.* prior of Catley

John son of William Pampyng' of Worstead, dioc. Norwich, *ad tit.* St. Mary's Hospital, Cripplegate, London

Roger Hexham of Keresley, dioc. Lincoln, *ad tit. domus* of Sopwell

Henry Mason of Sherington, dioc. Lincoln, *ad tit.* prior of Caldwell

William Thoury of Eastwick, dioc., Lincoln, *ad tit.* prior of Sandown

John Maycok' of Higham Ferrers, dioc. Lincoln, *ad tit.* St Mary Delapré, Northampton

Nicholas Waryn of Higham Ferrers, dioc. Lincoln, *ad tit.* abbot of St James outside Northampton

Thomas Coupul of Holme, dioc. Lincoln, *ad tit.* prior of St Peter, Dunstaple

William Morel of Bocking, of immediate jurisdiction of the archbishop
of Canterbury, *ad tit.* prior of [Earl's] Colne
Adam de Estbrouk, rector of Poulshot, dioc. Salisbury
Thomas Chef of Buckland, dioc. Lincoln. *ad tit.* prior of Snelshall
John Marechal of Lathbury, dioc. Lincoln, *ad tit.* prior of Caldwell
William Croxton of Shelton, dioc. Lincoln, *ad tit.* prior of Holy Trinity,
London
Richard Lymesy of Ware, dioc. Lincoln, *ad tit.* abbot of Thame
Fratres: John de Fenglesham, Carmelite Friar
Walter de Forde, Augustinian Canon
William de Neuport, John Burgoynon, Roger de Ware, monks of
Bermondsey
Robert Gyle, Jocelin de Gillyngham, Walter Lose, Friars Minor
Walter de Banham, Richard Bomstede, Carmelite Friars
Henry de Brutona, Dominican Friar
Roger Boulge, dioc. Norwich, *ad tit.* Prior of Holy Trinity London

706 *Priests*
Alexander de Dungre, rector of Ewelme, dioc. Lincoln.
Henry Kynthorp of Thurning, dioc. Lincoln, *ad tit.* prior of Bushmead
Thomas son of Richard de Wich' of London, *ad tit.* prior of Leeds
William atte Bush of Hadleigh, deanery of Bocking, *ad tit. domus* of
Kersey, granted for all the orders
Edmund son of Edmund Stokkere of Dean, dioc. Lincoln, *ad tit.* prior
of Bushmead
Thomas Fareman of Wrotham, dioc. Rochester in deanery of Shoreham,
ad tit. abbot of Lesnes
Walter de Medwe of Hadleigh, deanery of Bocking, *ad tit. domus* of
[Great] Bricett
John de Berton', dioc. Hereford, *ad tit.* prior and brethren of Hospital
of St James, near Westminster
William Dallyng', vicar of Tortington, dioc. Chichester
Robert Bourgham, dioc. Rochester, *ad tit.* prioress of St Mary Magdalen,
Combwell
William de Irton, dioc. Coventry and Lichfield, *ad tit. domus* of Rocester,
entered in the registry of the bishop of Coventry and Lichfield
John de Depedene, perpetual vicar of Hoo St Werburgh, dioc. Rochester
Thomas son of Warinie Clement of Kirton in Holland, dioc. Lincoln *ad
tit. domus* of Kirkstead
John Herdyng' of North Petherton, dioc. Bath and Wells, *ad tit.* prior
of St Mary, Southwark
John son of Simon of Algarkirk, dioc. Lincoln, *ad tit.* prioress of
Gokewell
432   Peter Clerc of Wycombe, dioc. Lincoln, *ad tit.* abbot of Medmenham
John son of Richard Imaygne of 'Bykenersworth', by dimissory letters
from the abbot of St Albans directly subject to the Holy See *ad tit.*
prioress of Markyate
Ralph Avestetoune, dioc Chichester, *ad tit.* prior of Tortington
John Samitere of Iford, dioc. Salisbury, *ad tit.* prior of Holy Trinity,
London

Thomas de Partenay of Louth, dioc. Lincoln, *ad tit. domus* of Minting

Thomas Bunch' of Terrington, dioc. Norwich, *ad tit.* prior of St Mary, Southwark

Thomas Foby of Climping, dioc. Chichester, *ad tit.* prior of Tortington

Thomas son of Robert le Rotur of Berkswell, dioc. Coventry and Lichfield, *ad tit.* abbot of Rocester

Hugh Mape of Clenton, dioc. Hereford, *ad tit.* patrimony approved by his ordinary

John Ude of Stotfold, dioc. Lincoln, *ad tit.* prior of Sempringham

Richard Mile of Weedon, dioc. Lincoln, *ad tit.* prior of Daventry

William Botiler of Bovington, dioc. Lincoln, *ad tit.* provision made by the abbot of Westminster

John Hullyng' of Burton, dioc. Lincoln, *ad tit. domus* of Ashridge

Thomas Gygel of Fenny Compton, dioc. Coventry and Lichfield, *ad tit. domus* of Ossulveston

Robert atte Stokkes, of Westmill, dioc. Lincoln, *ad tit.* the master brethren of Hospital of St James, Charing.

John le Parkere of Fenny Stratford, dioc. Lincoln, *ad tit.* prioress of Harrold

Andrew son of William atte Cros of [Newton in the] Wold, dioc. Lincoln, *ad tit.* abbot of Pipewell

Robert son of John Smith (*Fabri*) of [Newton in the] Wold, dioc. Lincoln, *ad tit.* abbot of Sulby

Peter de Knyghtecote, dioc. Coventry and Lichfield, *ad tit. domus* of St Michael, Warwick

Diocese of Winchester: Robert Hughet of Sele, *ad tit.* prior of Newark of 5 marks from the chantry of Ashstead

John de Ichenestok' rector of Abbotsworthy

John Trenchend', *ad tit.* prior and fraternity of St Peter, Winchester

John Trenchefeil, *ad tit.* prior of Ivychurch

Robert Robyn of 'Andeide', *ad tit.* prior of Mottisfont

John Dantry, *ad tit.* prior of St Mary Kalendar, Winchester

Nicholas de Halle, *ad tit.* prior and Fraternity of St Peter, Winchester

John Pravy of Selborne, *ad tit.* prior of Selborne

John de Colvedon, *ad tit.* provision made by the abbot of Hyde

Fratres: William de Bradeley, Augustinian

Thomas de Gormecestre, canon of Merton

Henry de Bruynton', monk of Chertsey

Adam le Walshe, John de Stormonch', Walter de Mordon', Friars Minor

John Spyng', John de Hertford', John Wytlok', Carmelite Friars

John de Colby, Robert de Swantona, Dominican

707 *Dimissory Letters etc.*

22 June 1346, Southwark, for Henry de Shirefeld, subdeacon, for the diaconate and priesthood

23 June 1346, for Thomas de Heyton, rector of Ewell, clerk, for minor orders and subdiaconate

2 July 1346, for Reginald Foylet of Exbury, dioc. Winchester, for minor orders not yet received and all holy orders

Sunday, 23 July 1346, in his chapel at Southwark, the bishop ordained
as acolyte John de Dagworth', rector of Ock, dioc. Lincoln, tonsured
clerk

433 Sunday, 30 August 1346, the bishop gave the first tonsure to Henry son
of Henry Graspays, *literatus* of London

8 September 1346, Southwark, dimissory letters for Robert le Wayte,
acolyte, for all orders

16 September 1346, Southwark, dimissory letters for monks of Beaulieu:
Walter de Farnhulle Thomas de Forde, John Leynte, tonsured, for the
minor orders not yet received and the subdiaconate; Robert de Burgate,
for the subdiaconate; Robert de Milkesham, John de Forde for the
diaconate; Richard de Merwell', John de Osmynton' and Ralph de
Dounton for the priesthood

21 September 1346, Southwark, dimissory letters for Thomas de
Wokhurst', deacon for the priesthood

14 September, Southwark, for Gerald de Farges of Southampton, for
the minor and all other orders

708 ORDERS conferred in the conventual church of St Mary, Southwark,
by Benedict, bishop of 'Cardicen', by authority from the bishop of
Winchester, Saturday in Ember Week, 23 September, 1346.

Acolytes
Thomas de Heyton, rector of Ewell
Philip Payn of Winchester
Simon de Stonham
Hamo de Chikwelle, rector of Fonthill Bishop, dioc. Salisbury
Henry de Titynge of the parish of St Martha
Nicholas de Drokenesford'
Reginald Note of Burford, dioc. Lincoln
Fr. Alexander de Ereswell', Augustinian
William Borgeys of Wycombe, dioc. Lincoln
John son of Adam son of Ralph of Walsoken, dioc. Norwich
Henry de Swafham, dioc. Ely
Robert son of Peter de Wysebech', dioc. Ely
Fratres: Simon de Wydersfeld, John de Bereford, Friars Minor
William Mereworth', canon of Newark
John de Dunstaple, canon of Missenden, dioc. Lincoln

709 *Subdeacons*
Richard de Farlee, *ad tit.* prior of Mottisfont
John de Dagworth, rector of Ock, dioc. Lincoln
John Heynot, rector of Chalton
John de Brikeville of Andover, *ad tit.* prior of St Mary Kalendar,
Winchester
John de Bynham, rector of Baughurst
John Kyrkehowe of Burgh, rector of Shipdham, dioc. Norwich
Stephen le Gardiner, of the Isle of Wight, *ad tit.* prior of St Peter,
Winchester
Walter de Depham, rector of Elden

John Russel of Worthy, *ad tit.* prior of St Mary Kalendar, Winchester

Thomas de Wykhurst, *ad tit.* abbot of Waverley

William Pay of Basingstoke, *ad tit.* prior of St Denys, Southampton

Richard Mede, *ad tit.* prior of St Mary Kalendar, Winchester

Richard Doubleday of Colecote, dioc. Salisbury, *ad tit.* prior of Bermondsey

William atte Reye of Chatham, dioc. Canterbury, *ad tit.* prior of St Gregory, Canterbury

William Barew, dioc. Salisbury, *ad tit.* prior of Maiden Bradley

John Hygeleye, rector of Thrandeston, dioc. Norwich

David Bonvill', dioc. St Davids, *ad tit.* prior of the hospital of St John, Burford

434 Walter son of Solomon le Groos of Burford, dioc. Lincoln, *ad tit.* abbot of Tilty

William Werour of Drayton near Daventry, dioc. Lincoln, *ad tit. domus* of [Temple] Bruer

Nicholas de Blaston', dioc. Lincoln, *ad tit.* abbot of Ossington

Walter Robynes of 'Greneburgh', *ad tit.* prior of Luffield, by dim. letters of abbot of St Albans

Fratres: Peter de Secthethe, Roger de Denham, monks of Lewes

John Dene, Dominican

John de Brich', John de Kerseye [Carmelite Friars]

Edmund de Cantuar', canon of Bilsington, dioc. Canterbury

Thomas Darre, Augustinian

710 *Deacons*

John le Frend of Woodhampton, dioc. Salisbury, *ad tit.* monastery of Ivychurch

M. John Llandaf of Usk, rector of St Martin outside Westgate, Winchester

William atte Puynde of West Woodhay, *ad tit.* abbot of Notley

John son of Gilbert de Wenham. *ad tit.* prior of St James, Thremhale

William le Monck' of Peniton, *ad tit.* prior of St Mary Kalendar, Winchester

Hamo de Somery, rector of Leybourne, dioc. Rochester

John de Badyngham of Ringwood, *ad tit.* monastery of Ivychurch

John le Greyn of Breamore, *ad tit.* prior of Breamore

John Moune of Southampton, *ad tit.* prior of St Denys, Southampton

Simon Saltewlle of Preston near Wingham, dioc. Canterbury, *ad tit.* prior of Leeds

John de Tudenham, dioc. Norwich, *ad tit.* prior of Bermondsey

William called de Yerdele, of Tanworth, dioc. Worcester, *ad tit.* prior of Newark

Richard de Badelkyng', dioc. Salisbury, *ad tit.* prior of Poughley

William Swan of Horton, dioc. Salisbury, *ad tit.* abbess of Tarrant

John de Tigehale, rector of Blendworth

John de Hardres, dioc. Canterbury, *ad tit.* prior of St Gregory, Canterbury

Edmund Reynald of [Fen] Ditton, dioc. Ely, *ad tit.* prior of Swavesey

Geoffrey Hegham of Northampton, dioc. Lincoln, *ad tit.* prior of Holy Trinity, London
John de Burbath' of Highworth, dioc. Salisbury, *ad tit. domus* of Bindon
John Baynel of Hampton, dioc. Lincoln, *ad tit. domus* de [Temple] Bruer
M. William Boulge, rector of Farnborough
Fratres: Robert Treweman, John Dacre, monks of Lewes
John Gyles, Friar Minor
John de Tenterdown, canon of Bilsington, dioc. Canterbury
John de Toucetre of Ashridge, dioc. Lincoln
Thomas de Werminstre, Dominican
John de Lamburn', John de Asshe, Augustinian canons.
Ralph de Chivele, Thomas de Cantuar', Clement de Sellyng', Carmelite Friars
Richard de Malmesbury, canon of Waltham
Henry de Schirefeld, *ad tit.* prior of Thremhall

711. *Priests*
M. Roger de Fulford', rector of Kaerwent, dioc. Llandaff
Thomas le White, *ad tit.* prior of Breamore
William son of Andrew le Cook' of Micheldever, *ad tit.* prior of St Denys, Southampton
435 Fr John de Burgoyne, monk of Bermondsey
William Jurdan, dioc. Rochester, *ad tit.* prior of Leeds
Philip de Barton', rector of Blisland, dioc. Exeter
Robert Payn of Newport Pagnell, dioc. Lincoln, *ad tit.* prior of Chipley
M. John de Overton, rector of Upham
Nicholas de Langeford, rector of Chale, Isle of Wight
M. John le Gulden', rector of [East] Stoke by Bindon, dioc. Salisbury
Richard atte Welle of Somborne, *ad tit.* prior of St Mary Kalendar, Winchester
Henry Goulde of Ringwood, *ad tit.* prior of [Christchurch] Twynham
John le Bokke of Alton, *ad tit.* prior of Selborne
Philip le Taillour of Micheldever, *ad tit.* prior of Andwell
William of Worthy Mortimer, *ad tit.* prior of St Mary Kalendar, Winchester
Richard de Eston of 'Ludeshulle', *ad tit.* prior of Selborne
Thomas Mundeleye of Farnham, *ad tit.* prior of [Monk] Sherborne
William Elys, dioc. Winchester, *ad tit.* prior of St Mary Kalendar, Winchester
David son of Adaf Duy of Ab' de Conieto Ayllachwed uthof, dioc. Bangor *ad tit.* 3 marks from the patrimony of David Seys ap Gronow his relative, entered in the registry of the bishop of Bangor
John Eylm', rector of St Michael, Wallingford, dioc. Salisbury
Roger le Hore of Chitterne, dioc. Salisbury, *ad tit.* prior of Maiden Bradley
Roger Hokesham of Kearsley, dioc. of Lincoln, *ad tit. domus* of Sopwell
Richard Waryn of Staunton, dioc. Salisbury, *ad tit.* prior of Ivychurch
William son of Thomas Borlof of Pilton, dioc. Lincoln, *ad tit.* prior of Thoby

Alexander atte Welle of Harlton, perpetual vicar of St John Baptist in Milne Street, Cambridge, dioc. Lincoln

John Wyscard of Pulloxhill, dioc. Lincoln, *ad tit. domus* of Dunstaple

Roger Boulge, dioc. Norwich, *ad tit.* prior of Holy Trinity, London

Stephen Alkham of Perry, dioc. Canterbury, *ad tit.* abbot of Lesnes

Hugh Carpenter of Markyate, dioc. Lincoln, *ad tit.* prioress of Markyate

Thomas Hulet of Caddington, dioc. Lincoln, *ad tit.* prioress of Markyate

John de Swyndon, dioc. Salisbury, *ad tit.* prior of [Monkton] Farleigh

Thomas Sadok, rector of South Warnborough

Hugh son of Gilbert Lovesson' of Stainby, dioc. Lincoln, *ad tit. domus* of Buckingham

Fratres: Alexander de Pydele, William Redynges, John Gamene, Richard de Hanyngdon', monks of Hyde

Gocelin de Kyngescle, Robert Wyle, Thomas de Honstanton', Friars Minor

Gilbert de Dallynge, Adam de Redborne, John de Watford, William atte Dene, monks of St Albans, with dimissory letters from that abbot

Thomas de Bumstede, Nicholas Walton', John de Micheldevere, John de Fenglesham, Carmelite Friars

Fr Richard de Merwelle, monk of Bealieu

Fr John Yeldyng', Augustinian

Fr Thomas de Stotevile, canon of Missenden, dioc. Lincoln

Fr John de Maydenstan, brother of the hospital of St Bartholomew in Smithfield, London, by dimissory letters from the bishop of London

Fr Thomas de Haywode, Dominican

Fr John de Maydenstan, Carmelite Friar

John Robekyn, dioc. Salisbury, *ad tit.* prior of hospital of Lechlade

436 **712.** *Dimissory Letters etc*

23 October 1346, Southwark, for Hugh Goudewyne of Kingston, for the first clerical tonsure

18 November 1346, Southwark, for John de Hurselegh', acolyte, for all orders

1 December 1346, Southwark, for Fr Thomas de Brokhurst and Hugh de Basynge, acolytes, Nicholas de Wygford, subdeacon, and Henry Imbert and Philip de Farnham, monk deacons of Winchester cathedral, for subdiaconate, diaconate and priesthood respectively

Same date, for William de Burgham, canon of Christchurch Twynham, for diaconate and priesthood

6 December 1346, Southwark, for Robert Pen of Petersfield, for first clerical tonsure

1 November 1346, Southwark, the bishop conferred the first clerical tonsure on Richard de Kendale, of the parish of St Leonard, London, under the immediate jurisdiction of the archbishop of Canterbury

713. ORDERS conferred in the conventual church of St Mary, Southwark, by Benedict, bishop of Carddicen', as authorized by the bishop and by virtue of a commission from M. John de Usk, vicar-general in the absence of the bishop in foreign parts, Saturday in Ember-week,

23 December 1346

714. LETTER of invitation from M. John de Usk, rector of Burghclere, to bishop Benedict, to confer orders in the bishop's absence.

Southwark, 22 December 1346

715. *Acolytes*
Winchester diocese: John Raison of Merton
Thomas Berton of Farleigh
Simon Stonham of Tandridge,
Richard Horton of Ewell
Richard Snodenham of Shalford
William de Middleton of Carshalton
Fratres: John de Notyngham, John de Mylton', William de Sarum, Augustinians
Ralph de Faryndon', John Chamberlayn, Thomas de Aumondesham, John Oulep, Walter Blesby, John de Kyngeseye, Friars Minor

437   **716.** *Subdeacons*
Winchester diocese: Roger de Action', rector of Thornbury, dioc. Hereford
Henry Tityng', *ad tit.* prior of Newark
John Serle of Hursley, *ad tit.* prior of hospital of Lechlade
Robert son of Robert le Wayte of Winchester, *ad tit.* master of St James hospital, Charing
Philip Payn of Winchester, *ad tit.* abbess of Wherwell
Peter Redynge of Cobham, *ad tit.* guardian of hospital of Sandown
John atte Crouche of Wallop, *ad tit.* prior of Breamore
Hamo de Chikewell', rector of Fonthill Bishop, dioc. Salisbury
Edmund de Kyngton', dioc. Worcester, *ad tit.* abbot of Dorchester
Fratres: John de Dunstaple, canon of Missenden, by dimissory letters from the bishop of Lincoln
Henry de Colynburn', canon of St Mary, Southwark
Richard de Merston, Henry de Clifton', Richard de Biriton', Hugh Hertwelt, William de Torseye, Walter de Warfeld', William Southfeld', John Herle, Richard de Kingeston'

717. *Deacons*
Thomas de Wykhurst, *ad tit.* abbot of Waverley
Walter de Depham, rector of Eldon
John le Creek', rector of Little Berkhampstead, dioc. Lincoln
Fratres: John de Assh', John de Hastynge, John de Kerseye, John Munymouth', John de Kersaulton', John de Oresfenham, John de Vinetria

718. *Priests*
William le Monck of Peniton, *ad tit.* prior of Kalendar, Winchester
John de Sakevill', rector of [West] Bergholt, dioc. London
Simon le Saltewelle, dioc. Canterbury, *ad tit.* prior of Leeds
William le Yerdele of Tanworth, dioc. Worcester, *ad tit.* prior of Newark
Fratres: Walter de Ford, Augustinian

Thomas de Maydenston', Robert de Leyre, Thomas de Cant', Clement de Sellynge

719. *Dimissory Letter* 9 February 1347, Southwark, for John atte Vyne, rector of Chalton, clerk, for minor orders not yet received and all major orders.

720. ORDERS conferred by the bishop in his manor chapel at Southwark, Ember-Saturday in the first week of Lent.

St Matthias (24 February) 1347

721. *Acolytes*
Winchester diocese: William de Waverle, rector of Ewell
William Sparwe of Wyke
Peter Ken of Albury
John Trosseloue
John son of John Sharp of the parish of St Vedast, dioc. Canterbury
Frater John Grouncourt, Friar Minor
Robert Sexteyn, dioc. Canterbury
Roland de Lerdynton', dioc. Chichester
Fratres: John de Buklonde, Peter de Milton, Walter de Balshale, monks of Chertsey
William de Donyngton', Carmelite Friar
Walter Gerard, Dominican

438 **722.** *Subdeacons*
Thomas de Enham, rector of Froyle
Philip le Veysi, *ad tit.* prior of Hamble, procurator of abbot of Tiron
Richard Umfrey of Wherwell, *ad tit.* abbot of Netley
Robert Everard of Sherborne St John, *ad tit.* prior of Andwell
John Chuere of Clandon, *ad tit.* prior of St Mary, Southwark
William de Middelton', vicar of Carshalton
Robert Martyn of Bourne, *ad tit.* prior of St Mary, Southwark
John le Tannere of Alresford, *ad tit.* prior of Selborne
Fratres: Thomas de Brokhurst, Hugh de Basynge, monks of Winchester cathedral
John Roe of Eyworth, dioc. Lincoln, *ad tit.* prior of Caldwell
Richard Scardeyn, dioc. Canterbury, *ad tit.* prior of St Mary, Southwark
Henry la Zousch', dioc. Lincoln, *ad tit.* prior of Bushmead
Roger atte Hull', dioc. Lincoln, *ad tit.* prioress of Studley
John natus Willelmi Moolde, dioc. Coventry and Lichfield, *ad tit.* prior of St Sepulcre, Warwick
John Hugones of Warmington, dioc. Coventry and Lichfield, *ad tit.* prior of Thoby
John son of William le Skynnere of Bure, dioc. Norwich, *ad tit.* prior of St Mary, Thetford
John le Smyth of Newnham in the jurisdiction of the abbot of St Albans, *ad tit.* prior of Caldwell
William del Shawe, dioc. Coventry and Lichfield, *ad tit.* prior of Caldwell

Thomas de Lyndewode, dioc. Exeter, *ad tit.* abbot of Hartland, entered
in the registry of the bishop of Exeter
William Dugger of Buckingham, dioc. Lincoln, *ad tit.* prior of Snelshall
John de la Lee of Bletchley, dioc. Lincoln, *ad tit.* prioress of Harrold
Vincent Suel of Newport Pagnell, dioc. Lincoln, *ad tit.* prior of Snellshall
John de Neubury, dioc. Salisbury, *ad tit.* abbot of Robertsbridge
Fr William de Merewell', canon of Newark
Fratres: William de Tringe, Robert de Bromore, Friars Minor
Thomas son of Richard de Sandon', dioc. Lincoln, *ad tit.* prior of
Wymondley
Thomas Archer, dioc. Canterbury, *ad tit.* his own pension
Hugh Carpenter of Wavendon, dioc. Lincoln, *ad tit.* prior of Snelshall
John Sweyn, dioc. Hereford, *ad tit.* prior of St Gregory, Canterbury
John son of Adam Radulfi of Walsoken, dioc. Norwich, *ad tit.* prior of
Caldwell
Thomas Underhull', dioc. Canterbury, *ad tit.* prior of Leeds
John Rok, dioc. Canterbury, *ad tit.* prior of St Gregory, Canterbury

723. *Deacons*
Winchester diocese: Fr Nicholas de Wykford', monk of Winchester
cathedral
Fr Thomas de Croyndon', canon of Tandridge
John Berlee of Hursley, *ad tit.* prior of the hospital of Lechlade
Fr Henry de Colyngbourn', canon of St Mary, Southwark
Henry de Titynge, *ad tit.* prior of Newark
William Pox of Basingstoke, *ad tit.* prior of St Denys, Southampton
Philip Payn of Winchester, *ad tit.* abbess of Wherwell
John atte Crouche of Wallop, *ad tit.* prior of Breamore
Robert le Wayte of Winchester, *ad tit.* master of the hospital of St
James, Charing
Stephen le Gardiner of Carisbrooke, *ad tit.* prior of St Peter, Winchester
Roger de Acton', rector of Thornbury, dioc. Hereford
William atte Rye of Chartham, dioc. Canterbury, *ad tit.* prior of St
Gregory, Canterbury
William Westeby of Tong, dioc. York, *ad tit.* Fr Philip de Thame, prior
of St John of Jerusalem in England
John Facy of Bridgewater, dioc. Bath and Wells, *ad tit.* prior of St Mary
Cripplegate, London
Robert de Wyke, rector of Steepleton Iwerne, dioc. Salisbury
John de Petcham, dioc. Canterbury, *ad tit.* apolstolic grant to him of a
benefice at the disposal of the prior of Leeds
Roger de Shipbrok', rector of Gnosall, dioc. Conventry and Lichfield
439 William de Merton', dioc. Lincoln, *ad tit.* prior of Snelshall
John de Irford, rector of Rodepeyton, dioc. St Davids
Adam Fynacourt, dioc. Salisbury, *ad tit.* prior of St Frideswide, Oxford
Thomas Michel, dioc. Lincoln, *ad tit.* abbot of Medmenham
John Kyng, dioc. Lincoln, *ad tit.* prior of Snelshall
Henry Bruton' of Eton, dioc. Lincoln, *ad tit.* prior of Snelshall
Edmund de Kington, dioc. Worcester, *ad tit.* abbot of Dorchester

Thomas Streche, dioc. Coventry and Lichfield, *ad tit. domus* of St Michael, Warwick

John de Stapelford', dioc. Salisbury, *ad tit.* master of the hospital of St John, Lechlade

Robert Poosser of Cranbrook, dioc. Canterbury, *ad tit.* prior of Leeds

John atte Crouche of Boughton under Blean, dioc. Canterbury, *ad tit.* abbot of Langdon

John Domerham, dioc. Salisbury, *ad tit.* abbot of Bindon

Robert de Natyndon', dioc. Canterbury, *ad tit.* prior of St Gregory, Canterbury

Robert Wyke of Dover, dioc. Canterbury, *ad tit.* Maison Dieu of Dover

Walter Robyns of Grandborough, dioc. Lincoln, *ad tit.* abbot of Biddlesden, by dim. letters of the abbot of St Albans

Robert Leg' of Holme, dioc. Lincoln, *ad tit.* prior of Caldwell

Simon Bynyng', dioc. Lincoln, *ad tit.* prior of Dunstaple

John de Corby, dioc. Lincoln, *ad tit.* prior of St Mary, Southwark

Fratres: John de Herle, William de Southfeld, Augustinians

Roger de Boston, canon of Wymondley, dioc. Lincoln

724. *Priests*

Winchester diocese: Fratres Henry Imbert, Philip de Farnham, monks of Winchester Cathedral

M. William Boulge, rector of Farnborough

Fr John de Chadeslee, canon of Newark

John de Tygehale, rector of Blendworth

Thomas de Wykhurst, *ad tit.* abbot of Waverley

Henry de Shirfeld', *ad tit.* prior of St James, Thremhall

John Hendeman, *ad tit.* prior of Andwell

John Wenham, of Eastleach South, *ad tit.* prior of Reigate

John de Sutton, rector of Elworthy, dioc. Bath and Wells

Henry Stecheden' of Sherington, dioc. Lincoln. *ad tit.* prior of Canons Ashby

John Cokay of Maidstone, dioc. Canterbury, *ad tit.* abbot of Combwell

Robert son of John Fleg' *orundus* of the town of Bury, by dim. letters from the abbot of Bury St Edmund, by title of his own patrimony

John son of [   ] Pampynge of Worstead, dioc. Norwich, *ad tit. domus* of St Mary, Cripplegate, London

Richard Chalfhunte of Aylesbury, dioc. Lincoln, *ad tit.* abbot of Thame

Henry atte Noke of Frindesbury, dioc. Rochester, *ad tit.* Fr Philip de Thame, prior of St John of Jerusalem

Robert Norton' of Winterton, dioc. Lincoln, *ad tit.* prior of [Monk] Sherborne

William Modbury, rector of West Quantoxhead, dioc. Bath and Wells

John Everard of St Neots, dioc. Lincoln, *ad tit.* prior of Bushmead

Nicholas le Smyth of 'Ieoneldon' dioc. Lincoln, *ad tit.* prior of Caldwell

Richard atte Well' of 'Ieoneldon' dioc. Lincoln, *ad tit.* prior of Bushmead

Roger Onger, dioc. Exeter, *ad tit.* prior of St Germans

Thomas Maloly, dioc. Coventry and Lichfield, *ad tit. domus* of St Michael

Thomas Haukyn of Hockley, Lincoln, *ad tit.* prior of St Peter, Dunstaple

Stephen Stabbe of Tregony, dioc. Exeter, *ad tit.* abbot of Rewley near
    Oxford
William Thenry of Eastwick, dioc. Lincoln, *ad tit.* prior of Caldwell
John Hyde of Thrapston, dioc. Lincoln, *ad tit.* prioress of Harrold
John Bray of Shitlington, dioc. Lincoln, *ad tit.* prior of Dunstaple
Fr Henry de Bruton', Dominican
Fr John de Tenkdenn', canon of Bilsington
440   Fr Richard de Hatfeld, Dominican
Fratres Alexander Dabtot, John de Karleel, Thomas de Wychom, John
    Bersey, Ralph de Chinele, John Briche, Carmelite Friars
John Creyk', rector of Little Berkhampstead, dioc. Lincoln
John Godybour of Canterbury, *ad tit.* prioress of St Sepulcre, Canterbury

725. ORDERS conferred at St Mary, Southwark, by Benedict bishop of
Cardicen', Saturday *Sitientes,* 17 March 1347

Acolytes
William de Horneby, rector of Wootton, dioc. Lincoln
John Yillynge of Southwark
William le Conestable of Frismarsh, dioc. York
Thomas de Hadlegh, dioc. Winchester
Thomas Godard of London
Fratres William Todyngton', Carmelite Friar
Thomas Bysshop, John de Canisale, Dominicans

726. *Subdeacons*
William de Waverlee, rector of Ewell
Roger Gondgrom of Overton, *ad tit.* prior of the fraternity of St Peter,
    Winchester
John de Retford, rector of Welton, dioc. Lincoln
William de Swafeld', rector of Brigsley, dioc. Lincoln
Edward Chaumberlayn, rector of Portland, dioc. Salisbury
William de Hawe, rector of half the church of [Monk] Up Wimborne,
    dioc. Salisbury
Robert son of Peter de Wysebech', dioc. Ely, *ad tit.* prior of Caldwell
John de Rendlesham, dioc. Norwich, *ad tit.* prior of Bermondsey
Roger Peek' of Maidstone, dioc. Canterbury, *ad tit.* prior of Leeds
John le Yonge of Sheepbridge, dioc. Salisbury, *ad tit.* prior of St
    Frideswide, Oxford
William Orger of Thorganby, dioc. Lincoln, *ad tit.* abbot of Thornton
Robert de Bromfeld, rector of Melmerby, dioc. Carlisle
John Ponnt of Newbury, dioc. Salisbury, *ad tit.* Fr Philip de Thame,
    prior of St John of Jerusalem
Fratres: William de Clyve, monk of Lesnes
John de Pykworth, Carmelite Friar
Luke de Bourn', Walter Gerarder, Dominicans

727. *Deacons*
John de Weston', dioc. York, *ad tit.* prior St Mary, Southwark
John Chervere of Clandon, dioc. Winchester, *ad tit.* prior of St Mary,
    Southwark

William de Bradlegh', rector of Eynsford, deanery of Shorham, of immediate jurisdiction of the archbishop of Canterbury

M. William de Fenton, rector of Ackworth, dioc. York

William de Shawe, dioc. Coventry and Lichfield, *ad tit.* prior of Caldwell

William de Middulton', perpetual vicar of Carshalton

Alexander Flemmyng, rector of Hadleigh, dioc. London

Nicholas de Throkenesford', rector of Stapleford Tawny, dioc. London

441 William Serle, rector of Baddesley Clinton, dioc. Coventry and Lichfield

William Poleyn of Ayot, dioc. Lincoln, *ad tit.* prior of Launde

Fratres: Roger de Beoston', canon of Wymondley

William Pack', monk of Bermondsey

Reginald atte Wode, William de Hethe, monks of Lesnes

728. *Priests*

Thomas de Waleton, rector of Southchurch, of Bocking in the immediate jurisdiction of the archbishop

John de Irford of Rodbaxton, dioc. St Davids

Walter de Depham, rector of Eldon, dioc. Winchester

Roger de Acton, rector of Thornbury, dioc. Hereford

John Edward, rector of Offord Cluny, dioc. Lincoln

Simon Johannis rector of Cronware, dioc. St Davids

John Berlee of Hursley, *ad tit.* prior of the hospital of St John, Lechlade

Fratres: William de Neuport, monk of Bermondsey

John de Bello, William de Child, Peter de Tefford, Dominicans

Geoffrey Bondstres, John de Lammborne, William de Southfeld, Augustinians

Caduanus Nydan, Friar Minor of Oxford

Richard de Badelkyng', dioc. Salisbury, *ad tit.* prior of Poughley

Richard Doubeday of Colcote, dioc. Salisbury, *ad tit.* prior of Bermondsey

John atte Crouche of Boughton under Blean, dioc. Canterbury, *ad tit.* abbot of Langdon

729. *Commissions*

28 March 1347, Esher, to Benedict, bishop of Cardicen', to ordain William de Swafeld rector of Brigsley, dioc. Lincoln, as deacon on Easter Saturday, 31 March 1347, in any suitable place in the diocese

29 March 1347, Esher, to the same to ordain in St Mary's, Southwark or elsewhere, on the same day, Edward le Chaumberlayn rector of Portland, dioc. Salisbury, and Robert de Bromfeld rector of Melmerby, dioc. Carlisle, as deacons.

Same date, to the same to ordain William de Horneby rector of Wootton, dioc. Lincoln, as subdeacon and William de Hawe rector of half the church of [Monk] Up Wimborne, dioc. Salisbury, as deacon, at the place and time as above

Memorandum that bishop Benedict in St Mary's Southwark, conferred the orders according to the above commissions, 31 March 1347

442 **730.** *Dimissory Letters*

12 May 1347, for Robert Dolre, Richard de Stoke and Richard de Shireburn', and also William Martyn, canons of Christchurch

Twynham, i.e. Robert, Richard and Richard for all minor orders not yet received; William for the diaconate—from any bishop
14 May 1347, Southwark, for William Coterun, deacon, of Kingsclere, for the priesthood

731. ORDERS conferred by the bishop of Winchester pontifically in his manor chapel at Southwark: minor orders on William de Lamheth, clerk, and John Heryng' of Winterborne Herringston, vicar of Sopley, both having the first tonsure.

Whitmonday, 21 May 1347

732. ORDERS conferred by the bishop in his manor chapel, Southwark, Ember Saturday, vigil of Trinity Sunday, i.e. 26 May 1347

Acolytes
William de Whatton' of Stoke, dioc. York
John de Trehsk', prebendary of the prebend of Itchen
Fratres: Roger de Mesehale, monk of Rochester
Roger de Howynge, Alan de Estwell', William de Heneford, Friars Minor
Peter atte Mersh', John Camsale, Edmund de Mepham, John de Barstaple, Richard atte Grove, Dominicans
John Bernard', Richard de Certeseye, Thomas de Graveleye, John de la Mote, William de Flamstede, John de Mentenore, monks of St Albans

733. *Subdeacons*
John de Neubury, rector of Pentridge, dioc. Salisbury
William de Burstall', dioc. York, *ad tit*. prior of St Mary, Southwark
John Heryng' of Winterborne Herringston, vicar of Sopley, dioc. Winchester
Thomas le Brun of Burton, dioc. Lincoln, *ad tit*. rector and brethren of Ashridge
John le Vyne, rector of Chalton, dioc. Winchester
Richard de Northcreyk', rector of Siddington, dioc. Worcester
John Gyngel of Warter, dioc. York, *ad tit*. prior of St Mary, Southwark
Henry Jakes of Winchester, *ad tit*. prior of St Deny's, Southampton
Thomas Martyn of Farnham, dioc. Winchester, *ad tit*. prior of Selborne
Fratres: John de Bokelond', Peter de Milton, John de Shotesbrok', Walter Balsale, monks of Chertsey
Thomas Bisshop, William de Ripple, Thomas de Chedyngdon', Dominicans
John Briche, Friar Minor
Thomas Bruyn, monk of Rochester
William de Dodyngton', Carmelite Friar

443   **734.** *Deacons*
Winchester diocese: M. Thomas de Enham, rector of Froyle
William de Waverlee, rector of Ewell
Richard de Elyng', *ad tit*. prior of St Mary Kalendar, Winchester
Richard Umfrey, *ad tit*. abbot of Netley
John de Brikevill of Andover, *ad tit*. prior of St Peter, Winchester

Thomas Mareschal, precentor of St Mary, Southampton
William de Horneby, rector of Wootton, dioc. Lincoln, by dimissory
  letters from M. William Bachiler, canon of Lincoln, *sede vacante*
Robert de Depedale, rector of Culford, dioc. Norwich
William de Knytekote, dioc. Coventry and Lichfield, *ad tit.* domus St
  Michael, Warwick, entered in the registry of the bishop
Fratres: Peter de Secthithe, Roger de Dunham, monks of Bermondsey
  John Vale, Henry Cnolle, John Ridden, William Tringe, Friars Minor
Richard de Kyngeston, Carmelite Friar
William Bocher, canon of Lesnes
Roger Polcaron, Dominican
John de Oxon', Augustinian

735. *Priests*
Edward le Chaumberlayn, rector of Portland, dioc. Salisbury
William Pygot of Wath, dioc. York
John de Welburn', rector of Raunds, dioc. Lincoln
Walter le Tornour, rector of Frinsted, dioc. Canterbury
John Testard, dioc. Chichester, *ad tit.* prior of Tortington
Edmund de Kington, dioc. Worcester, *ad tit.* abbess of Dorchester
John son of Ad' son of Ralph of Walsoken, dioc. Norwich, *ad tit.* prior
  of Caldwell
Thomas de Chadeleshunte, dioc. Coventry and Lichfield, *ad tit. domus*
  of Cold Norton
Richard de Chadeleshunte, dioc. Coventry and Lichfield, *ad tit. domus*
  St John, Lichfield
John de la Lee of Bletchley, dioc. Lincoln, by dimissory letters from
  M. William Bachiler, *sede vacante, ad tit.* prioress of Harrold
John de Petham, dioc. Canterbury, *ad tit.* the provision of a benefice
  belonging to the prior of Leeds
John atte Crouche of Wallop, *ad tit.* prior of Breamore
William de Donmowe, *ad tit,* prior of Newark, for the chantry of
  Ashstead
Robert le Wayte of Winchester, *ad tit.* master of the hospital of St
  James, Charing
Henry Tityng', *ad tit.* prior of Newark
John Payn, *ad tit.* abbess of Wherwell
Stephen le Gardiner of Carisbrooke, *ad tit.* prior of St Peter, Winchester
John Facy, dioc. Bath and Wells, *ad tit.* prior of hospital of St Mary,
  Cripplegate, London
Fratres: John de Resa, John de Schorna, Reginald de Sutton', monks of
  Rochester
John de Hastynges, Thomas de Thurgarton', Carmelite Friars
John Bertelot, William de Hanigfeld, Richard de Horton', Richard de
  Hogstaple, Dominicans
Reginald atte Wode, canon of Lesnes
Stephen de Blyburgh', Friar Minor
Thomas de Croyndon', canon of Tandridge

444 **736.** *Certificatory letter, etc*

Notification that Adam de Lymbergh, rector of Adel, dioc. York, was raised to the diaconate by Richard, bishop of Ossory, Ember Saturday, vigil of Trinity, 1344, in the conventual church of Bermondsey, by authority of Adam, late bishop of Winchester.

Southwark, 8 July 1347

Dimissory Letters for Thomas Marescall', *custos* or precentor of the church of St Mary, Southampton, deacon, for the priesthood

19 August 1347

Licence granted to Benedict, bishop of Cardicen', to confer minor orders on John de Pecham, now with first tonsure, rector of Mereworth, dioc. Rochester, in any church

4 September 1347

Dimissory Letters for M. Thomas de Enham, rector of Froyle, deacon, for the priesthood

4 October 1347

737. ORDERS conferred by the bishop at the parish church of South Waltham, Ember Saturday, 22 September 1347

Acolytes
Robert Takewell of Bourne
John Trokkende of Winchester
John Kyrkeham of Winchester
John atte Watere of Southampton
Severin de Tyntagel, dioc. Exeter
John Trente of Andover
John Marlebergh' of Andover
John Bernard of Compton
Thomas Holm of Compton
John Platfot of Winchester
James de Burghton'
John Laurens of Broughton
Richard Palmere of Winchester
Richard Arnewode
John Trossel of Ringwood
Richard Hampton' of Ringwood
William Belle of Bramley
John Edward of Winchester
John Selede of Wallop
John Gilot of Winchester
Nicholas Lude
Thomas de Leckforde
John Michel, dioc. Exeter
Robert le Longe of Winchester
Walter Gibbe of Winchester
John Salesbury of Ringwood
Roger Herman of Alresford

Fr Theobald Brokhurst, canon of Titchfield
Ralph Sylvestre of Sherborne St John
John le Smyth of Ford [ingbridge]
John de Helle of Winchester
Henry atte Brok' of Kington, dioc. Worcester
William Whitberd of Mapledurham
Laurence Muleward of Sheet
Thomas Uppehull' of Mapledurham
John de Wycchebury of Basingstoke
Richard Gigge of Worting
Bartholomew de Shipton'
Thomas de Farlee
William Sperner of Romsey
Robert Shete of Mapledurham
Fratres: John de Herierd, John de Glastyngbury, John de Guldeford', William Skyllyng, monks of St Swithun's
William de Selewode, John Hendyng', Friars Minor
Stephen de Sarum, canon of Breamore
Peter de Brakenham, monk of Beaulieu
Daniel de Brokhale, Carmelite Friar
Geoffrey Gyngot, John atte Ryede, William de Watercombe, monks of Quarr
John Wodelok', John Bardolf, Nicholas de Upton', Thomas de Kendale, monks of Hyde
Thomas de Brokhampton, Nicholas Dye, Dominicans
John de Berkstede, Friar Minor
Thomas de Aulton', canon of Selborne

738. *Subdeacons*
Robert de Wyngreworth', rector of half the church of Kirkby Laythorpe, dioc. Lincoln
Peter de Farnham, vicar of Thatcham, dioc. Salisbury
Roger atte Gardine of Offham, dioc. Chichester, *ad tit.* prior of Shulbred
William Westmere, rector of Mappowder, dioc. Salisbury
Roger Otery of Winchester, *ad tit.* prior of St Denys, Southampton
Thomas Draghesper, dioc. Salisbury, *ad tit.* prior of Andwell
Edward Salemon of Winterborne, dioc. Salisbury, *ad tit.* prior of Merton
John Rande, dioc. Winchester, *ad tit.* prior of St Mary Kalendar, Winchester
Robert son of Robert Ede of Merstham, dioc. Salisbury, *ad tit. domus* of Dorchester
Thomas *dictus* Preest of Nether Wallop, *ad tit.* prior of Breamore
William son of Richard Molendinar' of Stockton, dioc. Hereford, *ad tit.* prior of Hurley
Thomas Berton' of Tisted, *ad tit.* prior of St Mary Kalendar, Winchester
John Pycard, *ad tit.* 5 marks from Ashstead, by grant of the prior of Newark
William atte Wyfold of Sheepbridge, dioc. Salisbury, *ad tit.* prior of Andwell
Henry Styangre of Basing, *ad tit.* prior of Selborne

Thomas Tassel of Godshill, *ad tit.* prior of the confraternity of St Peter, Winchester

M. Thomas Blount, rector of All Saints, Southampton

Robert Swenlond, rector of Wootton

Walter Morys, *ad tit.* prior of St Denys, Southampton

Thomas Bysshop of Romsey, *ad tit.* prior of Mottisfont

Thomas le Smyth of Wittenham, dioc. Salisbury, *ad tit.* prior of Dorchester

Fratres: John Leente, monk of Netley

John de Hatfeld, William de Aulton, John de Cicestr', canons of Durford, dioc. Chichester

John de Grenstede, William Garet, William de Slyndefeld, John de Barstaple, Dominicans of Chichester

Walter de Farnhull', Thomas de Forde, monks of Beaulieu

Richard *ad crucem*, monk of Quarr

Roger de Compton', Richard Talemache, Carmelite Friars

John Pyges, Dominican

John Exston', monk of Hyde

Robert Dolre, Richard de Stoke, Richard de Shireborne, canons of Christchurch Twynham

Stephen atte Mulle, brother of St Nicholas hospital, Portsmouth

John de Keynesham, Dominican

739. *Deacons*

Walter de Mersham, rector of Limpsfield

William Boycote, dioc. Lincoln, *ad tit.* abbot of Titchfield

Philip Veisy of Maplederwell, *ad tit.* prior of St Mary Kalendar, Winchester

Robert Martyn of Bourne, *ad tit.* prior of Southwark

Peter Wodelond' of West Preston, dioc. Chichester, *ad tit. domus* de Medmenham

Peter Redyng' of Cobham, *ad tit.* hospital of Sandown

William Abbedesbury, dioc. Salisbury, *ad tit.* abbot of Beaulieu, entered in the registry of the bishop of Salisbury

John le Tannere of Alresford, *ad tit.* procurator of the abbey of Lyre

446   Henry Jakes of Winchester, *ad tit.* prior of St Denys, Southampton

Richard Mede of Winchester, *ad tit.* the brethren of St Mary Kalendar, Winchester

Richard de Pottesham, dioc. Chichester, *ad tit.* abbot of Bindon

John Rossel of Worthy, *ad tit.* prior of St Mary Kalendar, Winchester

John de Newebury, dioc. Chichester, *ad tit.* abbot of Robertsbridge

John Sweyn, dioc. Hereford, *ad tit.* prior of St Gregory, Canterbury

Maurice son of Henry Lanathly, dioc. St Davids, *ad tit.* prior of Ivychurch

William Richer of Yatendon, dioc. Salisbury, *ad tit.* prior of Hurley, entered in the registry of the bishop of Salisbury

Roger Godgron of Overton, *ad tit.* fraternity of St Peter, Winchester

Richard de Northcrek', rector of Siddington, dioc. Worcester

Thomas de Mopelton, dioc. Salisbury, *ad tit.* abbot of Bindon, entered in the registry of the bishop of Salisbury

John de Newbury, rector of Pentridge, dioc. Salisbury
Robert Everard of Sherborne, *ad tit.* prior St Denys, Southampton
Thomas Queyntrel of Yeovil, dioc. Bath and Wells, *ad tit.* prior of
    Tortington
John le Yonge of Sheepbridge, dioc. Salisbury, *ad tit.* prior of St
    Frideswide, Oxford
John Heryng', vicar of Sopley
John le Brut, rector of Stock Gaylard, dioc. Salisbury
John de Bynham, rector of Baughurst
Thomas Morys of Winterborne, 'Styvynton', dioc. Salisbury, *ad tit.*
    abbot of Bindon, entered in the registry of the bishop of Salisbury
Fratres: Thomas de Brokhurst, Hugh de Basynge, monks of St Swithuns
Gilbert de Perschute, canon of Mottisfont
Robert Burgate, monk of Beaulieu
John atte Stone, monk of Quarr
Thomas Fachel, Thomas de Coberlegh', John Sarum, Carmelite Friars
Thomas Park', canon of Selborne
Thomas de Keynsham, Dominican
John de Mannygford, monk of Hyde
Adam de Byndon, John de Langeford, canons of St Denys, Southampton
William Martyn, canon of Christchurch

740. *Priests*
William de Waverlee, rector of Ewell
John Doberham, dioc. Salisbury, *ad tit.* abbot of Bindon
Thomas Crompe of Redberth, dioc. St Davids, *ad tit.* prior of Ivychurch
William atte Wode of Lancing, dioc. Chichester, *ad tit.* prior of
    Tortington
William de Middleton', vicar of Carshalton, dioc. Winchester
Reginald Foncente, dioc. Salisbury, *ad tit.* prior of Breamore
John le Forest' of Cheriton, *ad tit.* prior of St Mary Kalendar, Winchester
John Moune of Southampton, *ad tit.* prior of St Denys, Southampton
John Pyket, *ad tit.* prior of St Mary Kalendar, Winchester
Nicholas de Evesham, rector of Capel, dioc. Norwich
Thomas son of Roger le Dieghere of Reading, dioc. Salisbury, *ad tit.*
    abbot of Dorchester
Thomas de Duffeld, dioc. York, *ad tit.* hospital of St Nicholas,
    Portsmouth
William atte Rye of Chatham, dioc. Canterbury, *ad tit.* prior of St
    Gregory, Canterbury
Robert *dictus* Merke, dioc. Glasgow, *ad tit.* prior of Ivychurch
John Brikevile of Andover, *ad tit.* fraternity of St Peter, Winchester
Adam de Ertham, dioc. Chichester, *ad tit.* prior of Shulbred
Richard de Farlee, *ad tit.* prior of Mottisfont
Richard atte Cote of Tonge, dioc. Canterbury *ad tit.* [   ]
447   Thomas Mareschal, precentor of St Mary, Southampton
Fratres: John de Christi Ecclesie, William de Wynton, monks of Netley
John de Catterleston, Simon de Sancto Albano, Friars Minor
Robert de Tichefeld, monk of Quarr
John de Wylton, canon of Breamore

Robert de Milkesham, John de Forde, monks of Beaulieu
Walter de Sparkeford, monk of Hyde
Nicholas de Wykford, monk of St Swithuns
Walter de Hadham, canon of Bisham, dioc. Salisbury
Philip de Wodefolde, canon of Ivychurch, dioc. Salisbury
Walter de Burgham, canon of Christchurch

741. ORDERS conferred by the bishop in his manor chapel, Southwark, all minor orders not received, on M. Godfrey Fromond, rector of Dadington, dioc. Winchester, with dim. letters from the bishop of Lincoln.

All Saints (Nov. 1) 1347

conferred by Benedict, bishop of Cardicen', by authority of the bishop of Winchester, in the manor chapel of Southwark, minor orders on William de Farlee, clerk.

St Luke (Oct. 18) 1347

742. *Dimissory Letters*
12 December 1347, Southwark, for Nicholas Giffard, William Haket and John Lech', canons of Southwick: Nicholas for the subdiaconate, William and John for the priesthood
Same date, for Thomas Hardyng' of Mere, clerk, for minor orders 2 June, 1348 Southwark, for John de Herierd, John de Glastyngbury, John Nicole, William Skyllyng, Hugh de Basynge and Thomas de Brokhurst, professed monks of the cathedral church of Winchester: the first four for the subdiaconate, Hugh and Thomas for the priesthood
5 December, 1348, for M. Walter de Merstham, rector of Limpsfield, for the priesthood
18 December 1348 for John Romy of Fordingbridge, deacon, for the priesthood
19 December 1347, Southwark, for Thomas Heved, acolyte for all holy [orders], Thomas *dictus* le Preost of Wallop for the diaconate, John de Bynham, rector of Baughurst for the priesthood
20 December 1347, for Richard Fyg' of Great Bookham and William le Bakere of Petersfield, acolytes, for the subdiaconate

448   **743.** ORDERS conferred by the bishop in his manor chapel, Southwark, Ember Saturday, 22 December 1347

Acolytes
Richard de Donecastre, rector of Farway, dioc. Exeter
John de Ditton, rector of Sharnford, dioc. Lincoln
Roger de Barneburgh', rector of Siddington, dioc. E Worcester
Henry de Waleton', rector of Llanelly, dioc. St Davids
Adam de Arblaster of Hasfield, dioc. Worcester
John de Codyngton', dioc. York
Fratres: Geoffrey Otery, canon of Newark
Adam de Berkyng', canon of Southwark

744. *Subdeacons*
William de Farlee, canon and prebendary of the conventual church of
Nunnaminster, Winchester
John de Alkebarewe, rector of half the church of Cotgrave, dioc. York
John de Bellerby, rector of St Rowald, Shaftesbury, dioc. Salisbury
Peter de Sancto Paulo, rector of Wolves Newton, dioc. Llandaff
M. Godfrey Froumond, rector of Doddington, dioc. Lincoln
William de Bollewyk', rector of Irthlingborough, dioc. Lincoln
M. Simon de Otteley, dioc. York, *ad tit.* warden and scholars of St
Mary, Oxford
Henry de Boggeworth, rector of Cold Overton, dioc. Lincoln
William de Dunstaple, dioc. Lincoln, *ad tit. domus* St Peter, Dunstaple
Fratres: Henry de Tykesone, Richard de Stanton', Roger Onynge, Friars
Minor

745. *Deacons*
Philip Gylde of Wallingford, dioc. Salisbury, *ad tit.* abbot of Dorchester,
entered in the registry of the bishop of Salisbury
Peter de Normandeby, rector of Burgh Castle, dioc. Norwich
Robert le Smyth of East Garston, dioc. Salisbury, *ad tit.* prioress of
Amesbury
Robert de Wyngreworth', rector of half the church of St Denis, Kirkby
Lathorp, dioc. Lincoln
Robert de Swanlond, rector of Wootton, dioc. Winchester
Philip de Leylond, dioc. Coventry and Lichfield, *ad tit.* domus of
Combermere
M. Thomas de Bakenhull', rector of Eastnor, dioc. Hereford
William atte Wyfold of Sheepbridge, dioc. Salisbury, *ad tit.* prior of
Andwell, procurator for abbot of Tiron
Frater Milliam de Mereworth', canon of Newark

746. *Priests*
John Heyren of Basingstoke, *ad tit.* prior of Selborne
John le Yonge of Sheepbridge, dioc. Salisbury, *ad tit.* prior of St
Frideswide, Oxford
John de Cannteton', rector of Penbryn, dioc. St Davids
Richard de Northcreyk, rector of Stoke by Eye, dioc. Norwich
Walter de Merstham, rector of Limpsfield, dioc. Winchester
William de Burstall, vicar of Kingston, dioc. Winchester
John Ponnt of Newbury, dioc. Salisbury, *ad tit.* prior of St John of
Jerusalem in England
John de Newbury, rector of Pentridge, dioc. Salisbury
Walter de Boycote, dioc. Lincoln, *ad tit.* abbot of Titchfield
William Pax of Basingstoke, dioc. Winchester, *ad tit.* prior of St Denys,
Southampton
John Chevere of Clandon, dioc. Winchester, *ad tit.* prior of Southwark
Fratres: Nicholas Hardcourt, Robert Botiller, John Vale, Geoffrey de
Sancto Edmundo, John Gyles, John de Santone, Friars Minor

449

747. *Dimissory Letters*

3 January 1348, Southwark, for Richard son of Richard Fykeys of Portsmouth, dioc. Winchester, for all minor orders

24 February 1348 for John Seys, rector of Shalfleet, Isle of Wight, for all minor orders not yet received

11 March 1348 for Fratres John de Thoneye and Theobald de Brokhurst, acolytes, for the subdiaconate; Walter de Oxon', deacon, for the priesthood, canons of Titchfield

748. ORDERS conferred by the bishop in his manor chapel, Southwark, Ember-Saturday, in first week of Lent, 15 March 1348

Acolytes

Robert de Wymondeswold, rector of Thurlow, dioc. Norwich

William de Sutton', rector of Colveston, dioc. Norwich

William Wolf' of Edington, dioc. Salisbury

Simon Goman of Tunbridge, dioc. Chichester

Adam Neubolt, rector of Northborough, dioc. Coventry and Lichfield

Robert de Wylford, rector of Niton, [Isle of Wight] dioc. Winchester

749. *Subdeacons*

John de Yepeswich', rector of Bliston, dioc. Exeter

Richard de Donecastre, rector of Farway, dioc. Exeter

John de Ludham, rector of St Mildred, Canterbury, by letters dimissory from the archbishop

Richard de Tyffyngton', presented to the vicarage of Bramfield, *ad tit.* hospital of St Giles outside the bar of the Old Temple, London

Robert de Wakefeld, rector of Lee, dioc. Lincoln

Peter de Sancto Paulo, rector of Wolves Newton, dioc. Llandaff

William Sperner of Romsey, dioc. Winchester, *ad tit.* prior of Ivychurch

Severin de Tyntagel, dioc. Exeter, *ad tit.* prior of Launceston

John de Derby, rector of Hempstead, dioc. Norwich

450 Robert Lovekyn of Adlington, dioc. Worcester, *ad tit.* abbess of Polesworth

John de Ditton, rector of Sharnford, dioc. Lincoln

John de Luda, rector of St Cross, York

John de Copham, rector of Shipton Beauchamp, dioc. Bath and Wells

Henry de Walton', rector of Llanelly, dioc. St Davids

John de Stafford', rector of Hannington, dioc. Salisbury

John Mer of Weymouth, dioc. Salisbury, *ad tit.* abbot of Bindon

William le White, dioc. Lincoln, *ad tit.* abbot of Dorchester

Fratres: Thomas de Aulton, canon of Selborne

Adam de Berkynge, canon of St Mary, Southwark

John de Tonnebrugg', brother of hospital of St Mary, Ospringe, dioc. Canterbury

Stephen de Guenor, Carmelite Friar

750. *Deacons*

William de Farlee, dioc. Winchester, canon and prebendary of Nunnaminster

Henry de Bagworth, rector of Cold Overton, dioc. Lincoln

John de Alkebarghe, rector of half the church of Cotgrave, dioc. York

William Whatton' of Stoke, rector of the chapel of St James, near Seaford, dioc. Chichester

John de Bellerby, rector of St Rowald, Shaftesbury, dioc. Salisbury

Hugh de Corbrugg', rector of Hunstaneworth, dioc. Durham

Simon Mason, rector of Sudbrooke, dioc. Lincoln

Henry Walet, dioc. Salisbury, *ad tit.* prior of Poughley

John Staundene of Hungerford, dioc. Salisbury, *ad tit.* prior of Poughley

Stephen de Swanton', of Dover, dioc. Canterbury, *ad tit.* prior of St Martin, Dover

Robert de Notyngham, rector of Brancaster, dioc. Norwich

M. Godfrey Froumond, rector of Doddington, dioc. Lincoln

John de Huntyngton', dioc. Lincoln, *ad tit.* prior of Bushmead

William *dictus* le Clerc of Penshurst, dioc. Canterbury, *ad tit.* abbot of Lesnes

Thomas Langeton', rector of Somercotes, dioc. Lincoln

Thomas atte Berton, dioc. Winchester, *ad tit.* prioress of Kington [St Michael]

Fratres: John Sannford, Carmelite Friar

John de Boklond', Peter de Mylton', John Shotesbeak, Walter Balsale, monks of Chertsey

751. *Priests*

M. Thomas de Bokenhull', rector of Farley, dioc. Winchester

John *natus* Thomae Johannis of Spaldwick, vicar of Sawston, dioc. Ely

Robert de Wyngreworth', rector of half the church of St Denis, Kirkby Laythorp, dioc. Lincoln

John Romy of Ford[ingbridge], dioc. Winchester, *ad tit.* prior of Ivychurch

John Veisy, dioc. Winchester, *ad tit.* prior of the Kalendar, Winchester

John Rook of Stalisfield, dioc. Canterbury, *ad tit.* prior of St Gregory, Canterbury

Roger Wyke of Dover, dioc. Canterbury, *ad tit.* master of the hospital, Dover

Robert Posse of Cranbrook, dioc. Canterbury, *ad tit.* prior of Leeds

Benedict Skardeyn of Canterbury, *ad tit.* prior of St Mary, Southwark

John de Newbury, dioc. Salisbury, *ad tit.* abbot of Robertsbridge

Robert de Swanlond', rector of Wootton, dioc. Winchester

M. John Barnet, rector of Westwell, dioc. Canterbury

451 Thomas de Wodeford', dioc. Salisbury, *ad tit.* prior of Lega

Peter de Normandeby, rector of Burgh Castle, dioc. Norwich

Fratres: John Asshe, Augustinian

John de Rougham, Thomas de Bylingham, Carmelite Friars

John de Kersaulton', John de Cressyngham, Richard de Mershton, Henry de Cliston, Hugh de Herthwell', monks of Westminster

752. GRANT OF FIRST CLERICAL TONSURE by the bishop of his manor chapel, Southwark, 17 March 1348

John Savage of Grimley, dioc. Worcester

John Ballard of Watford, of the exempt jurisdiction of St Albans.
  Diocese of Winchester: Henry Coc of Egham

Roger Cheseman of Guildford   Peter Carpentarius of Cobham
Richard Passour of Chertsey   and Laurence his brother
Robert Ferour of Chertsey   Thomas Mulleward of Eversley
Ralph Prince of Thorp   John Bratford of Streathem
Simon Barbour of Chertsey   Richard Croydon of Southwark

753. GRANT OF FIRST TONSURE at Esher to John Salle of Winchester,
Thomas de Cherteseye, John de Cherteseye, William Janyn of Kingstone
and John de Wynton'

                                                        1 April 1348

754. *Dimissory Letters*
6 April 1348, Southwark, for William de Wynton, clerk, for minor orders
  and Walter de Porteswode, subdeacon for the diaconate
12 April 1348 for Richard de Houghton', of the Isle of Wight, for minor
  orders
16 April 1348 for John Seys, rector of Shalfleet, Isle of Wight, acolyte,
  for all holy orders

755. ORDERS conferred by the bishop in his manor chapel, Southwark,
Holy Saturday, 19 April 1348

Deacons
Robert de Wymondeswold', rector of Little Thurlow, dioc. Norwich
Fr Thomas de Brokhampton', Dominican

Priests
William de Farlee, dioc. Winchester, canon in the conventual church of
  Nunnaminster
Henry de Waleton rector of Llanelly, dioc. St Davids
John de Ditton', rector of Sharnford, dioc. Lincoln
John de Ludham, rector of St Mildred, Canterbury
Richard de Doncastre, rector of Farway, dioc. Exeter
Richard de Tyffyngton', dioc. Coventry and Lichfield, *ad tit.* hospital of
  St Giles outside the bar of the Old Temple, London
Ralph de Notyngham, rector of Mirfield, dioc. York
Peter de Sancto Paulo, rector of Wolves Newton, dioc. Llandaff
John de Derby, rector of Hempstead, dioc. Norwich
Fr William de Dadyngton', Capucin

452   **756.** *Tonsure and Dimissory Letters*
24 April 1348, Southwark, letters for Thurstan Godstrode of
  Chiddingfold, dioc. Winchester, for first tonsure and minor orders
19 May 1348 for Fr Robert Dolre, Richard de Stoke, Richard de
  Shireborne, canons of Christchurch Twynham, sudbeacons for the
  diaconate
12 May 1348, Esher, the bishop conferred the first tonsure on John
  Partrich', William Twyners, Thomas Twynersh', William Sheremannes,

John de Reigate, Thomas Passour, John Storie, William Hakstall' and Thomas Smyth' of Walton

18 May 1348, Southwark, the bishop conferred the first tonsure on Robert de Appleby, dioc. Lincoln, showing his dimissorial letters

20 May 1348, letters for Richard Herbert, acolyte, of Hayling, dioc. Winchester, for all holy orders

25 May 1348, for John Chivaler, clerk, of Wolknestede (Godstone), dioc. Winchester, for all minor orders

9 June 1348, the bishop conferred the first tonsure on Nicholas *dictus* le Clerc of Walton, Andrew Bondy, John de Shirewode, Robert Eliot and Robert de Asshewell, dioc. Winchester

757. ORDERS conferred by the bishop in the parish church of Esher, Ember Saturday in Whitweek, 14 June 1348

Acolyte
Fr John de Melborne, Augustinian

Subdeacon
John de Codynton', rector of Beighton, dioc. Norwich

Priests
Robert de Wymondeswold', rector of Little Thurlow, dioc. Norwich
Robert de Wylford, rector of Niton, Isle of Wight
John Sharp of the parish of St Vedast, London, in the jurisdiction of the archbishop, *ad tit.* prior of Stratford atte Boghwe, near London
William de Dunstaple, dioc. Lincoln, *ad tit.* prior and canons of St Peter, Dunstaple
Denis de Taucestre, prebendary in the collegiate chapel of St Mary in the Fields, Norwich

758. *First Tonsure*
21 June 1348, Chertsey, first tonsure for William Hale of Chertsey, Simon de Wodeham; William atte Hide and John Herm of Wisley, with letters of authorization from Edward prince of Wales; Thomas de Rokesbury, John *dictus* Lovender, John Lutewyne, Richard de Wokkyng', Robert Mounteyn, William Pentecost and John le Barbour—all of the diocese

759. *Dimissory Letters*
15 July 1348, Southwark, for John Perket of Chiddingfold, for all minor orders
11 July, for Rogert de Toveton', rector of Tunworth, acolyte, for the subdiaconate

453 **760.** *First tonsure*
Friday, feast of the Assumption, 15 August 1348, Esher, John Doni of Bletchingley, John de Bodesham, John Danyel, Alexander Daniel, John de Geyton, Bartholomew Cnollere of Bletchingley
Sunday, 17 August 1348, Farnham, Thomas Giles of Hascombe, John de Mussynden', Walter atte Cnolle, John de Rudyngshers and William

his brother, Thomas le Teslere, Richard de Godalmyng', William Tannere also of Godalming, John Harscombe, from the same—all of the diocese

21 August 1348, Farnham, William Andrew, John de Bereford, William de Bereford, Richard Yst, Thomas Dyere, Thomas de Redesle, John de Blebbelee and William his brother, Robert Copyn

24 August 1348 [Bishops] Waltham, Thomas Megg', dioc. Lincoln

25 August, Waltham, Edward Suleman, Walter le Barber, Richard Spenser, John atte Haler

761. *Dimissory Letters*

16 August 1348, Farnham, for M. John de Evyton, dioc. Winchester, acolyte, for all holy orders

762. *First Tonsure*

8 September 1348, [Bishops] Waltham, John Retherfeld, dioc. Winchester, and John de Gorewy, dioc. Worcester

9 September, 1348, Waltham, Melchisar Wodelok'

7 September 1348, Houghton, John Walshe and John Kyng, of the diocese

11 September 1348, Hambledon, William Gervays, rector of Westcote, William Wake and John Trendenham, of the diocese

14 September 1348, in the manor chapel of the abbot of Beaulieu called Beufre, Nicholas le Whit', John le Frye, Walter Bryan, Nicholas Schus, Robert Avere, John Sawyare, John de Marlebergh', Robert Barbour, Thomas Helyan, Robert Flemmyng', Thomas Rannvile, Robert Botre, Nicholas Imbert, John Seman, Richard de Assheden', Robert le Courter, William de Langeford, Robert Stalmer and Thomas Stryde— of the diocese

15 September 1348, in the chapel of Wells, near Romsey, Richard de Perschute, Nicholas Bedel, John de Chelworth, Nicholas le Forest and John de Tichborne—of the diocese

Same date, John atte Crouche of Ringwood received dimissory letters for the priesthood

17 September 1348, in the manor chapel of Highclere, first tonsure for Richard Alvish', William Michel, Thomas de Farnham, John White, John Bailly, Johne atte More—of the diocese

763. *Dimissory letters etc.*

17 September 1348, Highclere, letters for Fr. John de Manyngford for priesthood, John de Exton' for diaconate, Nicholas de Bourton', John Bardolf, Thomas de Candale and John de Wodelok' for subdiaconate— all monks of Hyde

Same date, for Robert de Wolfreton, warden of the chapel of Limerstone, Isle of Wight, acolyte for all holy orders and Peter de Wolfreton, clerk, for minor and all holy orders—both of the Isle of Wight

14 September 1348, Beaulieu, for Fr Walter Kyngot, John Ride, William de Watercombe and Philip de Pokelchirch' for subdiaconate, Richard Balam for diaconate and John Stone for priesthood—all monks of Quarr

18 September 1348, Highclere, for John de Langeford of the diocese, for first tonsure and minor orders and all holy orders

454 18 September 1348, Highclere, for Robert Everard of Sherborne St John, deacon, for priesthood

Same date, grant of first tonsure to Nicholas Copinor of Albury, Thomas Botesham, John Warner, John Huchun of Woodhay, John Goudhire— of the diocese

13 September 1348 Beaulieu, dimissory letters for Robert de Dolre, Richard de Schireborne and Richard de Stok', deacons, for priesthood—canons of Christchurch Twynham

18 September 1348, Southwark, for Roger Otery, dioc. Winchester, for diaconate and priesthood

Same date, for Robert Pyk' of Reigate for first clerical tonsure

29 September, 1348, Southwark, grant of first tonsure to Matthew Henrici, student (*scolar*) of Cologne, with dimissory letters from the archbishop of Cologne

27 October 1348, Southwark, dimissory letters for John Chanu of Walton-on-Thames for all minor orders

764. ORDERS conferred by the bishop in the manor chapel, Southwark, Ember Saturday, 20 December 1348

Acolytes
William de Barneby, rector of Hardwick, dioc. Lincoln
Richard de Derby, rector of Hodnet, dioc. Coventry and Lichfield
William Rethewelle, rector of Potterspury, dioc. Lincoln
Roger de Cestrefeld, dioc. Coventry and Lichfield
William de Ingelby, rector of Wootton, dioc. Winchester
Richard Chapman of Hale Street, dioc. Canterbury
Thomas de Bridelynton, dioc. York
John Alisanndre of Guildford
Robert atte Brugg' of Lambeth
Thomas de Hornyngtoft, rector of Gressenhall, dioc. Norwich
Peter de Croydon', dioc. Canterbury
John Wode of Coulsdon
Reginald Husee
John Pecok' of Chiddingfold
Giles de Wynage, canon of Middleburg, dioc. Utrecht
Thomas Madefrai, rector of Langathen, dioc. St Davids
Fratres: John de Seton, Dominican
Peter de Bedyngfeld, John de Southbury, Carmelite Friars
John de Malmesbury, canon of St Mary, Southwark

765. *Subdeacons*
Richard de Wath', rector of Stibbington, dioc. Lincoln
Thomas de Oldyngton', rector of Haltwhistle, dioc. Durham
Thomas de Walfyngham, rector of All Saints, Barnwell, dioc. Lincoln
Richard de Whitbergh', rector of Fletching, dioc. Chichester
M. Ralph West, rector of Greatford, dioc. Lincoln
Richard Cayli of Bradfield, rector of Little Sampford, dioc. London

Thomas Elyot of Wonersh, *ad tit.* prior of Newark
Bartholomew de Cranebrok', dioc. Canterbury, *ad tit.* prior of Leeds
John Bolt of Southampton, rector of St Michael in Fleshmonger Street,
    Winchester
John Edelyne of Peniton, *ad tit.* monastery of Ivychurch
Richard Monk of Wallop, *ad tit.* prior of Breamore

455   William son of Roger le Smyth atte Rude of Worplesdon, *ad tit.* prior
    of Newark
Walter Frank' of Docking, dioc. Norwich, *ad tit.* prior of Leyes
Roger Herman of Alresford, *at tit.* monastery of Chertsey
Ralph de Croyland, rector of Norton Bavant, dioc. Salisbury
Henry Forest, rector of Water Eaton, dioc. Salisbury
Robert de Newnenham, rector of Nunney, dioc. Bath and Wells
John de Nessefeld, rector of Foston, dioc. York
Thomas de Hierne, rector of Willesborough, dioc. Canterbury
John Ewe of Uxbridge, dioc. London, *ad tit. domus* of Keynsham
Peter de Marisco of Winchester, *ad tit.* prior of Newark
John Abbe of Steyning, dioc. Chichester, *ad tit.* prior Holy Trinity,
    London
John son of William of te Halle of Westwick, dioc. Ely, *ad tit.* prior of
    St Mary, Sulby (?)
William Arnald of Ripple, dioc. Canterbury, *ad tit.* prior of St Gregory,
    Canterbury
John Saney of Sholden, dioc. Canterbury, *ad tit.* abbot of St Radegund
Richard de Bolessort, rector of Culrath, dioc. Connor
William Mate of Meopham, dioc. Canterbury, *ad tit. domus* Holy
    Trinity, London
Fratres: Matthew de Horle, Dominican
John de Fenton, Ralph de Wrangle, Richard de Gutyng', John de
    Hadenham, canons of Holy Cross, Waltham
John de Haddon', canon of the prior of St Bartholomew, Smithfield
Walter de Remesbury, Baldwin de Brynkele, Robert de Sancto Mamueo
William de Lond', Robert de Wyndlesore, John de Shapeye, canons of
    Merton
Geoffrey Otery, canon of Newark

766. *Deacons*
Peter son of Richard Aldewyk' of Rattlesden, dioc. Norwich, *ad tit.*
    domus of Bromehill, which is entered in the register of the bishop of
    Salisbury
Robert Bonensannt of Scropton, dioc. Coventry and Lichfield, *ad tit.*
    prior of hospital of St John of Jerusalem
William Aleyn of Womenswold, dioc. Canterbury, *ad tit.* abbot of St
    Radegund
William Langhogg of Chelmondiston (?), dioc. Norwich, *ad tit.* prior of
    St Mary, Dodnash
Alexander Gilles of Dover, dioc. Canterbury, *ad tit.* prior of Combwell
Robert de Haytfeld, rector of Coln St Dennis, dioc. Worcester
John de Kendale, rector of Caldecote, dioc. Norwich

Robert son of Peter de Wysebech', dioc. Ely, *ad tit.* prior of St Mary, Southwark

Thomas Tassel, dioc. Winchester, *ad tit.* prior and brethren of St Peter, Winchester

Thomas Blount, rector of All Saints, Southampton

Thomas Lamb of Strood, dioc. Rochester, *ad tit.* prior of Prittlewell

Reginald atte Welle of Walton, dioc. Lincoln, *ad tit.* prioress of Sopwell

John Becwell of Halstow, dioc. Rochester, *ad tit.* prior of Bayham

Richard Sulgrave of Ashwell, dioc. Lincoln, *ad tit.* prior and canons of St John Baptist, Latton

Michael Wodizere of Chatham, dioc. Rochester, *ad tit.* prior of Leeds

M. Robert de Wyntryngham, dioc. Lincoln, *ad tit.* dean of the royal free chapel of St Martin-le-Grand, London

Robert Sok' of Swaffham, dioc. Ely, *ad tit.* prior of Anglesey

John Pikard of Guildford, *ad tit.* prior of Newark

M. Thomas Michel, rector of Holme, dioc. Norwich

Thomas *dictus* le Preest of Nether Wallop, *ad tit.* prior of Breamore

456 Warin, rector of Weston Colville, dioc. Ely

William son of John le Bakere of Petersfield, *ad tit.* prior of Tortington

John Andreu of Cerne, dioc. Salisbury, *ad tit.* abbot of Cerne

Fratres: John de Reynham, John de Coggeshale, monks of Stratford, dioc. London

Richard de Cornubia, Dominican

Thomas de Neweby, Friar Minor

Robert de Mershton, canon of St Bartholomew, Smithfield, London

Thomas de Aulton, canon of Selborne

Adam de Berkynge, canon of St Mary, Southwark

John de Oxebury, William de Ludham, Robert Swan, John de Pykeford', Carmelite Friars

John de Welles, canon of Bilsington, dioc. Canterbury

767. *Priests*

Robert Everard, perpetual vicar of the prebendal church of Preston, dioc. Salisbury

Adam de Newbold, rector of Northborough, dioc. Coventry and Lichfield

M. Thomas de Clipston', rector of Great Ponton, dioc. Lincoln

John Tannere, dioc. Winchester, *ad tit.* abbot of Lyre

John de Ledes, rector of Burstow, dioc. Canterbury

John Smith' of Hollingborne, dioc. Canterbury, *ad tit.* prior of Leeds

William atte Wyefold, dioc. Salisbury, *ad tit.* prior of Andwell

Henry de Wetynge, dioc. Norwich, *ad tit.* prior of Thetford

John Jour of Milton, dioc. Ely, *ad tit.* prior of Bushmead

Richard Umfrai, dioc. Winchester, *ad tit.* abbot of Netley

Richard de Elynge, *ad tit.* prior and fraternity of St Mary Kalendar, Winchester

Simon Byndynge of Leighton Buzzard, dioc. Lincoln, *ad tit.* monastery of St Peter, Dunstaple

William Sprittok' of Sutton, dioc. Norwich, *ad tit. domus* St Mary, Woodbridge

John Amifleis son of Robert Amifleis of Girton, dioc. Ely, *ad tit. domus* of Tiptree

Robert atte Cherch of Staple, dioc. Canterbury, *ad tit.* abbot of Langdon

Robert Martyn of Bourne (?), dioc. Winchester, *ad tit.* prior of St Mary, Southwark

Henry Jakes of Winchester, *ad tit.* prior of St Denys, Southampton

John Badyngham, dioc. Winchester, *ad tit.* prior of Selborne

Walter Selot of Guildford, dioc. Winchester, *ad tit.* prior and brethren of Sandown

Simon Edyman of Brisley, dioc. Norwich, *ad tit. domus* of Bilsington

Philip de Legh, rector of Leigh, dioc. Coventry and Lichfield

John de Codyngton', rector of Weighton, dioc. Norwich

John Seys, rector of Shalfleet, Isle of Wight, dioc. Winchester

John de Pekham, rector of Mereworth, dioc. Rochester

Thomas Alyndon' of Maidstone, dioc. Canterbury, *ad tit.* prior of Leeds

John Russel of Headbourne Worthy, dioc. Winchester, *ad tit.* prior of St Mary Kalendar, Winchester

Roger Gondgrom of Everton, dioc. Winchester, *ad tit.* prior of St Peter, Winchester

John son of Thomas son of Hugh of Ratcliffe on Trent, dioc. York, *ad tit.* abbot of Darley, which is entered in the register of the archbishop of York

Thomas de Berton, rector of the chapel of Frobury, dioc. Winchester

Hugh son of Robert Symond of Alvington, dioc. Worcester, *ad tit.* abbot of Osney

Henry de Hegham, rector of Ditton, dioc. Rochester

William Lenur of Great Thurlow, dioc. Norwich, *ad tit.* prior of Chipley

Peter son of Richard Aldewyk' of Rattlesden, dioc. Norwich, *ad tit. domus* of Bromehill

Fratres: Henry de Colyngburn', canon of St Mary, Southwark

Thomas de Henle, monk of Stratford, dioc. London

Gilbert de Perschute, Walter de Derneford, canons of Mottisfont

457   John de Sannford, John de Ferynge, Richard de Hidelesdon', Carmelite Friars

John de Martlesham, Thomas de Staneweie, Friars Minor

768. *First Tonsure and Dimissorial Letters*

23 December 1348, Southwark, first tonsure conferred on John de Berkham, dioc. Chichester

11 January 1349, Farnham, conferred on William Reynald of Fordingbridge

2 February 1349, Esher, Candlemas, on John de Edyndon', warden of the hospital of St Nicholas, Portsmouth, and on M. Walter de Sevenhampton', rector of Worting, raised to acolytes

Same date, dimissory letters for monks of Quarr: William de Boklond' for minor orders, for William de Caresbrok' and John de Cosham for the subdiaconate, Geoffrey Kyngot, John Ride and William de Watercombe for the disconate and Richard Balam for the priesthood

7 March 1349, for Hugh Mareschal of Reigate for minor and holy orders

19 March 1349, Farnham, received the first clerical tonsure:

Robert Makaye of Abbotstone
Robert Truttesworth of Chertsey
John Pokefeld of Chiddingfold
Robert de Kyngesleye and John Salmon of Ewhurst
John Brompton' of Stoke d'Abernon
Robert atte Vonne of Eversley
Thomas Bochard of Nately
Richard atte Berton' of Heckfield
Richard de Odyham
Thomas atte Hethe of Odiham
William Wydenhale of Headley
Nicholas Chauyn of Alton
John Colyere of Pirbright
Richard Loteron of Up Nately
William Hovet of 'Ludlyng'
William Battescroft of Puttenham
Walter Imworth of Witley and John atte Halle of Hursley
12 May 1349, dimissory letters for Walter Frelond, rector of Ockham, for minor and all holy orders
13 April 1349, Farnham, first tonsure conferred on John atte Chirche and Thomas Peneke of Rotherwick

769. ORDERS conferred by the bishop in the parish church of Cobham, Ember Saturday in Lent, 7 March 1349

Acolytes

Thomas de Stanford, rector of St Pancras, Winchester
M. John de Ware, rector of Bishopstone, dioc. Salisbury
John Maiheu of Godshill
Richard Kinet of Basing
John Styangre of Basing
Thomas Litherere of Andover
John Benstede of Clatford
William Jolyf of Leatherhead
John Benstede
Peter Guldon of Heckfield
M. Walter Cole, rector of St Rumwold, Winchester
John Mone of the Isle of Wight
William Husee of Romsey
Walter Dykfyn of Winchester
John de Buryton'
William Fynyngleye of Odiham
458 Walter Frille of Walton
Nicholas Follere of Woking
John Stynt of Farnham
John Farman of Shere
John de Schirefeld
John London' of Houghton

Henry de Froyle
Thomas Marschal of Alton
Nicholas Berton Sacy of Hurstbourne Priors
Nicholas atte Bergh'
Stephen Frenssh
Thomas Frank of Waltham
John Andrew of Mottisfont
Walter Herman of Guildford
John Syre of Catherington
Peter Taillour of Guildford
Richard Sewelle of Albury
John Bakere of Alresford
Bartholomew Lucas of Guildford
Henry Petleye
Walter filius Lecester of Thirsk, dioc. York
John Bussewelle of Shere
Adam atte Wath', dioc. York
Peter Rogier of Shere
John de Rippele
Robert atte More
Fr. Nigel de Waltham and John de Wynton', monks of Waverley

John le Smyth of Walton
Walter Brakestoke, rector of
  Wield, dioc. Winchester

Fr. Bartholomew Drukas,
  Dominican of Guildford
  convent
Thomas Magger of Brill, dioc.
  Lincoln

770. *Subdeacons*
William de Barneby, rector of Hardwick, dioc. Norwich
M. Henry de Lutegarshale, rctor of 'Westundeworth'
William Tangele, *ad tit*. prior of St Peter, Winchester
Walter de Upton', rector of St Clement, Winchester
Richard Commere of Bedhampton, *ad tit*. prior of Newark
William Beegh of Wallop, *ad tit*. prior of Mottisfont
John Parsones of Upclatford, *ad tit*. prior of St Peter, Winchester
William Poors of Worplesdon, *ad tit*. prior of Newark
M. John de Lemynton, rector of Appleford, Isle of Wight
M. John de Snecott, *ad tit*. prior of Newark
William de Engulby, rector of Wotton
Walter de Brokhampton', rector of Steventon
John Chalkeberd of Cheriton, *ad tit*. prior of St Mary Kalendar,
  Winchester
John de Wicchebury, *ad tit*. prior of Bisham Montagu
Nicholas Bisshop' of Wherwell, *ad tit*. prior of St Denys, Southampton
Nicholas Chaun of Walton, *ad tit*. prior of the hospital of Sandown
John Kyng' of Langley Marsh, dioc. Lincoln, *ad tit*. prior of Merton
Walter Chapman of Merrow, *ad tit*. prior of Newark
Thomas Cuppyng' of Liss, *ad tit*. abbot of Netley
Walter Plenice of Clive, dioc. Hereford, *ad tit*. prior of Sandown
John Clomere of Shepperton, dioc. London, *ad tit*. prior of Sandown
William Frylond of Petersfield, *ad tit*. prior of Tortington
John Reyson of Merton town, *ad tit*. prior of Merton
William Cranemore, Isle of Wight, *ad tit*. prior of Carisbrooke
John Peek', *ad tit*. prior of Breamore
Robert atte Hethe of Kingsclere, *ad tit*. prior of Mottisfont
Richard son of John of Llandenny, dioc. Monmouth, *ad tit*. prior of
  Hurley
John Monck of Guildford, *ad tit*. prior of Boxgrove
Richard Fig' of Great Bookham, *ad tit*. prior of Reigate
Mark le Booe of South Waltham, *ad tit*. abbot of Hyde
William le White of Yateley, *ad tit*. prior of Hurley
John Michel, dioc. Exeter, *ad tit*. prior of St German, Cornwall, which
  is entered in the registry of the bishop of Exeter
Adam le Frere, *ad tit*. prior and fraternity of St Mary, Winchester
John Frere of Winchester, *ad tit*. prior of St Mary Kalendar, Winchester
William Herefu of Winchester, *ad tit*. prior of St Peter, Winchester
John atte Wode of Coulsdon, *ad tit*. prior of Newark
John son of John of Yelling, *ad tit*. prior of St Mary, Southwark
John Thome called Lecester of Thrisk, prebendary of the prebend of
  Itchen
William Grym of Sele, *ad tit*. prior of Selborne

John Trokkende of Winchester, *ad tit.* prior of St Denys, Southampton
Peter Reyn' of Farnham, *ad tit.* prior of Merton
Ralph Tristram, rector of Greatham
Richard Kynet of Basing, *ad tit.* prior of Hamble, procurator of abbot of Tiron, dioc. Chartres
William Bronnyng' of Colmer, *ad tit.* prior of Hayling, procurator of abbot of Jumièges
Thomas de Eykeringe, rector of Abbots Ann

459 Thomas Lumbard of East Oakley, *ad tit.* prior of St Mary Kalendar, Winchester
Roger de Cesterford', rector of Bradford Peverell, dioc. Salisbury
John de la Dale, rector of Hendon, dioc. London
Thomas de Bodleston, dioc. Lincoln, *ad tit.* hospital of St Mary Magdalen, Southwell
William Richard of Stoke-by-Guildford, *ad tit.* [   ]
M. Walter de Sevenhampton, rector of Worting
John son of Augustin of Hemington, dioc. Lincoln, *ad tit.* apostolic provision at collation of the abbot of Crowland
William de Rothewelle, rector of Pottersbury, dioc. Lincoln
William Ware, rector of St Mary Magdalen, Bermondsey
Fratres: John de Glastyngbury, John Nichol and William Skillyng, monks of the cathedral church
Robert Dawe, monk of Waverley
Adam de Dunmowe, Dominican of Winchester convent
John de Burstede, Dominican of Guildford
Peter de Brakenham, monk of Beaulieu

771. *Deacons*
Richard Manek, of Wallop, *ad tit.* prior of Breamore
Severin de Tintagel, dioc. Exeter, *ad tit.* prior of Launceston
Peter Marreys, rector of St Alphege at the corner of Calpe Street, Winchester
Henry Stiangre of Basing, *ad tit.* prior of Selborne
John Courneys of Wokingham, dioc. Salisbury, *ad tit.* abbot of Medmenham
John Bolt of Southampton, rector of the church in Fleshmonger Street, Winchester
John Vyne, rector of Chaldon
John Roude, rector of St Peter without the Southgate, Winchester
Robert de Willardlye, dioc. York, *ad tit.* master of the hospital of Burton Lazars
John Hertford of St Albans, with dim. letters from the abbot, immediately subject to the Holy see, *ad tit.* prioress of Sopwell
Thomas Elyot of Wonersh, *ad tit.* prior of Newark
Robert de Newenham, rector of Nunney, dioc. Bath and Wells
Roger Hereman of Alresford, *ad tit.* abbot of Chertsey
Richard de Wath', rector of Stibbington, dioc. Lincoln
William son of Roger le Smyth' of Worpleston, *ad tit.* prior of Newark
John Abbe of Steyning, dioc. of Chichester, *ad tit.* prior of H. Trinity, London

Fratres: Thomas de Forde, monk of Beaulieu

Stephen de Molendinis, professed brother of St Nicholas, Portsmouth

Geoffrey Otery, canon of Newark

William de Rammesbury, Baldwin de Brinkele, Robert de Sancto Manifeo, William de London, Robert de Windesore and John de Shepeye, canons of Merton

772. *Priests*

Thomas Tassel, *ad tit.* prior of St Peter, Winchester

Thomas de Bourn', *ad tit.* prior of Selborne

Thomas le Preest of Nether Wallop, *ad tit.* prior of Breamore

John Waleys of Rotherfield Peppard, dioc. Lincoln, *ad tit.* abbot of Thame

John le Greyn of Breamore, *ad tit.* prior of Breamore

William son of John le Bakere of Petersfield, *ad tit.* prior of Tortington

Robert son of Peter de Wysbech, dioc. Ely, *ad tit.* prior of Southwark

Roger de Bernes, nominated to be subdeacon in the chapel of St Elizabeth, Winchester, *ad tit.* prior of St Peter, Winchester

460 William Gaterugg', vicar of Alton

Thomas Blount, rector of All Saints, Southampton

M. Philip de Lend', rector of Crundale, dioc. Canterbury

Walter Morys of Portswood, *ad tit.* prior of St Denys, Southampton

John Pikard of Guildford, *ad tit.* prior of Newark

Henry de Schutlynden', vicar of Banstead, dioc. Winchester

Reginald atte Welle of Walton, dioc. London, *ad tit. domus* of Sopwell

Richard de Clere, *ad tit.* prior of the hospital of Sandown

Fratres: Hugh de Basynge, monk of the cathedral priory

John de Langeford, canon of St Denys, Southampton

Thomas de Wolveleye, monk of Waverley

Thomas de Aulton, canon of Selborne

Robert de Burgate, monk of Beaulieu

Luke de Bourn', Dominican of the Winchester convent

Stephen de Forde, canon of Breamore

773. *Letters dimissory and first tonsure*

5 March 1349 Esher, letters for Fr. Robert Wylmyn, canon of Southwick for all holy orders

6 March 1349, first tonsure conferred on Ralph Tristram, William de Edyndon', John Dale and William Richer, all of the diocese

Same date, letters for Adam de Berkyng' for the priesthood and John de Malmesbury for the subdiaconate

10 March, Southwark, letters for Thomas de Eykeryng', rector of Abbots Ann, subdeacon, for the diaconate and priesthood

20 March 1349, Farnham, letters for William Ware, rector of St Mary Magdalen, Bermondsey, subdeacon, for the diaconate and priesthood

461 **774.** ORDERS conferred by the bishop in the chapel of Farnham Castle, Saturday when *Sitientes* is sung (Saturday before Passion Sunday), 28 March 1349

Acolytes

William Veysi of Mapledurwell
John de Brokenhull, dioc.
Hereford
Richard Hayward of
Bedhampton
Walter de Muryden', dioc.
Lincoln
John Mayheu of the Isle of Wight
John Donnere of Sherfield
John Adcok' of Sherfield
John Laurence of Overton
John de Husselborne
John Lond' of Andover
John Neumann of Broughton
Richard Parker of Farnham
Walter atte Broche of Guildford
John de Alresford'
Richard de Weston, rector of
West Clandon
Simon Freman of Chertsey
Richard le Vans of South
Warnborough

John Smyth of Itchenstoke
Robert Berys of Wickham Scures
Richard Neulyn of Kingsley
John Seward of South Waltham
John Spicer of Alton
John Makerel
Thomas Tourgys, rector of
Stratfield Turgis
Robert de Bukyngham, rector of
Puttenham
Henry de Hoo
Henry atte Park' of Hursley
William de Bukkebrugge, rector
of Farley
M. John de Tetteford
Hugh Mareschal
Fr. Robert Whiten', canon of
Titchfield

775. *Subdeacons*

M. John de Edyndon', warden of the hospital at Portsmouth
William Wolf, rector of Houghton
William *dictus* Monck of Kempsford, dioc. Worcester, *ad tit.* prior of
Mottisfont
Thomas Madefray, rector of Bradninch, dioc. Exeter
Stephen le Frenssh' of Tandridge, *ad tit.* prior of Tandridge
William Archer of Sherborne St John, *ad tit.* prior of Selborne
Walter Herman, *ad tit.* prior of Selborne
William le Eorl, *ad tit.* prior of Newark
Edward atte Putte, *ad tit.* prior of Selborne
Nicholas de Wambergh', dioc. Salisbury, *ad tit.* abbot of Hyde
Nicholas son of John atte Bergh' of Oxted, *ad tit.* prior of Tandridge
Robert atte Moure, *ad tit.* prior of St Mary and St John, [Monk]
Sherborne
M. Walter Cole, rector of St Rumbold, Winchester
Walter Dyksyn, *ad tit.* abbess of Wherwell
John de Bynstede, *ad tit.* prior of St Mary Kalendar, Winchester
William Husee, *ad tit.* prior of Mottisfont
Richard Athelarde, *ad tit.* prior of Andwell, procurator of the abbot of
Tiron
Thomas Fysshere of Kings Somborne, *ad tit.* prior of St Mary Kalendar,
Winchester
Walter de Brankescombe, rector of St Mary, Wield
Thomas Mareschal, *ad tit.* prior of Selborne
James Lumbard of Broughton, *ad tit.* abbot of Hyde

William Donk', *ad tit.* abbot of Waverley
John London' of Hinton, *ad tit.* prior of Southwark
William Jolyf of Leatherhead, *ad tit.* prior of Newark
John le Stubbare, *ad tit.* abbot of Waverley
John Stynt of Farnham, *ad tit.* prior of Selborne
Robert de Hampton', rector of St Laurence, Winchester
Fratres: John de Wynton'. Nigel de Waltham, monks of Waverley
Richard de Sylchestre, Richard de Herdynge, canons of Titchfield

462   **776.** *Deacons*
Thomas de Roldeston', *ad tit.* hospital of St Mary Magdalen, Southwell,
    with dimissory letters from the archbishop of York
Richard son of John de Lawadyn, dioc. St Davids, *ad tit.* prior of Hurley
William de Cranemere of the Isle of Wight, *ad tit.* prior of Carisbrooke
Richard de Dommere, *ad tit.* prior of Newark
Thomas Lumbard' of East Ockley, *ad tit.* prior of St Mary Kalendar,
    Winchester
John de Everton', *ad tit.* prior of Newark
William de Engulby, rector of Wotton
Thomas Cuppyng' of Liss, *ad tit.* abbot of Netley
John Frere of Winchester, *ad tit.* prior of St Mary Kalendar, Winchester
John de Wicchebury, *ad tit.* prior of Bisham Montagu
William Frilonde of Petersfield, *ad tit.* prior of Tortington
Walter de Brekhampton', rector of Steventon
Nicholas Bysshop of Wherwell, *ad tit.* prior of St Denys, Southampton
John Peck, *ad tit.* prior of Christchurch Twynham
John Parsones of Upclatford, *ad tit.* prior of St Peter, Winchester
William Brouning of Colmer, *ad tit.* prior of Hayling, procurator of the
    abbot of Jumièges
John Chalkelerd of Cheriton, *ad tit.* prior of St Mary Kalendar,
    Winchester
M. Walter de Upton, rector of St Clement, Winchester
Mark leBoor of Waltham, *ad tit.* prior of St Mary Kalendar, Winchester
John Kyng', of Langley Marsh, dioc. Lincoln, *ad tit.* prior of Merton
Nicholas Chaun of Walton, *ad tit.* prior of hospital of Sandown
John Trokkemere of Winchester, *ad tit.* prior of St Denys, Southampton
William le White, *ad tit.* prior of Hurley
M. John de Lemynton', rector of Appleford, Isle of Wight
William Poors of Worplesdon, *ad tit.* prior of Newark
John atte Wode of Coulsdon, *ad tit.* prior of Newark
M. Walter de Sevenhampton, rector of Worting
John Rayson of the town of Merton, *ad tit.* prior of Merton
William Tangele of Andover, *ad tit.* prior of St Mary Kalendar,
    Winchester
John Monck of Guildford, *ad tit.* prior of Boxgrove
Stephen Clomere of Shepperton, dioc. London, *ad tit.* prior of hospital
    of Sandown
William Begh' of Wallop, *ad tit.* prior of Mottisfont
Ralph Tristram, rector of Greatham
William Grym, *ad tit.* prior of Selborne

Robert atte Heth' of Kingsclere, *ad tit.* prior of Mottisfont
John Thome dictus Lecester de Thresk', prebendary of the prebend of
Itchen
William Richer, rector of Stoke-by-Guildford
John Dale, rector of Hendon, dioc. London
Walter Chapman of Merrow, *ad tit.* prior of Selborne
William Barneby, rector of Hardwick, dioc. Norwich
Roger de Chesterfeld, rector of Bradford Peverell, dioc. Salisbury
Fratres: Adam de Donmowe, Dominican
John Bardolf, John Wodelok', monks of Hyde
John de Thorneye, Theobald de Brokhurst, canons of Titchfield
Robert de Asshe, monk of Waverley

777. *Priests*
John Corneys of Wokingham, dioc. Salisbury, *ad tit.* abbot of
Medmenham
John Abbe of Steyning, dioc. Chichester, *ad tit.* prior Holy Trinity,
London
Robert de Wyllardby, dioc. York, *ad tit.* hospital of Burton Lazars,
dioc. Lincoln
John Rande, rector of St Peter outside Southgate, Winchester
John Bolt, rector of St Michael in Fleshmonger Street, Winchester
463   William son of Roger Smyth atte Rude of Worplesdon, *ad tit.* prior of
Newark
Richard Opnek' of Wallop, *ad tit.* prior of Breamore
Peter Marreys, rector of St Alphege at the corner of Calpe Street,
Winchester
John Verrier of Winchester, *ad tit.* prior of Selborne
Thomas Elyot of Wonersh, *ad tit.* prior of Newark
William de Benham, *ad tit.* prior of Bisham Montagu
Robert de Wolferton', rector of the chapel of Limerstone, Isle of Wight
Stephen atte Mulle, professed brother of St Nicholas hospital, Portsmouth
Roger Herman of Arlesford, *ad tit.* abbot of Chertsey
Severin de Tyntagel, dioc. Exeter, *ad tit.* prior of Launceston
John Vyne, rector of Chaldon
M. William de Polmorna, rector of Watley
Fratres: Geoffrey Kyngot, John atte Ryde, monks of Quarr
John Park', canon of Selborne
Thomas de Forda, monk of Beaulieu
Peter de Middelton', John de Shotesbrok', monks of Chertsey
Robert de Newenham, rector of Nunney, dioc. Bath and Wells

778. ORDERS conferred by the bishop in the chapel of Farnham castle,
Holy Saturday, 11 April 1349

Subdeacons
John Fareman of Ash, *ad tit.* abbot of Chertsey
Richard Lovekyn, *ad tit.* prior of Selborne
William Laurence of Overton, *ad tit.* prior of Selborne
Robert de Bukyngham, rector of Puttenham

John Frye, rector of the chapel of Yaverland, Isle of Wight
John Neweman of Broughton, *ad tit.* prior of Breamore
William Carpenter, *ad tit.* Fr. James Pasquier, prior of Andwell
Richard Weston, rector of West Clandon
Frater Robert de Whiton', canon of Titchfield

779. *Deacons*
James Lumbard' of Broughton, *ad tit.* prior of St Mary Kalendar, Winchester
Walter Herman, *ad tit.* prior of Selborne
Walter Dyksyn, *ad tit.* abbess of Wherwell
Thomas de Eykeringe, rector of Abbots Ann
Stephen le Frenssh' of Tandridge, *ad tit.* prior of Tandridge
John Stubbare, *ad tit.* abbot of Durford
John de Bynstede, *ad tit.* prior of St Mary Kalendar, Winchester
Robert atte Moure, ad tit. prior of St Mary and St John Baptist, Monk Sherborne
William Eorl, *ad tit.* prior of Newark
M. Nicholas de Wambergh', dioc. Salisbury, *ad tit.* abbot of Hyde
John Stynt, *ad tit.* prior of Selborne
William le Monck' of Kempsford, dioc. Worcester, *ad tit.* prior of Mottisfont
Robert de Hampton, rector of St Laurence, Winchester
John London' of Hinton, *ad tit.* prior of St Mary, Southwark
William Jolyf of Leatherhead, *ad tit.* prior of Newark
Thomas Madefray, rector of Bradninch, dioc. Exeter
Walter de Brankestoke, rector of St Mary, Wield
Frater John de Wynt', monk of Waverley

464   780. *Priests*
William White of Yateley, *ad tit.* prior of Hurley
Thomas Lumbard of East Ockley, *ad tit.* prior of St Mary Kalendar, Winchester
John Trokkereme of Winchester, *ad tit.* prior of St Denys, Southampton
John Chalkeberd of Cheriton, *ad tit.* prior of St Mary Kalendar, Winchester
M. Walter de Sevenhampton, rector of Worting
Richard son of John de Lawadyn, dioc. St Davids, *ad tit.* prior of Hurley
William Grym of Sele, *ad tit.* prior of Selborne
William Poors of Worplesdon, *ad tit.* prior of Newark
Walter de Brokhampton', rector of Steventon
John atte Wode of Coulsdon, *ad tit.* prior of Newark
Thomas Cuppying' of Liss, *ad tit.* abbot of Netley
Nicholas Bysshop of Wherwell, *ad tit.* prior of St Denys, Southampton
William Frylonde of Petersfield, *ad tit.* prior of Tortington
William Cranemore of the Isle of Wight, *ad tit.* prior of Carisbrooke
M. Walter de Upton', rector of St Clement, Winchester
William de Engulby, rector of Wotton
John Monck' of Guildford, *ad tit.* prior of Boxgrove
Richard de Wath', rector of Steventon, dioc. Lincoln

William Brouning' of Colmer, *ad tit*. prior of Hayling
William Begh' of Wallop, *ad tit*. prior of Mottisfont
Richard Frere, *ad tit*. prior of St Mary Kalendar, Winchester
Mark Boor of [Bishops] Waltham, *ad tit*. prior of St Mary Kalendar, Winchester
John Parsones, *ad tit*. prior of St Peter, Winchester
William Barneby, rector of Hardwick, dioc. Norwich
John Kyng of Langley Marsh, perpetual vicar of Godshill, Isle of Wight
M. John de Lemynton', rector of the chapel of Appleford, Isle of Wight
M. John de Everton, *ad tit*. prior of Newark
John Thome *dictus* Lecester of Thrisk, prebendary of the prebend of Itchen
Thomas de Roldeston', *ad tit*. hospital of St Mary Magdalen, Southwell, dioc. York
Ralph Tristram, rector of Greatham
Robert atte Hethe of Kingsclere, *ad tit*. prior of Selborne
Frater Adam de Donmowe, Dominican of the Winchester convent

781. ORDERS conferred by the bishop in the chapel of the hospital of St Mary, Sandown, Ember Saturday, vigil of Trinity Sunday, 6 June 1349

Acolytes

Ralph de Cornhulle, rector of Lamarsh, dioc. London
Roger de Beautre, rector of Highclere
Andrew de Bekensfeld, rector of Wisley
John Chaun of Walton
Hamond atte Solere of Alresford
Robert Pesshen of Monxton
Robert de Snoxhulle
John atte Rouberne of Effingham
Robert Mohent of Kingston
John de Sandford, rector of Eldon
Robert Sprynget of Carshalton
Peter de Beronden', rector of half of Abinger
Thomas Folk', rector of Kingsgate, Winchester
Frater Roger Coumbe, monk of Quarr

Richard *dictus* Clerc of Chaddesley, rector of St Mary, Guildford
M. John Peverel, rector of Uttoxeter, dioc. Čoventry and Lichfield
Thomas de Gyppewyz, rector of King's Ripton, dioc. Lincoln
Thomas Rouz, rector of Whippingham
John Chapelayn of Basingstoke
John de Kyngeston' rector of Great Marlow, dioc. Lincoln
Hugh, rector of "Lammas", dioc. Bangor
Thomas *dictus* Smyth of Walton
Adam Deghore of Tiverton, dioc. Exeter
Fratres: Geoffrey Gillyng'. John atte Beure, canons of Merton

465   **782.** *Subdeacons*

M. John de Totteford', rector of Long Ditton
John *dictus* Wyn of Alton, rector of St James without Winchester
Thomas de Stannford', rector of St Mary of the Valleys, Winchester
Richard de Wokkyng' rector of St Petroc, Winchester
Simon Freman of Chertsey, *ad tit*. prior of Newark

John Waleys, rector of Ibstone, dioc. Lincoln
Bartholomew Lucas of Guildford, *ad tit.* prior of Newark
Henry Pittelye of Clanfield, *ad tit.* prior of St Mary Kalendar, Winchester
Richard Snodenham, *ad tit.* prior of Newark
John Sewel, *ad tit.* prior of Newark
William Dorsete of Lockerley, *ad tit.* prior of Selborne
Richard de Farham, *ad tit.* prior of Selborne
Batholomew Spernen, dioc. Exetor, *ad tit.* abbot of Hartland, which is
   entered in the registry of the bishop of Exeter
John Godyng, *ad tit.* abbot of Hyde
William Potum of Ewhurst, *ad tit.* prior of Newark
John de Blebury, rector of Houghton
Thomas de Rasen, rector of All Saints, Wallingford, dioc. Salisbury
John Trys of Southampton, *ad tit.* prior of the hospital of St Mary,
   Bishopsgate, London
John de Bokenhull', dioc. Hereford, *ad tit.* prior of St Mary, Southwark
Richard de Perschore, *ad tit.* his own patrimony, with one corrody in
   the cathedral church of Winchester, valued at 5 marks
Frater William de Boukelonde, monk of Quarr

783. *Deacons*
Richard Athelard, *ad tit.* Fr James Pasquier, prior of Andwell, procurator
   in England of the abbot of Tiron
John Migreyn, rector of the chapel of Henley, dioc. Winchester
Thomas le Fisshere of King's Somborne, *ad tit.* prior of St Peter,
   Winchester
William Husee of Romsey, *ad tit.* subprior of Breamore, the priory being
   vacant
Henry, rector of Waterston, dioc. Salisbury
Walter Noght rector of Dibden
John Fareman of Ash, *ad tit.* abbot of Chertsey
Robert de Bokyngham, rector of Puttenham
Fratres: John de Cosham, monk of Quarr
Richard Whiton', canon of Titchfield
John de Malmesbury, canon of St Mary, Southwark
John Nichol, William Skillyng', monks of Winchester cathedral

784. *Priests*
William de Rothewelle, rector of Pottersbury, dioc. Lincoln
Walter Herman, *ad tit.* prior of Selborne
Robert atte Moure, *ad tit.* prior of St John Baptist, Sherborne
Walter Chapman of Merrow, *ad tit.* prior of Newark
M. Nicholas de Wambergh', vicar of Micheldever
Robert de Hampton', rector of St Laurence, Winchester
M. Thomas de Farnylawe, dioc. Durham, *ad tit.* warden and scholars of
   Merton Hall (*aula*), Oxford
John de Wycchebury, *ad tit.* prior of Bishop Montagu
John Gogh', rector of Ash, dioc. Winchester
Thomas Madefray, rector of Bradninch, dioc. Exeter
Walter Dyksyn, *ad tit.* prior of Newark

William Jolyf of Leatherhed, *ad tit.* prior of Newark
William de Urlee of Steep, *ad tit.* prior of Newark
John London' of Hinton, *ad tit.* prior of St Mary, Southwark
466   Walter de Brankescombe, rector of St Mary, Wield, dioc. Winchester
Nicholas Thame, *ad tit.* prior of the hospital of Sandown
Roger de Cesterfeld', rector of Bradford Peverell, dioc. Salisbury
John de Bynstede, *ad tit.* prior of St Mary Kalendar, Winchester
Fratres: William de Remmesbury, Baldwin de Brinkele, William de
London, canons of Merton
Robert de Thorney, canon of Titchfield

785. *First Tonsure and Dimissorial Letters*
Trinity Sunday, 7 June 1349, the bishop conferred the first tonsure on
William Goudyng', John Foul, John Fantag, William atte Rude of the
Winchester diocese, and Walter Chiese, dioc. Salisbury
26 July 1349, Highclere, letters for Adam de Lichefeld, rector of Hartley,
Winchester diocese, acolyte, for all holy orders
25 July 1349, Highclere, first tonsure conferred on John Geron of
Burghclere
7 September 1349, Downton, letters for Roger de Stannford, rector of
Church Oakley, for minor and all holy orders

786. ORDERS conferred by the bishop in the manor chapel of [Bishops]
Waltham, Ember Saturday, 19 September 1349

Acolytes
John de Tunnbregg', rector of
Oxted
John Waker, rector of Orchard,
dioc. Bath and Wells
John de Fulford, rector of Froyle
Thomas de Wolverton', rector of
Upham
John Gary of Longstock
William Sopard of Chertsey
Richard Vaus of South
Warnborough

M. Robert de Lemynton'
Thomas Hildesle of Basingstoke
Fratres: Richard de Tichefield,
canon of Titchfield
William Channterel, Carmelite
Friar
John Bonde, canon of Breamore
John Bourdevile, Friar Minor

787. *Subdeacons*
M. John de Ware, rector of Crawley
Robert Sutheroy, dioc. Worcester, *ad tit.* prior of St Denys, Southampton
John Baron of Newport, Isle of Wight, *ad tit.* prior of St Peter,
Winchester
Peter de Berondon', rector of half of Abinger
John Brikevile of Romsey, *ad tit.* prior of St Peter, Winchester
Robert de Snokeshull', perpetual chaplain of the chapel of la Vacherie
Andrew de Bekenesfeld', rector of Wisley
Ralph de Cornhull, rector of Lamarsh, dioc. Lincoln
Hamond Solere of Alresford, *ad tit.* prior of Tortington

Thomas Tourgys, rector of Stratfield Turgis
John de Sannford, rector of North Waltham
William de Bokkebrugge, rector of Farley near Winchester
John Capeleyn of Basingstoke, *ad tit.* prior of Selborne
John Forst of Basing, *ad tit.* Fr. James Pasquier, prior of Andwell

467   Thomas Folk, rector of St Pancras, London, in the immediate jurisdiction
of the archbishop of Canterbury, by dimissorial letters from the prior
of Christchurch, Canterbury, *sede vacante*
Fratres: Thomas de Langeford', Dominican
John Boure, Geoffrey Gillynge, canons of Merton

788. *Deacons*
Bartholomew Lucas, *ad tit.* prior of Newark
Henry de Putteleye of Clanfield, *ad tit.* prior of Tortington
John Nieweman of Broughton, *ad tit.* prior of Ivychurch
Bartholomew Sperven, dioc. Exeter, *ad tit.* abbot of Hartland, which is
entered in the register of the bishop of Exeter
William Dorsete of Lockerley, *ad tit.* prior of Selborne
Richard de Wokkyng', rector of St Mary Kalendar, Winchester
Simon Freman of Chertsey, *ad tit.* prior of Newark
John Godyng, *ad tit.* prior of Selborne
Richard de Perschore, *ad tit.* prior of St Peter, Winchester
Richard de Farham, rector of Abbotstone
John de Blebury, rector of Houghton
Thomas de Stannford, rector of St Mary in the Vale, Winchester
John Waleys, rector of Ibstone, dioc. Lincoln
Fratres: John de Burton, monk of Winchester cathedral
John Mercer, Friar Minor
Walter de Boklonde, monk of Quarr
Nicholas Gyffard, canon of Southwick
Richard Sewel, *ad tit.* prior of Newark

789. *Priests*
John Migrem, rector of the chapel of Henley
Richard Dommere of Bedhampton, *ad tit.* prior of Newark
William Husee of Romsey, *ad tit.* prior of Breamore
Richard Athelard, *ad tit.* Fr James Pasquer, prior of Andwell, procurator
in England for the abbot of Tiron
Thomas le Visshere of Somborne, *ad tit.* prior of St Peter, Winchester
John Peck, *ad tit.* prior of Christchurch Twynham
Robert de Bokyngham, rector of Puttenham
James Lumbard, *ad tit.* prior of St Mary Kalendar, Winchester
Walter Nhot, rector of Dibden
Fratres: John de Guldeford, William de Skellynge, John Wodelok',
monks of Winchester cathedral
Walter de Balsale, monk of Chertsey
John de Malmesbury, canon of Southwark
Adam Canon, canon of Southwick
John de Lake, canon of St Denys, Southampton
Robert Whiton', canon of Titchfield

790. *Dimissorial letters, first tonsure and ordination of acolytes*

19 September 1349, [Bishops] Waltham, letters for Thomas de Chynham, dioc. Winchester, acolyte, for all holy orders

20 September 1349, first tonsure conferred on John Stryneyn of Southampton and Laurence Horder from the same, dioc. Winchester

25 October 1349, Southwark, first tonsure conferred on Thomas Scharp of Pewsey, dioc. Salisbury

468 Sunday, All Saints Day, 1 November 1349 the bishop ordained as acolytes John de Middelton', rector of Minchinhamton, dioc. Worcester, John Dolveys, rector of Eddlesborough, dioc. Lincoln and William Hanley, rector of Marsh, dioc. Lincoln, in his manor chapel of Southwark; and Stephen de Whitecroft and Walter de Longehurst, dioc. Winchester received the first tonsure

16 December 1349, Southwark, letters for Thomas de Clopton, rector of Blendworth, for minor and all holy orders

791. ORDERS conferred by the bishop in his manor chapel of Southwark, Ember Saturday, 19 December 1349

Acolytes
Richard Laurance of South Waltham
Richard Chamberleyn of Basing
Thomas de Sengesdon of the Isle of Wight
Walter Wenyat of the same
Robert Page of Alresford
John Payn of Carshalton
Robert Curteys of Whitchurch
Henry le Welder of Send
William de Ranby, rector of Newnham
John de Carren, rector of Herbrandston, dioc. St Davids
John de Harewedon', rector of Thorner, dioc. York
William de Cave, rector of Chevening, deanery of Shoreham, under the immediate jurisdiction of the archbishop, with letters from the prior of Christchurch, *sede vacante*
John Lok, rector of Compton
Frater William de Preston, monk of Bermondsey
Henry de Tatton, rector of Waddon, dioc. Ely, with dimissorial letters from John de Oo, vicar general for the bishop in foreign parts
William de Ulcote, rector of Great Mongeham, dioc. Canterbury, with letters from the prior of Christchurch
Thomas Feder of Winchester
Nicholas Bernard of Sparkford
William Dymeyn of Heckfield
John de Wolyngham, rector of Bramwith, dioc. York
Geoffrey de Rannvile, rector of All Saints, Ellisfield
John Vyncent, rector of Cloughfold, dioc. Hereford
Fratres: Laurence de Storteford, Nicholas de Cantebrugg', Henry de Yakesle, canons of Holy Cross, Waltham

792. *Subdeacons*
Richard Vaus of South Warnborough, *ad tit.* prior of Selborne

Roger de Beautre, rector of Highclere
John de Colne, rector of Ecton, dioc. York
Robert Pesshoun of Monkston, *ad tit.* prior of St Mary Kalendar, Winchester
Thomas de Querlee, *ad tit.* prior of St Mary, Southwark
Thomas Jekyn of Stalisfield, dioc. Canterbury, by letters from the prior of Christchurch, *sede vacante, ad tit.* prior of Tandridge
Henry Holforde, *ad tit.* abbot of Robertsbridge
Edmund Heron of Pentney, dioc. Norwich, *ad tit.* brethren and sisters of St Katherine by the Tower, London
John de Hedyndon', rector of the church or chapel of Sezincote, dioc. Worcester
Thomas de Wolverton', rector of Upham
Richard de Babynton' of Gamlingay, dioc. Ely, with letters from M. John de Oo, *ad tit.* prior of St Neots
Walter de Freland, rector of Ockham
John de Kyngeston, rector of Great Marlow, dioc. Lincoln
William Whiteberd, *ad tit.* prior of Christchurch, London
William de Reygate, *ad tit.* prior of Tandridge
William de la Chambre of St Neots, dioc. Lincoln, *ad tit.* prior of St Neots

469   Robert de Pleselegh', rector of Polstead, dioc. Norwich
Richard de Eccleshale, rector of South Hill, dioc. Exeter
M. Richard Wodelond', rector of Niton, Isle of Wight
Thomas le Coc, rector of Taplow, dioc. Lincoln
John de Tunnbregg', rector of Oxted, dioc. Winchester
John Bulveys, rector of Edlesborough, dioc. Lincoln
William de Hanley, rector of Marsh, dioc. Lincoln
Almaric de Schirland, rector of Wymondham, dioc. Lincoln
William de Tamworth, rector of Moulton, deanery of Bocking, under the immediate jurisdiction of the archbishop of Canterbury, with letters from the prior of Christchurch
Nicholas Ysenurst, *ad tit.* prior of Selborne
John de Saxton', rector of Hartfield, dioc. Chichester
William de Lambhyth', rector of Boxworth, dioc. Ely, with letters from M. John de Oo, T[homas], bishop of Ely absent in foreign parts
John Hanecok' of Pitney, dioc. Bath and Wells, *ad tit.* prior of Prittlewell
John de Middelton', rector of Minchinhampton, dioc. Worcester, with letters from the prior of Worcester, *sede vacante*
John Hanberst of Buxted, deanery of South Malling, under the immediate jurisdiction of the archbishop, with letters from Simon de Islep', the elect of Canterbury
John Haket of Ickleton, dioc. Ely, with letters from John de Oo, vicar general, *ad tit.* prioress of Ickleton

793. *Deacons*
Thomas Rouz, rector of Whippingham, Isle of Wight
Ralph de Cornhull', rector of Lamarsh, dioc. London
John de Brykevile, *ad tit.* prior of St Peter, Winchester
William de Bokkebrugg', rector of Farley

John Forest' of Basing, *ad tit.* Fr James Pasquer, prior of Andwell
John Odyn of Prittlewell, dioc, London, *ad tit.* abbot of St Osyth
Robert de Snokeshull', perpetual chaplain of the chantry of la Vacherie
Richard de Snodesham, *ad tit.* prior of Newark
Hamo atte Solere of Alresford, *ad tit.* prior of Tortington
Robert Sutherbi, *ad tit.* prior of St Denys, Southampton
Richard Lenelyn of Binstead, *ad tit.* prior of Selborne
Andrew de Bekenesfeld', rector of Wisley
Peter de Berondon', rector of half the church of Abinger
Thomas de Eccleshale, rector of Potton, dioc. Lincoln
M. John de Totteford', rector of Long Ditton
Peter de Lucy, rector of St Saviour, Winchester
Thomas Torgys, rector of Stratfield Turgis
John Wyn, rector of St James without Winchester
Thomas Folk', rector of St Pancras, deanery of the Arches, London,
    under immediate jurisdiction of the archbishop of Canterbury, by
    letters from the prior of Christchurch, *sede vacante*
M. John de Ware, rector of Crawley
Fratres: Reginald de Sutton', Walter de Lecestr', canons of Holy Cross,
    Waltham

794. *Priests*
John de Bleobury, rector of Houghton
John de Norwich' of Laleham, dioc, London, *ad tit.* abbot of Chertsey
Bartholomew Sperven, dioc. Exeter, *ad tit.* abbot of Hartland. which is
    entered in the registry of the bishop of Exeter
Walter Pipere of Salvington, rector of Halstead, deanery of Shoreham,
    with letters from Simon elect of Canterbury
Richard de Farnham, rector of Abbotstone
Henry de Putteleye of Clanfield, *ad tit.* prior of Tortington
Richard de Perschore, *ad tit.* prior of St Peter, Winchester
Richard de Berdewell', dioc. Norwich, *ad tit.* monastery of Thetford,
    which is entered in the registry of the bishop of Norwich
William Dorsete, rector of Widley
Richard Sewel of Byfleet, *ad tit.* prior of Newark
Richard de Wokkynge, rector of St Mary Kalendar, Winchester
Clement de Batefford, rector of All Saints, Farnham, dioc. Norwich
William Hardyng', *confrater* of the hospital of Sandown
John Godyng, *ad tit.* prior of Selborne
Simon Freman of Chertsey, *ad tit.* prior of Newark
William Richer, rector of Stoke-by-Guildford
John Fareman of Ash, *ad tit.* abbot of Chertsey
Fratres: Nicholas de Burton, monk of Hyde
John de Netheravene, canon of Mottisfont

470 **795.** *Ordination of acolytes and dimissorial letters*
Sunday, 17 January 1350, at pontifical mass in the manor chapel,
    Southwark, the bishop ordained as acolytes John de Kendale, rector
    of Kings Ripton, dioc. Lincoln, and John Ferrers of West Reedham,
    dioc. Norwich

3 February 1350, Southwark, letters for fratres William de Boklonde and
John de Cosham, monks of Quarr, for the priesthood from any bishop

796. ORDERS conferred by the bishop in his manor chapel at Southwark,
Ember Saturday in the first week of Lent, 20 February, 1350

Acolytes
M. Walter de Stracton, rector of Dunsfold
Robert Shirlee of Cranleigh
Bartholomew de Donnyngworth, Isle of Wight
George de Appulderlee
Thomas Oysel of Heckfield
John de Adderleye, rector of Bonsall, dioc. Coventry and Lichfield
John de Uppyngham, rector of Warmington, dioc. Coventry and Lichfield
William Bulneys, portioner of the church of Darley in the Peak, dioc.
    Coventry and Lichfield
William de Knaresburgh, dioc. York
Alexander de Dene
Richard de Burton', rector of Little Cove, dioc. Norwich
Reginald de Anne
John Birchovers of Alderwasley, dioc. Coventry and Lichfield
William de Tudderlee
Matthew de Torkeseye, rector of half the church of St Denis, Kirkby
    Laythorpe, dioc. Lincoln
Fratres: Richard Erle, canon of Reigate
William de Preston', Henry de Kynewardiston', Thomas Honyng, monks
    of Bermondsey
John de Chalgrave, William de Burstesham, monks of Westminster

797. *Subdeacons*
Richard le Chamberlayn of Basing, *ad tit.* prior of Hamble, procurator
    for the abbot of Tiron in England
John le Mays of Odiham, *ad tit.* Fr James Pasquier, prior of Andwell
William de Ranby, rector of Newnham
William Roke, rector of North 'Wokyndon', dioc. London
John Tunerich' of Middleton, dioc. Salisbury, *ad tit.* prior of Leeds
Robert Jakewell' of 'Petresburn', *ad tit.* prior of Selborne
Adam de Stonore, rector of half the church of Ermington, dioc. Exeter
M. Thomas de Luyton, rector of Sulhampstead Abbots, dioc. Salisbury
Richard de Chaddeslegh', rector of Curry Rivel, dioc. Bath and Wells
John Ferriers of West Reedham, dioc. Norwich, *ad tit.* prior of Coxford
John Kendale, rector of Kings Ripton, dioc. Lincoln
Roger Mohant of Kingston, *ad tit.* prior of Southwark
Walter Wenyat of Isle of Wight, *ad tit.* Fr Almaric, prior of Carisbrooke,
    procurator in England for the abbot of Lyre
John Ferour of Itchenstoke, *ad tit.* prior of Selborne
William de Hanleye, rector of Hardmead, dioc. Lincoln
John Fellesone, rector of Pleasley, dioc. Coventry and Lichfield
Henry de Tatton, rector of Whaddon, dioc. Ely
Thomas de Brettevill', rector of Saltfleetby, dioc. Lincoln

William de Sende, rector of Tilbury, dioc. London

William de Cave, rector of Chevening, deanery of Shoreham, under the immediate jurisdiction of the archbishop of Canterbury

471 Geoffrey de Raunvil', rector of All Saints, Ellisfield

John Lok, rector of Compton near Winchester

William de Sulecotes, rector of Great Mongeham, dioc. Canterbury

William Bryan of 'Wynchyngham', dioc. Ely, *ad tit.* hospital of St Mary, Bishopsgate, London

Nicholas Bernard of Sparkford, *ad tit.* prior of St Mary, Southwark

William de Tideswell, rector of Henton, dioc. Lincoln

John Wodeward of Hudecote, dioc. Worcester, *ad tit.* abbot of Chertsey

Thomas Budde of Belper, dioc. Coventry and Lichfield, *ad tit.* prior of Southwark

Fratres: Germanus de Jernemuta, monk of Bermondsey

Robert Solers, John de Wroteynge, Thomas de Piriton, Bartholomew de Tourseye, monks of Bermondsey

John Bounde, canon of Breamore

John de Paskeden', brother of St Thomas Hospital, Southwark, *ad tit.* the same hospital

Roger de Dorkynge, canon of Reigate

Robert de Bedeford, *confrater* of St Cross, next the Tower of London

John de Chesthunte, *confrater* of the same church

William de Thenford, canon of Missenden

798. *Deacons*

William de Lambehuth', rector of Boxworth, dioc. Ely, with dimissorial letters from Fr. Alan, prior, Thomas bishop of Ely being in foreign parts

John Bulneys, rector of Eddlesborough, dioc. Lincoln

John de Kyngeston', rector of Great Marlow, dioc. Lincoln

Robert de Pleselegh', rector of Polstead, dioc. Norwich

Nicholas de Amueneye, rector of Holwell, dioc. Salisbury

Roger de Beautre, rector of Highclere

John Cook' of Wey, rector of Ashreigny, dioc. Exeter

Almaric de Shirlond', rector of Wymondham, dioc. Lincoln

William de Hanley, rector of Marsh, dioc. Lincoln

Robert Pesshon of Monxton, rector of St Margaret next Westgate, Winchester

M. Richard de Wodelond', rector of Niton, Isle of Wight

Richard de Eccleshale, rector of Southill, dioc. Exeter

John de Sandford, rector of North Waltham

Thomas le Cook', rector of Taplow, dioc. Lincoln

Thomas de Querle, rector of St George, Winchester

Thomas de Wolverton, rector of Upham

Richard le Vaus, *ad tit.* prior of Selborne

Nicholas Isenurst, *ad tit.* prior of Selborne

Walter Fryland, rector of Ockham

William de Tamworth', rector of Moulton, deanery of Bocking, under the immediate jurisdiction of the archbishop of Canterbury, with letters from the prior of Christchurch, *sede vacante*

Henry Holford, dioc. Winchester, *ad tit.* abbot of Robertsbridge
Robert de Wytton', dioc. York, *ad tit.* abbot of Egglestone
John Baron, dioc. Winchester, *ad tit.* prior of St Peter, Winchester
William Whiteberd, *ad tit.* prior of Christchurch, London
John de Tunbregg', rector of Oxted
John de Saxton', rector of Hartfield, dioc. Chichester
John Capelayn of Basingstoke, *ad tit.* Fr James Pasquier, prior of
    Andwell, procurator for the abbot of Tiron
John Haket of Ickleton, dioc. Ely, *ad tit.* prioress of Ickleton
Fratres: John de Lond', monk of Westminster
472   Thomas de Hognorton', monk of Westminster
John de Peusey, Thomas de Thurmeston', canons of St Mary Hospital,
    Bishopgate, London

799. *Priests*
William de Wenlok', rector of St Peter, Berkhampstead, dioc. Lincoln
M. John de Farlee, rector of Stanton St Quinton, dioc. Salisbury, *ad tit.*
    of his benefice
Peter de Lucy, rector of St Saviour, Winchester
Thomas Turgys, rector of Stratfield Turgis
Bartholomew Lucas of Guildford, *ad tit.* prior of Newark
Richard de Snodenham, *ad tit.* prior of Newark
Ralph de Kestevene, rector of St Botolph without Aldergate, London
Robert Sutheray, dioc. Worcester, *ad tit.* prior of St Denys, Southampton
M. John de Ware, rector of Crawley
Thomas de Levemenstre, rector of St Martin, Ludgate, London
M. John de Totteford, rector of Long Ditton
John Bayson of Merton, *ad tit.*, prior of St Mary, Merton
M. Michael Marescal, rector of Bothaw, deanery of St Mary Arches,
    London, under the immediate jurisdiction of the archbishop of
    Canterbury
Henry le Longe of Seal, dioc. Rochester, *ad tit.* prior of hospital of St
    Mary, Cripplegate, London
John de Mussynden', dioc. Lincoln, *ad tit.* prior of Leeds
Peter de Berendon', rector of half of Abinger
John Forest of Basing, *ad tit.* Fr James Pasquier, prior of Andwell
John Neuman of Broughton, *ad tit.* prior of Breamore
Robert de Snokeshull', perpetual chaplain of la Vacherie
Andrew de Bokensfeld, rector of Wisley
William de Bokkebrugg', rector of Farley
Thomas Folk', rector of St Pancras, London, deanery of the Arches,
    London, under immediate jurisdiction of the archbishop
Ralph de Cornhull', rector of Lamarsh, dioc. Lincoln, *ad tit.* of his
    benefice
Fratres: Benedict Luganus, Dominican of the Winchester convent
John de Plumpton, confrater of St Cross next the Tower, London
John de Bokenhull', monk of Westminster
William de Boklond', John de Cosham, monks of Quarr

800. ORDERS conferred by the bishop in the parish church of Kingston,
Saturday when *Sitientes* is sung, 13 March 1350

Acolytes

Bartholomew de Dunningworth of the Isle of Wight

William de Borstowe

Fratres: John de Usk', John Beel, John de Abyndon', Ralph de Wedeneye, William de Canterbury, John de Hurlee, monks of Chertsey

801. *Subdeacons*

Alexander Denmun, dioc. Winchester, *ad tit*. prior of St Mary Kalender, Winchester

Thomas le Fader', rector of St Peter Whitebread, Winchester

473 William de Childerle *magna* dioc. Ely, with letters from M. John de Oo, canon of Hereford, vicar-general for Thomas bishop of Ely, absent in foreign parts, *ad tit*. prior of Merton

George de Apelderle, *ad tit*. prior of the hospital, Sandown

John de Penkeston', rector of Brighstone, Isle of Wight

William Demeyn *ad tit*. prior of the hospital of St Mary, Bishopgate, London

Fratres: Richard de Warnham, canon of Reigate

John de Chalgrave, William de Burstlesham, monks of the priory of Hurley, dependent on Westminster abbey, immediately subject to the Holy See

802. *Deacons*

William Rok', rector of 'Northwokyndon', dioc. London

Richard de Chaddeslegh' junior, rector of Curry Rivel, dioc. Bath and Wells

Nicholas de Sparkeford, *ad tit*. prior of St Mary, Southwark

John Lok, rector of Compton near Winchester

John Ferour of Itchenstoke *ad tit*. prior of Shulbred

Walter Wenyat of the Isle of Wight, *ad tit*. Fr Almaric, prior of Carisbrooke, procurator in England for the abbot of Lyre

John Mays of Odiham, *ad tit*. prior of Andwell, procurator for the abbot of Tiron

William de Ranby, rector of Newnham, dioc. Winchester

Roger Mohant of Kingston, *ad tit*. prior of St Mary, Southwark

John de Middelton, rector of Hampton, dioc. Worcester

Walter de Tideswell, rector of Henton, dioc. Lincoln

Fratres: Robert de Bedeford, John de Chestehunte, brothers of St Cross next the Tower of London

Roger de Dorkyng', canon of Reigate

John de Paskedon', brother of St Thomas hospital, Southwark

803. *Priests*

John Baron of Newport, Isle of Wight, *ad tit*. prior of St Mary Kalendar, Winchester (*juratus per W' de Farlee*)

Thomas de Wolverton, rector of Upham

Robert de Wytton', dioc. York, *ad tit*. abbot of Egglestone

William Wgeteberd, *ad tit*. prior of Christchurch, London

William de Lambheth', rector of Boxworth, dioc. Ely, with letters from Alan, prior, Thomas, bishop absent in foreign parts

Roger de Beautre, rector of Highclere
John *dictus* Wyn of Alton, rector of St James, Winchester
Nicholas Isenurst, *ad tit.* prior of Selborne
John de Kyngeston', rector of Great Marlow, dioc. Lincoln
Thomas de Querlee, rector of St George, Winchester
John de Tunnbregg', rector of Oxted
Henry Holforde, *ad tit.* abbot of Robertsbridge
John Capelayn of Basingstoke, *ad tit.* prior of Andwell, procurator in
England for the abbot of Tiron
Thomas le Cok', rector of Taplow, dioc. Lincoln
Robert Pesshon, rector of St Margaret near Westgate, Winchester
Robert de Pleselegh', rector of Polstead, dioc. Norwich
M. Richard de Wodelond, rector of Niton, Isle of Wight
John Hancok' of Pitney, dioc. Bath and Wells, *ad tit.* prior of Prittlewell
John Haket of Ickleton, dioc. Ely with letters from M. John de Oo,
canon of Hereford, vicar-general of Thomas bishop of Ely, absent in
foreign parts, *ad tit.* prioress of Ickleton
William de Tanworth', rector of Moulton, deanery of Bocking, under
immediate jurisdiction of the archbishop of Canterbury
John de Sanford', rector of North Waltham
Fratres: Thomas Crondere, John de Waldene, Dominican Friars

474   **804.** *Dimissorial letter*
13 March 1350, Kingston, for Robert de Cougham, rector of
Whippingham, Isle of Wight, acolyte, for all holy orders

805. ORDERS celebrated by the bishop in the manor chapel of Esher,
Saturday in Easter week, 27 March 1350

Subdeacons
William de Peykirk', rector of St Illegdon (? St Illogan, St Endellion),
Cornwall, dioc. Exeter
Bartholomew de Donnyngworth' of the Isle of Wight, *ad tit.* Fr Almaric,
prior of Carisbrooke, procurator for the abbot of Lyre
M. Walter de Stratton, rector of Dunsfold
John Waker, rector of Shefford [West], dioc. Salisbury
Fratres: John de Usk', John Beel, John de Abyndon', Ralph de
Wydeneye, monks of Chertsey

806. *Deacons*
Thomas Fader, rector of St Peter Whitebread, Winchester
George de Apperdeleye, *ad tit.* prior of Newark
John de Penkeston', rector of Brighstone, Isle of Wight
Matthew de Torkeseye, rector of half the church of Kirkby Laythorp,
dioc. Lincoln
William Demeyn of Heckfield, *ad tit.* prior of the hospital of St Mary,
Bishopsgate
Fratres: John de Chalgrave, William de Bustlesham, Bartholomew de
Tourseye, monks of the priory of Hurlee, dependent on Westminster
abbey, immediately subject to the Holy See

Richard de Warnham', canon of Reigate
William de Magna Childerle, dioc. Ely, with letters from M. John de
Oo, canon of Hereford, vicar-general for Thomas, bishop of Ely,
absent in foreign parts, *ad tit.* prior of Merton

807. *Priests*
William de Ranby, rector of Newnham
Walter Freland, rector of Ockham
William Rok', rector of 'Northwokyndon', dioc. London
William de Sende, rector of Tilbury, dioc. London
Richard Thoreon, rector of Barton, dioc. Lincoln
John Ferour of Itchenstoke, *ad tit.* monastery of Waverley
John de Neuport, rector of Paglesham, dioc. London
Nicholas Bernard of Sparkford, *ad tit.* prior of St Mary, Southwark
John Lok', rector of Compton near Winchester
Hamo atte Solere of Alresford, *ad tit.* prior of Tortington
Richard de Chaddeslegh Minor, rector of Curry Rivel, dioc. Bath and
Wells
Richard Gladier of Tysoe, dioc. Worcester, *ad tit.* prior of Sandown
John de Middleton, rector of Minchinhampton, dioc. Worcester
William de Tidesell', rector of Henton, dioc. Lincoln
Fratres: Robert Bedeford, John de Chesthunte, brothers of the hospital
of St Cross near the Tower of London
Roger de Berkynge, canon of Reigate
John de Paskeden, brother of St Thomas Hospital, Southwark, *ad tit.*
of the same
Ralph Mauricii, monk of Monk Sherborne

ORDERS celebrated by the bishop in the manor chapel of Southwark,
Ember Saturday, 22 May 1350, [*margin*] vigil of Trinity Sunday

475 **808.** *Acolytes*
Simon Robyn, rector of St Saviour, Winchester
Peter Ly of Hilborough, dioc. Norwich
Walter de Hethe, rector of Bromley, dioc. Rochester
Ralph Treiagn, rector of St Stephen-in-Brannel, dioc. Exeter
William Hartherne of Witley
M. William de Massyngham, rector of Camps, dioc. Ely
Adam Stranman of Good Easter
John de Oxted
Fratres: John Stoke, Bartholomew Wodelond', William de Wodeford',
Richard de Bocham
John de Certeseye, monk of Waverley

809. *Subdeacons*
Robert de Cougham, rector of Whippingham, Isle of Wight
John Adecok' of Sherfield, *ad tit.* prior of Tandridge
William *dictus* Belle of Bromley, *ad tit.* prior of Monk Sherborne
M. Stephen Treuaignon', rector of St Ladock, dioc. Exeter
M. John Dirworthy, rector of Ham, dioc. Exeter

M. Thomas de Bredon', rector of Donnington, dioc. Salisbury
Richard Laurence of South Waltham, *ad tit.* master and brethren of the
   hospital of St John, Oxford
John de Medborne, rector of Swanscombe, dioc. Rochester
Robert Froumond', rector of Brede, dioc. Chichester
Nicholas Northerne of Colmer, *ad tit.* prioress of Kilburn
William Sudde of Windsor, dioc. Salisbury, *ad tit.* abbot of Westminster
William de Lavenham, rector of Aldham, dioc. Norwich
John Markere of Sandy, dioc. Lincoln, *ad tit.* prior of Caldwell
John de Schipedham, rector of Kingsland, dioc. Hereford
John de Wodehall', dioc. London, *ad tit.* prior of Merton
Henry de Denton', dioc. Lincoln, *ad tit.* prior of Bushmead
John son of Ralph de Brikelsworth, dioc. Lincoln, *ad tit.* prior of St
   Thomas hospital, Southwark
M. John Wellewyk', rector of Gayton, dioc. Lincoln
Fratres: John de Burnham, canon of St Mary, Southwark
John de Eneford', monk of Waverley
Henry de Eynesham, monk of Netley
Henry Blount of Windsor, dioc. Salisbury, *ad tit.* abbot of Westminster

810. *Deacons*
Robert de Bakewell', of Bourne, *ad tit.* prior of Selborne
Alexander Denum of Stratfieldsaye, *ad tit.* prior of Monk Sherborne
Richard le Chaumberlain of Basing, *ad tit.* Fr James Pasquier, prior of
   Andwell
M. Thomas Mynot, rector of Northorpe, dioc. Lincoln
476   Geoffrey de Raunvill', rector of All Saints, Ellisfield
Bartholomew de Donnyngworth, *ad tit.* Fr Almaric, prior of Carisbrooke,
   procurator in England for the abbot of Lyre
William de Oulecotes, rector of Great Mongeham, dioc. Canterbury
Thomas de Clough', rector of Jevington, dioc. Chichester
John Birchovere of Alderwasley, dioc. Coventry and Lichfield, *ad tit.*
   [   ]
William de Hanleye, rector of Hardmead, dioc. Lincoln
Thomas Rudde of Belper, dioc. Coventry and Lichfield, *ad tit.* prior of
   Southwark
Richard de Burton', rector of Little Cove, dioc. Norwich
John Wodeward' of Hudecote, dioc. Worcester, *ad tit.* abbot of Chertsey
John de Purston, rector of Holy Trinity, Chester
M. Walter de Stratton, rector of Dunsfold
Fratres: John de Usk', John Beel, Ralph de Wedeneye
Peter de Alta Petra, monk of Bermondsey
William Brugge, Friar Minor

811. *Priests*
Thomas Fader, rector of [St Peter], Whitebread, Winchester
Thomas de Clyse of Wotton, dioc. Salisbury, *ad tit.* prior of Southwark
John de Sutton', rector of Freckenham, under the immediate jurisdiction
   of the bishop of Rochester
John de Adderlegh, rector of Bonsall, dioc. Coventry and Lichfield

William de Gofford, rector of Easton, dioc. Norwich
M. Geoffrey de Huneden', rector of Runcton, dioc. Norwich
John le Mays of Odiham, *ad tit.* Fr James Pasquier, prior of Andwell
John de Sporlee, rector of Carlton Colville, dioc. Norwich
Geoffrey de Lymbergh', rector of Brocklesby, dioc. Lincoln
William Dymeyn, dioc. Winchester, *ad tit.* prior of the hospital outside Bishopsgate
John de Uppyngham, rector of Warmington, dioc. Lincoln
William de Hanleye, rector of Marsh, dioc. Lincoln
Thomas Andrew, rector of Newton Nottage, dioc. Llandaff
Henry de Tatton, rector of Whaddon, dioc. Ely
Nicholas Asster of Good Easter, under the immediate jurisdiction of the dean of the royal free chapel of St Martin [-le-Grand], with letters from the dean, *ad tit.* master of the hospital of St James, Westminster
George de Aperdele, *ad tit.* prior of Newark
M. John de Penkeston', rector of Brighstone, Isle of Wight
William de Childerle Magna, dioc. Ely, *ad tit.* prior of Merton
Richard le Vaus of South Warnborough, *ad tit.* prior of Southwark
M. Adam de Wykemere, rector of 'Holewold', dioc. Norwich
John de Depyng', rector of Copmanford, dioc. Lincoln
Richard Levelyn, *ad tit.* prior of Selborne
Adam de Skypsee, rector of Playden, dioc. Chichester
Fratres: Thomas de Bromlegh', brother of the hospital of St Mary, Strood, dioc. Rochester
Thomas Ouyng', Henry Martyn, monks of Bermondsey
Richard de Warnham', canon of Reigate
Robert Herlyng', canon of St Peter, Ipswich, dioc. Norwich

812. *First tonsure*
23 May 1350, Southwark, in the manor chapel by the bishop for Thomas de Schardeburgh', dioc. York, with dimissorial letters from the archbishop

477 **813.** ORDERS conferred by the bishop in the manor chapel, Highclere, Ember Saturday, 18 September 1350

Acolytes
Walter Forde of Kingsclere
William de Wotton', rector of Warnford
John Bakere of Winchester
Fratres: John de Caresbrok', David de Bouklonde, John de Lemynton, John de Brakkele, monks of Quarr
Henry Payable, Friar Minor
John de Tyssbury, canon of Breamore
Thomas de Peueseye, Walter de Bretford', John de Eynsham, monks of Hyde
John de Dounton, John atte More, canons of St Denys [Southampton]

814. *Subdeacons*
Simon Robyn of 'Wateley', rector of St Saviour, Winchester
William Hartethorne, *ad tit.* prior of Shulbred

John Gary of Longstock, *ad tit.* prior of St Mary Kalendar, Winchester
M. Richard Paytyn, rector of Cronware, dioc. St Davids, by letters from
   M. Griffin de Caunton', archdeacon of Carmarthen, vicar for Reginald
   the elect of St Davids
John de Fulford', rector of Abbots Ann
John Warin', rector of Newton [Valence]
Fratres: John de Modeford', canon of Christchurch Twynham
Roger de Combe, John de Wynton', John de Hampton', monks of Quarr
Robert Russel, Nicholas le Leve, Robert Thurstayn, Richard de
   Merewell', John de Grandesburgh', John de Bruton', William
   Watford', monks of St Swithuns, Winchester
Robert de Ertham, canon of Southwick

815. *Deacons*
Richard Laurence of South Waltham, *ad tit.* master and brethren of St
   John's Hospital, Oxford
William Belle of Bromley, *ad tit.* prior of Hamble
John Walker, rector of Great Shefford, dioc. Salisbury
Nicholas Northerne of Colmer, rector of St Margarets outside Westgate,
   Winchester
Frater John Bonde, canon of Breamore
William de Eynesham, monk of Quarr

816. *Priests*
Alexander Demini of Stratfieldsay, *ad tit.* prior of Andwell
Richard Chaumberlayn of Basing, *ad tit.* prior of Hamble, procurator
   for the abbot of Tiron
John Wodeward of Hudecote, dioc. Worcester, *ad tit.* abbot of Chertsey
Bartholomew de Donnyngworth of the Isle of Wight, *ad tit.* prior of
   Carisbrooke, procurator for the abbot of Lyre (*margin* sworn by the
   rector of Chale)
Geoffrey de Raunville', rector of All Saints, Ellisfield
Fratres: Thomas de Elyndon', Alan de Estwell', Friars Minor

478   **817.** *Minor Orders and Dimissorial Letters*
Sunday, 5 September 1350, South Waltham, in his chapel, the bishop
   ordained as acolytes these monks of Winchester cathedral: Fratres:
   Robert Russel, Nicholas Lenf, Robert Thursteyn, Richard de Merewell',
   John de Brandesbury, John de Bruiton and William de Watford'
14 September 1350, Highclere, letters for canons of Merton: Fratres
   Geoffrey de Gyllynge and John de Froyle for the diaconate; for Robert
   Windlesore for the priesthood
11 October 1350, Esher, for Richard Bernard, clerk, of Winchester, for
   minor orders
21 November 1350, Southwark, for monks of Quarr: Fratres John
   de Caresbrok', David de Bouklond, John de Lemyngton' for the
   subdiaconate; Roger de Combe and John de Wynton for the diaconate

818. ORDERS conferred by John bishop of Worcester, Ember Saturday,
18 December 1350, in the manor chapel of the archbishop of Canterbury

at Lambeth, by licence from the archbishop and with the bishop's authority

Acolytes
Adam de Werplesdon, Thomas de Wymare, John Chillerton' of Reigate
Fratres: Philip de Blontesdon', Thomas Peythy, monks of Hyde
John de Saunderstede, canon of Southwark
Thomase de London, canon of St Mary, Merton

819. *Subdeacons*
John de Hurselee, *ad tit.* master and brethren of hospital of St Wulstan, Worcester
Robert Sprynget of Carshalton, *ad tit.* prior of St Mary, Merton
William de Wotton', rector of Warnford
Nicholas de Weston', *ad tit.* abbot of Waverley
John atte Wythege of 'Sonnyng' near Breamore, *ad tit.* prior of Breamore
Fratres: Simon de Howynge, Walter de Brutford', monks of Hyde
Thomas de Fytelton', canon of Southwark
John de Cherteseye, monk of Waverley

820. *Deacons*
Simon Robyn, rector of St Saviour, Winchester
John de Fulford, rector of Abbots Ann
John Gary of Longstock, *ad tit.* prior of St Mary Kalendar, Winchester
Fratres: John de Schirfeld, canon of Tandridge
John de Eneford, monk of Waverley
Geoffrey de Gyllyng, John de Froyle, canons of St Mary, Merton

479 **821.** *Priests*
M. Walter de Stratton, rector of Dunsfold
John Waker, rector of Great Shefford, dioc. Salisbury
Nicholas Northerne of Colmer, rector of St Margaret, Westgate, Winchester
Robert de Tekwell of Bourne, *ad tit.* prior of Selborne
Fratres: William de Preston, monk of Bermondsey
Robert de Wyndlesore, canon of St Mary, Merton
John Bounde, canon of Breamore

822. *Dimissorial letters*
8 February 1351, Southwark, for fr. John de Tissebury and William de Norton, canons of Breamore, for all holy orders
13 March 1351, Southwark, for John atte Celere of Winchester subdeacon, for the diaconate

823. ADMISSIONS OF CLERKS by the examiners of the bishop at Southwark, with others holding dimissorial letters from other dioceses, sent for ordination to Ralph, bishop of London, Saturday in the first week of Lent, 12 March 1351, in the church of St Paul, London

Acolytes
William Bekke, Roger atte Punde of Chipstead, Thomas Faukes of Leatherhead
Frater John Purie, canon of Newark

824. *Subdeacons*
Stephen Wyot, rector of Hatch
John atte Celere, *ad tit*. prioress of Kingston [St Michael,] dioc. Salisbury
Fratres: Thomas de London', canon of Merton
William de Bisshopeston', canon of Newark
William de Horlee, John de Crikkelade, monks of Chertsey

825. *Deacons*
Robert de Colyngborne, rector of Swarraton
John de Hursele, *ad tit*. master of the hospital of St Wulstan, Worcester
Robert Springet of Carlshalton, *ad tit*. prior of Merton
John Waren', rector of Newton Valence
Frater: John de Certeseye, monk of Waverley

826. *Priests*
John de Fulford', rector of Abbots Ann
Simon Robyn, rector of St Saviour, Winchester
William Belle of Bromley, *ad tit*. prior of Andwell, procurator of the
    abbot of Tiron
Richard Laurence of South Waltham, *ad tit*. master of the hospital of
    St John, Oxford
Fratres: Roger Coumbe, monk of Quarr
John de Schirfeld, canon of Tandridge
Geoffrey de Gylling', canon of Merton
John de Froille, canon of Merton
Ralph de Wydeneye, [monk of Chertsey]

480   **827**. ORDERS conferred by the bishop in his manor chapel of Esher,
Saturday when *Sitientes* is sung, 2 April 1351

Acolytes
Richard de Wantynge, dioc. Winchester
Edward de Chirdestok', dioc. Salisbury

Subdeacons
Roger Peuros, rector of St John of the Ivy, Winchester
William Bekke, rector of Colmer
Thomas Faukes *ad tit*. prior of St Mary, Merton (*added* for all orders)
Fratres: John de Oxon', Robert de Aston, monks of Reading, dioc.
    Salisbury
John de Hurlee, William de Canterbur', monks of Chertsey
John atte Pirie, canon of Newark

Deacons
William Cleygh of Treiorwerth, rector of St Peter, Calpe Street,
    Winchester
Robert de Alresford, holding the office of deacon in the chapel of St
    Elizabeth, Winchester, in view of that office
Stephen Wyot, rector of Hatch
Fratres: William de Horlee, John de Crikkelade, monks of Chertsey
John de Stanlak', monk of Reading
William de Bysshopeston', canon of Newark

Priests
John Warin, rector of Newton [Valence]
John de Hursele, *ad tit.* master of the hospital of St Wulstan, Worcester

828. *Dimissorial letter and commission*
31 March 1351, Esher, for canons of Southwark, to Thomas de Fitelton
for the priesthood, for John de Burnham for the diaconate and for
Walter de Thorneye for minor orders
Same date, commission to John bishop of Worcester, to hold ordinations,
Saturday of *Sitientes*, 2 April 1351, for any who show their dimissorial
letters

481   **829.** ORDERS conferred by the bishop in his manor chapel of Esher,
Saturday in Easter week, 16 April 1351

Acolytes
Fratres: William de Radynge, Walter Bouet, monks of Chertsey

Subdeacons
Richard de Wantynge, *ad tit.* abbot of Chertsey

Deacons
Thomas Faukes of Leatherhead, *ad tit.* prior of Merton for all orders
William Bekke, rector of Colmer
Roger Peuros, rector of St John of the Ivy, Winchester
William Mundele, rector of Essenden, dioc. Lincoln
Frater John Pirie, canon of Newark

Priests
Stephen Wyot, rector of Hatch
Robert Sprynget of Carshalton, *ad tit.* prior of Merton
Robert de Colyngbourne, rector of Swarraton
William Cleygh of Treiorwerth, rector of St Michael, Jewry Street,
Winchester
Robert de Alresford, *ad tit.* office of subdeacon at the chapel of St
Elizabeth, Winchester
Robert de Cougham, rector of Castle Rising, dioc. Norwich
Simon Crofton, dioc. London, *ad tit.* prior of Leeds, with letters from
the bishop of London
Frater William de Bisshopeston', canon of Newark

830. *Dimissorial letters and first tonsure*
29 April 1351, Southwark, letters for Fratres: Nicholas de Andevere,
John de Hameldon' and John de Soberton for all minor orders—
monks of Beaulieu; For John de Cristchirche, John de Candale for
minor orders, John de Brakkele for the subdiaconate, John de
Hampton' for the diaconate and William de Eynesham for the
priesthood—monks of Netley
29 May 1351, Southwark, for Fratres Nicholas de Andevere, John de
Hameldon' and John de Soberton, monks of Beaulieu, for all holy
orders

13 July 1351, Southwark, for Ralph de Mucheldevere, acolyte, for all holy orders

28 August 1351, Esher, William de Lungspee of the city of Winchester received the first tonsure and letters for minor orders

17 September 1351, Southwark, letters for fr. John de Caresbrok', David de Bouklond' and John de Lemyngton' for the subdiaconate; fr. John de Wynton' for the diaconate—monks of Quarr

14 October 1351, Southwark, letters for fr. Robert de Sancto Manifeo for the priesthood, Thomas de London' for the diaconate, Walter de Muchenhale for all orders—canons of Merton

482   Hugh atte Yate of Fenchurch, rector of St Saviour, Winchester for the priesthood

John Gary of Longstock, rector of St Alphege, Winchester for the priesthood

Fr. John de Merscham, canon of Reigate for the subdiaconate

Fr. Walter de Reigate, also canon of Reigate for minor orders

Osbert de Wimbervile, rector of St Petroc, Winchester, for the subdiaconate

Fr. Robert de Ertham, canon of Southwick, for the priesthood

Fr. Robert de Petresfeld, also canon of Southwick, for minor orders

M. Walter Benett, rector of Arreton, for the subdiaconate

William Bakere of 'Eastuderlegh', for the subdiaconate

Fr. John Pirie, canon of Newark, for the priesthood

Fr. William de Redynges, monk of Chertsey, for the subdiaconate

John Brikenvile of Romsey, for the priesthood, *ad tit.* prior of St Peter, Winchester

Thomas Faukes of Leatherhead, for the priesthood, *ad tit.* prior of Merton

27 November 1351, Southwark, letters for Fr. Robert de Petresfeld, canon of Southwick, acolyte, for all holy orders

30 November 1351, Southwark, letters for Fratres Robert Russel, Nicholas Loef and Robert Thurstayn for the priesthood—monks of Winchester cathedral

Fr. William Bondesdon', Thomas Peusey, Thomas Pethy, John Eynesham and Thomas Buryhull', for the subdiaconate; Simon Uynge and Walter Brutford for the diaconate—monks of Hyde

16 February 1352, Southwark, letters for M. Walter Beneyt, rector of Arreton, Isle of Wight, for the priesthood

18 February 1352, Southwark, for M. Robert de Wykford, rector of Avington for all minor orders

20 February 1352, Southwark, for Fr. Richard de Tichefeld' for the subdiaconate and Henry Cheny for minor orders—canons of Titchfield

Same date for M. Robert de Wykford, rector of Avington, for all holy orders

831. ORDERS conferred by John bishop of Worcester, in the conventual church of St Mary, Southwark, Ember Saturday in the first week of Lent, 3 March 1352

Acolytes
John de Rodmerton'
Robert de Abbotston'
Gervase Abraham
Richard de Elfeton', rector of the chapel of Appleford
John Coliere
Fr. Geoffrey de Rochis, monk of Bermondsey

Subdeacons
M. Philip de Codeford', rector of Corfe, dioc. Salisbury
Roger de Aumbresbury, rector of St John of the Ivy, Winchester
Peter Taillour of Guildford, *ad tit.* master and brethren of hospital of
   St Bartholomew in Smithfield, London
Fr. Richard de Colcestr', monk of Westminster

Deacons
William de Lungspeie of Winchester city, *ad tit.* prior of Leeds
Fr. John de Merscham, canon of Reigate
William de Wotton', rector of Warnford

Priest
Osbert de Wymbervile, rector of St Petroc, Winchester

483   832. ORDERS conferred by the bishop in his manor chapel of Esher,
Saturday when *Sitientes* is sung, 24 March 1352

Subdeacons
John de Rodmerton', rector of All Saints, Kingsgate, Winchester
Gervase Abraham, rector of St Peter outside Southgate, Winchester
John Coliere of Chilbolton, rector of St Margaret, High Street,
   Winchester

Deacons
Roger de Aumbresbury, rector of St John of the Ivy, Winchester
Fr. Walter de Radyng', monk of Chertsey

Priests
Fratres: William de Horlee, John de Crikkelade, monks of Chertsey
William de Wotton', rector of Warnford
William de Lungspee of Winchester city, *ad tit.* of a benefice to be
   provided by the abbot of Hyde

Dimissory letter
18 March 1352 for John Rousel of Somborne for all orders to the
   diaconate

833. ORDERS conferred by the bishop in the chapel of Farnham castle,
Saturday in Easter week, 7 April 1352

Acolytes

John Austyn of Farnham	Fratres: John de Redynge, John
John atte Hethe of Odiham	de Crawlee, William de
William de Tuderleye	Ottoworth—monks of Waverley

Subdeacons
Fr. Adam de Worplesdon', monk of Waverley
Richard de Elfeton, rector of the chapel of Appleford, Isle of Wight

Deacons
John de Rodmerton', rector of All Saints, Kingsgate Street, Winchester
Gervase Abraham, rector of St Peter outside Southgate, Winchester
John Coliare of Chilbolton, rector of St Margaret in the High Street, Winchester
Peter Taillour of Guildford, *ad tit.* abbot of Waverley

Priests
Roger de Aumbresbury, rector of St John of the Ivy, Winchester
Fratres: Thomas Petchi, John de Enesham and Thomas de Buryhullc—monks of Chertsey

484   **834.** *Dimissorial Letters*
31 May 1352, Esher, letters for
John Baker of Studley and Roger atte Pende for the diaconate
John de Middleton', rector of the chapel of Brook, Isle of Wight, for the diaconate
John de Rodmerton, rector of All Saints, Kingsgatestreet, Winchester, for the priesthood
John de Elfeton, rector of the chapel of Appleford, Isle of Wight, for the diaconate
Peter le Taillour of Guildford, for the priesthood
16 June 1352, Esher, for Nicholas Cokeswelle, monk of Beaulieu for all holy orders
26 August 1352, Southwark, for Robert Paye son of Geoffrey Paye of Blendworth, for all holy orders
18 September 1352, Wolvesey for Richard de Elfeton', rector of the chapel of Appleford, Isle of Wight, for the priesthood
19 September 1352, Wolvesey, for John Coliere of Chilbolton, rector of St Margaret outside Westgate, Winchester, and William Bakere of Studley, for the priesthood; and Peter Cheyne for minor orders to the diaconate
18 September 1352, Wolvesey, for Gervase Abraham, rector of St Peter outside Southgate, WInchester, for the priesthood
9 October 1352, Southwark, for Fratres John de Brakele for the diaconate and priesthood, John de Hampton for the priesthood, John de Christchirche and John de Kendale for minor and all holy orders—monks of Netley
22 October 1352, Southwark, for John Boreford of the New Forest, for the subdiaconate and diaconate
31 October 1352, Southwark, for Richard *natus* of Roger Chidham of Warblington for the first tonsure
11 December 1352, Southwark, for William Chival' of Titsey, for the subdiaconate and diaconate

835. ORDERS conferred by the bishop, Ember Saturday, 22 December 1352, in the manor chapel at Esher

Acolytes

Thomas de Percy, rector of Catton, dioc. York, with letters from the chapter of York, the dean being in distant parts, *sede vacante*

Robert Beneyt of the Isle of Wight

Richard Skyteby, dioc. York, with letters from the chapter

Nicholas de Thornhull', rector of Northchurch, near Berkhampstead, dioc. Lincoln

Nicholas Thedrich' of Sheepbridge, dioc. Salisbury

Fratres: William de Abyndon', William Hyldesleye, Walter Dabere, Dominicans

Henry de Bacherwyk', Nicholas de Westcote, monks of Chertsey

John de Grobham, dioc. Salisbury

485 **836.** *Subdeacons*

Robert de Bicton', dioc. Winchester, *ad tit.* a benefice by provision of the abbot of Hyde

John atte Roughbern, dioc. Winchester, *ad tit.* prior of Southwark

William Bertelot of Ringwood, *ad tit.* prior of Breamore

John Digan of Clent, *ad tit.* annual pension of 100s. from J', bishop of Worcester

John de Conyngesholme, dioc. Lincoln, *ad tit.* prior of St Frideswide, Oxford

Thomas de Eydon, dioc. Lincoln, *ad tit.* prior of St Mary outside Bishopsgate, London

John de Exon, rector of Whippingham, Isle of Wight

Thomas son of Elyas, rector of Kilbride, diocese of Limerick, Ireland

Robert de Bury, rector of Rothwell, dioc. Lincoln

Robert de Colston, rector of Fritton, dioc. Norwich

Fratres: John de Redynge, John de Craule, Henry de Wodeslok', monks of Waverley

Thomas de Heigham, Geoffrey Sturle, Henry Gleie, William Wurlee, Friars Minor

John de Rokesdon', John de Sutton', Carmelite Friars

John de Hovesdon', Dominican

Walter Beneyt, monk of Chertsey

837. *Deacons*

William Graunt of Didbrook, dioc. Worcester, *ad tit.* prior of Southwark

Richard de Oundell', dioc. Lincoln, *ad tit.* prior of Southwark

Walter de Topcliff', rector of Scarborough, dioc. York, with letters from the chapter of York

Nicholas de Weston, *ad tit.* prior of Southwark

Fratres: Walter de Iwode, canon of Reigate

Adam de Werplesdon', John de Barton, monks of Waverley

Walter de Muchenhale, canon of Merton

John de Hurle, monk of Chertsey

838. *Priests*

Roger Mohaut of Kingston, *ad tit.* prior of Southwark

Richard de Elfton, rector of the chapel of Appleford, Isle of Wight

John Caliare of Chilbolton, rector of St Margaret, Winchester
M. Robert Froumond', rector of Brede, dioc. Chichester
Fratres: Thomas de Aston', Robert Muscar, Friars Minor
John Wrytele, Dominican
Roger de Porynglond', Carmelite Friar

839. *Dimissorial Letters*
28 December 1352, letters for Fratres John atte More and John de
   Dounton', canons of St Denys, Southampton, for all orders
   Theobald Brokhurst and Richard de Tichefeld' for the priesthood, and
   Henry Cheny for the diaconate, canons of Titchfield
16 January 1353, Southwark, for M. Thomas David, rector of Shalfleet,
   Isle of Wight, for minor and all holy orders

486   19 March 1353, Southwark, for Thomas Quareor of Dorking, for the
   subdiaconate and diaconate

840. ORDERS conferred by the bishop in his manor chapel at Southwark,
Saturday when *Sitientes* is sung, 9 March 1353

Acolytes
John Harold of Wherewell
John Leys, rector of St Peter outside Southgate, Winchester
John de Bennebury, rector of Laverstoke
Thomas de Quareor of Dorking
Fratres: Richard Lovel, Friar Minor of the London convent
William Bouklond', Carmelite Friar

841. *Subdeacons*
John Serle of Faringdon, dioc. Winchester, *ad tit.* prior of Bruton
William de Stowe, dioc. York, *ad tit.* William, dean of St Martin-le-
   Grand, London
Fratres: John de Stapelford, canon of the hospital of St Mary,
   Bishopsgate, London
John de Bydenham, Friar Minor
Thomas de Percy, rector of Catton, dioc. York

842. *Deacons*
John de Exon', rector of Whippingham
John Russel of Somborne, *ad tit.* prior of Mottisfont
John atte Roughbern, *ad tit.* prior of St Mary, Southwark
John Pleistowe of Uffington, dioc. Salisbury, *ad tit.* prior of hospital of
   Lechlade
Robert de Bury, rector of Rothwell, dioc. Lincoln
Fratres: John de Saundersted', canon of St Mary, Southwark
Ralph de Bury, William de Foderyngeye, Friar Minor

843. *Priests*
William de Middelton', rector of Stanford Rivers, dioc. London
John Bureford of the New Forest, *ad tit.* prior of St Mary Kalendar,
   Winchester

William Graunt of Didbrook, dioc. Worcester, *ad tit.* prior of St Mary, Southwark

Thomas Eydon, dioc. Lincoln, *ad tit.* prior of the hospital of St Mary, Bishopsgate, London

Hugh de Grenewych', dioc. Lincoln, *ad tit.* prior of St Mary, Bishopsgate

Robert Northbury, dioc. Coventry and Lichfield, *ad tit.* abbot of Rocester

Walter de Topclif', rector of Scarborough, dioc. York

Robert Langthorn, dioc. York, *ad tit.* prioress of Goring

Nicholas Weston, dioc. Winchester, *ad tit.* prior of St Mary, Southwark

John Digan of Clent, dioc. Hereford, *ad tit.* annual pension of 100s. from the bishop of Worcester

Fratres: Walter Hysewode, canon of Reigate

Thomas Hugham, Henry Gren, Geoffrey de Stureye, Friars Minor

John Rokesdon', Carmelite Friar

487 **844.** MEMORANDUM that Saturday in Easter week, 25 March 1353, in the manor chapel of Esher the bishop conferred the subdiaconate on Edward de Chirdestok', rector of Rimpton, dioc. Bath and Wells, and Nicholas Thedrich' of Sheepbridge, scholar of the college (*aula*) de Vaux in the city of Salisbury

845. *Dimissorial Letters and First Tonsure*

5 May 1353, Esher, letters for Richard Elys, rector of Sherfield, for minor orders and the subdiaconate

14 May 1353, Esher, for Walter Saundre of Wherewell, for all minor orders and the subdiaconate

17 May 1353, for Fr. Walter Muchenhale, canon of Merton for the priesthood; and for John Leye of Silsoe, rector of St Peter outside Southgate, Winchester, for the subdiaconate

Same date, for John de Bennebury, rector of Laverstoke for the subdiaconate; for John de Exon, rector of Whippingham, for Fr. John Bel' and Walter de Redinge, monks of Chertsey, for the priesthood; and M. Robert de Lemynton' for the subdiaconate

1 September 1353, South Waltham, the bishop conferred the first tonsure on Walter de Braye, dioc. Salisbury, with letters from the bishop of Salisbury for all minor orders

18 September 1353, Esher, Letters for John Leye of Silsoe, rector of St Peter outside Southgate, Winchester, for the diaconate

22 August 1353, Waltham, for Fratres Walter Durant and Robert Beche for the subdiaconate; John de Brandesbury and John de Burton for the diaconate; Richard Merewell' and William Watford' for the priesthood—monks of Winchester cathedral

846. MEMORANDUM that on All Saints Day 1353, in the manor chapel, Southwark, the bishop conferred the first tonsure on Thomas de Bagshawe and Nicholas de Calton', dioc. Coventry and Lichfield, bearing letters for all minor orders

7 November 1353, Southwark, letters for John Benmond, dioc. Winchester, for minor orders

20 November 1353 for Fr. William de Boys, canon of Christchurch Twynham, for the diaconate and priesthood

Monday 9 December, feast of the Conception of the B.V.M., 1353, the bishop ordained as acolyte in his household chapel (*hospicii*) at Southwark, Giles de Wyngreworth', rector of Buckby, dioc. Lincoln, bearing letters for all holy orders

30 December 1353, Farnham, letters for Fr John Beaumond, canon of Titchfield, premonstratensian, for all holy orders

19 December 1353, Esher, for John Leye of Silsoe, rector of St Peter outside Southgate, Winchester for the priesthood

Same date, for Walter Saundre, dioc. Winchester, for the subdiaconate and the diaconate

488   21 February 1354, Southwark, for Fr Thomas de Peueseye for the diaconate and Fr William de Bluntesden' for the priesthood—monks of Hyde

5 March 1354, Southwark, for Fratres Robert de Watford and William de Wallop, canons of Selborne, for all holy orders

7 March 1354, Southwark, letters for William atte Halle of Yately, for minor orders; Roger Polwyn of South Moreton, rector of St Saviour, Winchester, for the subdiaconate and diaconate; Fr John de Burnham, canon of St Mary, Southwark, for the priesthood; Richard Pole of Guildford for minor orders

9 May 1354, Southwark, for Nicholas de Seyntlen and Roger atte Pende, dioc. Winchester for the priesthood

847. ORDINATION OF ACOLYTES, Holy Saturday, 10 April 1354, by the bishop in the chapel of Farnham castle: Henry le Wryghte of Portsmouth, Richard de Wortyng', John Brode of Overton and John de Fifhide

848. ORDERS conferred by the bishop in the manor chapel of Esher, Ember Saturday, 20 September 1354

Acolytes
John Muleward' of Bromley
Fratres: John de Mussynden', William de Norhampton', monks of Chertsey

Subdeacons
M. Thomas de Edyndon, warden of the hospital of St Nicholas, Portsmouth
Frater Henry Bladewyk', monk of Chertsey

Deacons
M. William Wolf', rector of Meonstoke
William Bertelot of Ringwood, *ad tit.* prior of Breamore
Edmund Cromhale, rector of Yatton, dioc. Salisbury
Hugh Vyneour, dioc. Norwich, *ad tit. domus* of Castle Acre
Walter Bonet, monk of Chertsey

849. *Priests*
John de Scapeys, dioc, Canterbury, *ad tit.* prior of Leeds
Thomas Ruston of Scarborough, dioc, York, *ad tit.* prior of Reigate
Thomas Bette of Lavenham, dioc. Norwich, *ad tit. domus* Holy Trinity, London

Richard Paty of Kedlington, dioc, Norwich, *ad tit.* prior of St Leonard, [Great] Bricett
Thomas le Smyth of Rendham, dioc. Norwich, *ad tit. domus* of Thetford
John Suthflete of Ash, dioc. Canterbury, *ad tit.* prior hospital of St John of Jerusalem in England
Frater John Bornham, canon of St Mary, Southwark
Dimissorial letter for Frater John de Saundrested' for the priesthood; for Walter de Thorney and William de Brakkelee for the subdiaconate

489 850. ORDERS conferred by the bishop in the manor chapel of [Bishops] Waltham, Ember Saturday, vigil of St Thomas (20 December) 1354

Acolytes
John Gyles of the Isle of Wight
Geoffrey Mone of Shorwell
William le Hore of Soberton
Thomas Coupere of Ripley
Fratres; John de Fostebury, canon of Titchfield
William Sarum, John de Stedham, canons of Mottisfont
William Symond, Edward de Morton, canons of Southwick
Robert atte More, Carmelite Friar

851. *Subdeacons*
John de Byssopeston', rector of Drayton Parslow, dioc. Lincoln
Walter Bussebrugg', dioc. Winchester, *ad tit.* prior of St Peter, Winchester
John Brode of Overton *ad tit.* abbess of Nunnaminster
John de Aston, dioc. Lichfield (*sic*), *ad tit.* prior of hospital of St Thomas, Southwark
Richard Aleyn, dioc. Salisbury, *ad tit.* prior of St Denys, Southampton
Fratres: John Herny, Dominican
Robert de Wyncheorvile, canon of Mottisfont
John de Craulee, Carmelite Friar
Walter Durant, William de Watford', monks of St Swithun, Winchester
Thomas atte More, rector of Elton, dioc. York

852. *Deacons*
Fratres: John de Brandesbury, John de Brynton', monks of St Swithun, Winchester
John de Xtiecclesia, monk of Netley
John de Pederton', Augustinian

Priests
William Bertelot of Ringwood, *ad tit.* prior of Breamore
Thomas de Quarrer', *ad tit.* prior of Tortington
Walter Saundre, rector of St Saviour, Winchester
Richard Pole of Guildford, *ad tit.* prior of the hospital of St Thomas, Southwark
Fratres; Richard de Merwell', Wiliam de Watford, monks of St Swithun
John de Wynton', canon of Mottisfont

John de Abyndon', Adam Albon, John Assh', John Preston, Friars
    Minor
John de Berwico, Augustinian

490   **853.** *Dimissorial Letters*
29 January, 1355, Southwark, for Edmund de Porteseye, for all holy
    orders
7 February 1355, Southwark, for Fratres William Symond and Edward
    Morton, for the subdiaconate—canons of Southwick

854. ORDERS conferred by the bishop in the manor chapel of Southwark,
Ember Saturday in the first week of Lent, 28 February 1355

First Tonsure
John Ferour of Clandon, Walter Scammel, Richard Monstede, William
    Skyrwhit, William Frelond, Peter Daniel, John Dawe of Shere, William
    Follore, John Honte of West Horsley, John atte Mere, Robert Smyth'
    of Alresford

855. *Acolytes*
Robert atte Welle of Chiddingfold
Robert le Ferr' of Chertsey
Richard atte Asse
Roger Cheseman
William Crok'
John Fynende of Kingston

856. *Subdeacons*
William de Tuderlee, *ad tit.* prior of St Denys, Southampton
Walter Baldewyne, dioc. Lincoln, *ad tit.* prior of Poughley
William atte Halle of Yateley, *ad tit.* prioress of Wintney
Fratres: Henry de Blechneshe, William de Marlyngford, Augustinians

857. *Deacons*
M. Robert de Nettelton', rector of Tarrant Monkton, dioc. Salisbury
Walter Adekyn, dioc. St Davids, *ad tit.* of his patrimony for this turn
John Beaumond, *ad tit.* abbot of Titchfield
Richard Aleyn, dioc. Salisbury, *ad tit.* prior of St Denys, Southampton
Walter Bussebrugg', *ad tit.* prior of St Peter, Winchester
Fratres: Walter de Thorney and Thomas Brakkelegh, canons of
    Southwark
Thomas de Petworth', John de Somborne and John Court, Augustinians

Dimissorial Letter
30 March 1355, Esher, for Simon de Brynton', rector of Headley, dioc.
    Winchester, for the priesthood

491   **858.** ORDERS conferred by the bishop, Holy Saturday, 4 April, 1355, in
the manor chapel of Esher

Deacons
D. Thomas de Percy, elect of Norwich, confirmed
William de Tuderleye, *ad tit.* prior of St Denys, Southampton
William atte Halle of Yateley, *ad tit.* prioress of Wintney
John Aston', dioc. Lichfield, *ad tit.* prior of hospital of St Thomas,
Southwark
Alan de Kyllum, dioc. York, *ad tit.* prior of the new hospital of St Mary,
Bishopsgate, London
Robert de Wentebrigg', rector of Thoresway, dioc. Lincoln

Dimissorial Letter
30 April, Southwark, for John son of Stephen Chivaler of 'Wolknestede',
for all minor orders

859. ORDERS conferred by the bishop in the manor chapel of Southwark,
Ember Saturday, Vigil of Trinity Sunday, 30 May 1355

Acolytes
Matthew son of Simon de Massyngham, dioc. Norwich, with letters from
M. Walter de Elvedon', vicar-general for Thomas, bishop-elect
John Campaign', dioc. London
M. John de Wylford, rector of Clown, dioc. Lichfield
Fratres: Robert de Bernham, James de Barsham, Godfrey de Avebury,
Friars Minor

860. *Subdeacons*
John de Bysshopeston', rector of Fen Stanton, dioc. Lincoln
John de Grobbeham, dioc. Bath and Wells, *ad tit.* prioress of Stratford
Robert de Halten, dioc. Lincoln, *ad tit.* prior of Brixworth
Walter Levenaunt, dioc. Exeter, *ad tit.* which the bishop says he holds
(*quem episcopus Exon, dixit se habere penes se*)
Walter atte Forde, *ad tit.* prior of Bisham Montagu
John de Ieveby, rector of Winford, dioc. York, with letters from
M. Thomas de Bucton, vicar-general for the archbishop in distant
parts
Robert atte Welle, dioc. Winchester, *ad tit.* prior of Merton
Fratres: Roger de Bedeford, monk of Bermondsey
William Howard', Friar Minor

861. *Deacons*
M. Walter Benet, rector of Arreton, Isle of Wight
Walter Fabri of Cerne Abbas, dioc. Salisbury, *ad tit.* abbot of Cerne
Geoffrey Geryn of Hillington, dioc. Norwich, *ad tit.* hospital of St John
of Jerusalem, remaining with the diocesan (*penes dictum dioces.*
residentem)
John Leve, dioc. Salisbury, *ad tit. domus* St Saviour, Bermondsey
Hugh de Walcote, dioc. Lincoln, *ad tit.* prior of Sempringham
Walter Baldewyne of Dean, dioc. Lincoln, *ad tit.* prior of Poughley
M. William de Trenelles, dioc. Exeter, *ad tit.* abbot of Tavistock which
the bishop of Exeter says he holds in his registry
John de Glaston, rector of Snettisham, dioc. Norwich

John de Norton', rector of Marsham, dioc. Norwich

Stephen atte Fen of South Elmham, dioc. Norwich, with letters from M. Walter de Elvedon', vicar-general for Thomas elect of Norwich, *ad tit. domus* of [Great] Bricett

Henry Champeneys of Everdon, dioc. Lincoln, *ad tit domus* Holy Trinity, London

Frater John de Houghton', monk of St Albans, with letters from the abbot

492   **862.** *Priests*

John atte Roughborne, dioc. Winchester, *ad tit.* prior of St Mary, Southwark

William atte Halle of Yateley, *ad tit.* prioress of Wintney

Geoffrey Annes of Felmingham, dioc. Norwich, with letters from M. Walter de Elvedon', vicar-general of Thomas elect of Norwich, *ad tit. domus* of Hickling, remaining with the said vicar

Nicholas Conwey of Sloley, dioc. Norwich, with letters from Fr. Laurence, prior of Norwich Cathedral, vicar-general for Thomas elect of Norwich, *ad tit.* abbot of Langley

Richard Aleyn, dioc. Salisbury, *ad tit.* prior of St Denys, Southampton

John atte Welle of Ginge, dioc. Salisbury, *ad tit.* prior of St Mary, Merton

William de Todenham, rector of Brandon Ferry, dioc. Norwich

William Dextere of Northwold, dioc. Norwich, *ad tit. domus* of West Dereham

Henry de Nethergate of Plumstead, dioc. Norwich, *ad tit.* hospital of St Giles, Norwich, remaining with the diocesan

Alan de Kylum, dioc. York, *ad tit.* prior of the new hospital of St Mary, Bishopsgate, London

John Godman of Fordham Heath, dioc. Norwich, with letters from the said M. Walter de Elvedon', *ad tit.* monastery of Thetford

Giles le Botilier, dioc. Lincoln, *ad tit.* prior of Snelshal

John Smyth of Waterden, dioc. Norwich, with letters from the said M. Walter de Elvedon', *ad tit. domus* of Coxford, remaining in the registry of William, late bishop

John Fox of West Bilney, dioc. Norfolk, with letters from the said M. Walter, *ad tit.* domus of West Dereham

Nicholas Wykham. dioc. Salisbury, *ad tit.* monastery of Ivychurch

Walter Adekyn, dioc. St Davids, *ad tit.* prior of the hospital of St Thomas the Martyr, Southwark

William de Tuderlegh', dioc. Winchester, *ad tit.* prior of St Denys, Southampton

John Beaumond of Titchfield, *ad tit.* abbot of Titchfield

Fratres: Tilman of Cologne, Giles de Preston, Thomas de Pecham, Friars Minor

Richard de Aston, monk of St Albans, with letters from the abbot

John de Rippes, monk of Bermondsey

Thomas de Lamborne, Dominican

Richard de Sculthorp', canon of Langley, Premonstratensian

John de Peterton', Augustinian

863. MEMORANDUM that the under-mentioned clerks of the diocese of Norwich, holding letters dimissory from Thomas elect of Norwich, whose status is set out below, were raised to the orders stated, at the date and place given, (*margin*) their titles remain in the registry of the elect of Norwich

Subdeacons
Geoffrey son of Edmund of Bishop's Lynn, *ad tit.* prior of St Mary Magdalen, Pentney
Edmund Coupere of Friston, *ad tit.* abbot of Leiston
William Gonty of Barton Bendish, *ad tit.* prior of Shouldham
Thomas Bulwere of Watlington, *ad tit.* abbot of West Dereham
John Maddy of Bridgham, *ad tit. domus* of Castle Acre

Deacons
Richard Gagge of Ipswich, *ad tit.* prior of Dodnash
John Porter of Coddenham, *ad tit. domus* of Scrucerois?
Gilbert Olyf of Waldingfield, *ad tit.* prior of Woodbridge

864. *Priests*
Thomas Pik of Merton, *ad tit.* prior and canons of Bromehill
John Radewynter of Chippenham, *ad tit.* Hospital of St John of Jerusalem
John Newelond' of Boxford, *ad tit.* prior of St Botolph, Colchester
William Maydes of Wilton, *ad tit.* prior and canons of Bromehill
John Schapman of Buckenham, *ad tit.* prior and canons of Buckenham
Thomas Atte Dele of Foston, *ad tit.* prior of Wormegay
John Harfrey of Shouldham, *ad tit.* abbot of West Dereham
Brice (*Bricius*) Galfridi Aylmer of Oxwick, *ad tit.* prior of St Stephen, Hempton
Thomas Rannild' of Barton Bendish, *ad tit.* prior and canons of Shouldham
M. Robert de Wentebrigge, rector of Thoresway, dioc. Lincoln

493
865. LETTER OF PRESENTATION for ordinations from Thomas elect of Norwich to the bishop—all from the diocese of Norwich:
(listing the 17 personal and place-names of 863 and 864, excepting the last)
For Ember Saturday, Vigil of Trinity Sunday, 1355
London, 29 June 1355

866. *Dimissorial Letters*
17 September 1355, Sutton, for Fratres John de Brandesbury, John de Bruton, for the priesthood; Walter Durant and Robert Beche for the diaconate—monks of Winchester cathedral
11 December 1355, Southwark, for William de Stodmersh, rector of Chiddingfold, for all holy orders
15 December 1355, Esher, for Frater John de Radyng, for the diaconate—monk of Waverley
17 February 1356, Southwark, Giles de Bromden', dioc. Winchester for all minor orders

867. ORDERS conferred by the bishop in his manor chapel at Southwark, Ember Saturday in the first week of Lent, 19 March 1356

Acolytes

Robert de Langeson' of Leire, dioc. Lincoln

William Chelaston, rector of 'Southfield', dioc. Norwich, with letters from M. Walter de Elvedon, vicar-general

John Chepman of Wandsworth

Henry Hendy, dioc. Salisbury

John Forster of 'Thorbey', dioc. Worcester

John de Comenore, dioc. Salisbury

William Burgh', rector of Babworth, dioc. York

868. *Subdeacons*

Richard de Derby, archdeacon of Nottingham, with letters from the archbishop of York

Thomas Herteshorn, rector of Horstead, dioc. Norwich

Wiliam Calewe of Iwerne, dioc. Salisbury, *ad tit.* abbot of Sherborne and canon of Salisbury

William Jakes of Ladbrooke, dioc. Coventry and Lichfield, *ad tit.* prior of Ivychurch

M. Robert de Lemyngton, *ad tit.* of his own patrimony

Fratres: Geoffrey, monk of Bermondsey

John Colneye, Friar Minor

Thomas Leveye, Carmelite Friar

869. *Deacons*

John Brode, dioc. Winchester, *ad tit.* abbess of Nunnaminster

Robert atte Welle of Chiddingfold, dioc. Winchester, *ad tit.* prior of St Mary, Merton

Roger atte Felde of Missenden, *ad tit. domus* of Missenden

494 Walter atte Forde, dioc. Winchester, *ad tit.* prior of Bisham Montagu

Nicholas de Maydenewynton', dioc. Salisbury, *ad tit.* prioress of St Helen, Bishopsgate

William de Wotton' of Claydon, dioc. Lincoln, *ad tit. domus* of Hospital of St John of Jerusalem

Fratres: Richard de Warburgh', Robert de Coteldon', canons of Dorchester, dioc. Lincoln

Robert Beneit, Tilemanus de Biddebrigg', Thomas de Cantuar', John de Preston', Carmelite Friars

William de Chudham, Friar Minor

Richard de Haryngworth, Dom.,

John de Wynchope, Augustinian

John de Insula of Kintbury, dioc. Salisbury, *ad tit.* master and brethren of St Bartholomew Hospital, Smithfield, London

870. *Priests*

John Aston, dioc. Coventry and Lichfield, *ad tit.* prior of the hospital of St Thomas the Martyr, Southwark

William Etmok of Avon Dassett, dioc. Conventry and Lichfield, *ad tit. domus* of Bruern

Robert de Sekynden', rector of Arlesey, dioc. Coventry and Lichfield
John de Chaddesden', rector of Drayton Parslow, dioc. Lincoln
John de Bisshepeston', rector of Fen Stanton, dioc. Lincoln
Fratres: Richard de Thame, canon of Dorchester, dioc. Lincoln
Thomas Peueseye, monk of St Swithun, Winchester
John Crauele, monk of Holy Trinity, Wallingford, dioc. Lincoln
John Radyng', monk of Waverley
John Tiryngton', Walter Wygan, Carmelite Friars
Simon de Leystona, Wiliam de Hurlee, Dominicans
John Dene, Friar Minor
M. Robert de Nettelton', rector of St Magnus, London, with letters from
  the bishop of London
Walter Baldewyne of Deene, dioc. Lincoln, *ad tit.* prior of Poughley
Richard de Stynynton' and Thomas de Mersch', canons regular of the
  Blood of Jesus Christ, Ashridge, dioc. Lincoln

871. ORDERS conferred by the bishop in the manor chapel of Esher,
Saturday when *Sitientes* is sung, 10 April 1356

Acolytes
John Skaret of Buckingham, rector of Stockton, dioc. Salisbury
Fratres: John Kent and Henry de Wyntreshull', monks of Chertsey

Subdeacons
John Chapman of Wandsworth, dioc. Winchester, *ad tit.* prior of
  St Mary, Merton
Maurice Ocorerry of Ballyclog, dioc. Armagh
Fratres: Nicholas de Weston', Thomas de Musseynden', monks of
  Chertsey

495 **872.** *Deacons*
Peter de Moumby, dioc. Lincoln, *ad tit.* abbot of Holy Cross, Waltham
William Calewe of Iwerne, dioc. Salisbury, *ad tit.* abbot of Sherborne
Simon Basset of Sutton Coalfield, dioc. Coventry and Lichfield
M. Robert de Lemynton', dioc. Winchester, *ad tit.* his own patrimony
Thomas de Herteshorn, rector of Horstead, dioc. Norwich
Fratres: Henry de Blatherwyk', monk of Chertsey
Walter Durant, Robert Beche, monks of St Swithun, Winchester

873. *Priests*
Walter atte Forde, dioc. Winchester, *ad tit.* prior of Bisham Montagu
John Brode of Overton, dioc. Winchester, *ad tit.* abbess of Nunnaminster
Roger atte Felde of Missenden, dioc. Lincoln, *ad tit.* abbot of Missenden
M. Peter Corragh, dioc. Dublin, scholar of the collegiate hall of Oxford
  with letters from the bishop of Lincoln
Fratres: John de Brandesbury, John de Bruyton, monks of Winchester
  cathedral
John de Hurlee, Walter Benet, monks of Chertsey
Mathias de Colonia, Friar Minor

874. *Dimissorial Letters*
13 June 1356, Stratfieldsaye, letters for Walter Durant, monk of
  St Swithun, Winchester, for the priesthood

8 August 1356, Southwark, for Fratres John de Usk' and Henry de Blatherwyk', monks of Chertsey, for the priesthood

18 September 1356, Marwell, for Fratres John de Forstebury for minor orders and Henry Cheym for the priesthood, canons of Titchfield

25 September 1356, Farnham, for Robert atte Welle of Chiddingfold, for the priesthood

27 October 1356, Southwark, for Peter de Chenny for all holy orders

5 November 1356, Southwark, for Thomas atte Hale and Ralph atte Orchard for the subdiaconate

17 December 1356, Southwark, for Richard de Chudeham, dioc. Winchester, for minor orders

875. ORDERS conferred by the bishop in the manor chapel of Southwark, Ember Saturday, 17 December 1356

Acolytes
William de Froille and John Someter of Tooting, dioc. Winchester

Subdeacons
Robert Beck', rector of Draycott, dioc. Coventry and Lichfield
Adam de Hylton, rector of Glatton, dioc. Lincoln
William Pykwell', of Ockham, rector of Foston, dioc. Lincoln
Richard Arnewode, dioc. Winchester, *ad tit.* prior of St Denys, Southampton (*margin*) Walter Rogeron of East Hendred, dioc. Salisbury, *ad tit.* abbot of Dorchester

Deacon
John Chapman of Wandsworth, dioc. Winchester, *ad tit.* prior of St Mary, Merton

496   **876.** *Priests*
M. William Wolf, rector of Meonstoke, dioc. Winchester
M. Edmund de Eston', rector of Ewell, dioc. Winchester
Thomas son of Bartholomew of Leverington, dioc. Ely, *ad tit.* prioress of St Michael, Stamford
John Forest of Thorley, dioc. Worcester, *ad tit.* prioress of Castle Headingham
John Langar, dioc. York, *ad tit.* prior of Leeds
Adam Brantyngham, dioc. York, *ad tit.* prioress of St Frideswide, Oxford
John Frensted of Ospringe, dioc. Canterbury, *ad tit. domus* of Dover
John Voirdire of Goodmanham, dioc, York, *ad tit.* abbot of Chertsey

877. ORDERS conferred by John, bishop of Rochester, by commission from the bishop, in the conventual church of St Mary, Southwark, Ember Saturday in the first week of Lent, 4 March 1357
Commission to the bishop of Rochester to ordain religious and beneficed clerks, bearing letters from their diocesan, duly examined by his commissaries and the chancellor of Winchester, also showing sufficient title and being of good repute

Southwark, 2 March 1357

878. *Acolytes*
Geoffrey atte Crouch of Bushey, of the exempt jurisdiction of St Albans, with letters from the abbot

Thomas Cotilere, dioc. Winchester
John Park' of Albury
John Gardyn, rector of Ashe near Overton
Walter Tigehale
William Nois, chaplain of Holy Trinity, Barton, Isle of Wight, with letters from the archpriest
Fratres: John de Delham, Stephen Wysebech', John de Certeseye, canons of Newark
Walter Thurbern of Saintbury, dioc. Worcester
John Berbury, rector of Bedwas, dioc. Llandaff
Roger de Wombewell, rector of Weston near Northampton, dioc. Lincoln
John James of Westwell, dioc. Lincoln
Fratres: Stephen de Sydemanton', monk of Reading, dioc. Salisbury
John Lake, Henry de Steynyng', Friars Minor
William Birley of Newark, dioc. York

879. *Subdeacons*
Robert de Abbotston', *ad tit.* prior of Poughley
John de Muleward of Bromley, *ad tit.* prior of Monk Sherborne
Thomas Derl of Fareham, *ad tit. domus* of Holy Trinity, London
497 M. Thomas de Islep, rector of Kirkby-on-Bain, dioc. Lincoln
John de Maydenburgh', dioc. Lincoln, *ad tit.* abbess of Barking
Adam Russel *alias* Vernon of Badminton, dioc. Worcester, *ad tit.* prioress of Clerkenwell
John Cursson of Berwick, *ad tit.* master of St Giles hospital outside the city of London
John Stone, dioc. Salisbury, *ad tit.* prioress of St Frideswide, Oxford
Robert de Bamburgh', dioc. Durham, *ad tit.* prior of St Martin, Dover
Fratres: Henry Pole, monk of Reading
John de Esschere, John Bercham, Dominicans

880. *Deacons*
Walter atte Riedesdich' of Binfield, dioc. Salisbury, *ad tit.* prior of Bisham Montagu
John le Thetchere of Hertford, dioc. Lincoln, *ad tit.* prior of St Mary hospital, Bishopsgate, London
John Richard of Billingborough, dioc. Lincoln, *ad tit. domus* of Beigham
Henry Medescroft of Wyck Rissington, dioc. Worcester, *ad tit.* exempt monastery of Chicksands
Adam de Hilton', rector of Glatton, dioc. Lincoln
William de Pikwell', rector of Foston, dioc. Lincoln
John Boydyn of Halstow, dioc. Rochester, *ad tit.* nuns of Minster
John de Whitclyve, dioc. Salisbury, *ad tit.* prior of Merton
Fratres: Alexander Botillier, Friar Minor
Richard de Yatelee, John de Leomunstre, monks of Reading
Nicholas de Chetham, William atte Biri, Carmelite Friars

881. *Priests*
John de Comenore, dioc. Salisbury, *ad tit* prioress of St Mary, Clerkenwell

Robert Gotegod of Derby, dioc. Coventry and Lichfield, *ad tit. domus* of St John, [Monks] Horton
Adam Colyn of Faversham dioc. Canterbury, *ad tit.* the nuns of St Sexburga, Minster
Fratres: William Wydeford, John Hotteford, Robert Bruton', John Mathey, Richard Lovel, John Hostiler, William Radyng', Friars Minor
William de Newbury, John de Wynkefeld, monks of Reading
John de Aston, Simon de Woderoue, John Trenge, Thomas de Wycombe, Bonhommes of Ashridge, dioc. Lincoln
William Upton, Thomas de Maldon, John Preston', Carmelite Friars

882. *Dimissorial Letters*
27 March 1357, Southwark, letters for Fr. Gilbert de Noys of Holy Trinity, Barton, Isle of Wight for the subdiaconate and John Rembaud of Gatcombe, for minor orders
3 May 1357, Southwark, for Philip Stedham and William de Salesbury, canons of Mottisfont, for all holy orders

498   883. ORDERS conferred by the bishop in the manor chapel of Southwark, Ember Saturday, vigil of Trinity Sunday, 3 June 1357

Acolytes
Thomas de Denton, dioc. Lincoln
Edmund atte Moure of Milton [Abbas], dioc. Salisbury
Richard atte Hille of Granchester, dioc. Ely
John Amice of Gaddesby, dioc. Lincoln
Adam Abraham of Wollaton, dioc. Coventry and Lichfield

884. *Subdeacons*
John Gyles of Shorwell, *ad tit.* abbot of Quarr
John Michel of Harrington, dioc. Lincoln, *ad tit.* prioress of Sopwell
Henry Coyne, dioc. Coventry and Lichfield, *ad tit.* prior of 'Hamelehok''
Reginald de Swynmore, rector of 'Lannarghell', dioc. St Asaph, with letters from M. David de Englefeld, guardian for spirituals in the dioc. and vicar-general, *sede vacante*, for Simon, archbishop of Canterbury
John Lorkyn of East Malling, deanery of Shoreham, of the immediate jurisdiction of the archibshop of Canterbury, *ad tit.* abbess of Malling
Roger de Wombewell', rector of Weston, dioc. Lincoln
Frater Edmund Wasteneys, Dominican

885. *Deacons*
M. John de Edyndon', archdeacon of Surrey
Thomas Eorl of Fareham, *ad tit. domus* of Holy Trinity, London
John le Clerc of Upavon, dioc. Salisbury, *ad tit.* abbess of Shaftesbury
Elias de Sutton', rector of Tunstall, dioc. Norwich
Robert de Abbotston', *ad tit.* prior of Poughley
John de Bulkynton', rector of Nether Wallop
Fratres: John de Bedefordia, John Muryet, John de Eshe, Dominicans

886. *Priests*
M. John Direworth', rector of Ham, dioc. Exeter
John Nichard of Billingborough, dioc. Lincoln, *ad tit. domus* of Bayham

Walter Rogeron of East Hendreth, vicar of the church of Steventon, dioc. Salisbury

John Mariner, dioc. Salisbury, *ad tit.* abbot of Stanley

John Chapman of Wandsworth, *ad tit.* prior of St Mary, Merton

William Albon, rector of Fen Drayton, dioc. Ely, with letters from MM. John Thursteyn, canon of Wells and Thomas de Elteslee, vicar-general for Thomas the bishop, in remote parts

William Wayte of Cornwell, dioc. Lincoln, *ad tit.* prior of Bicester

John Lodere of East Malling, dioc. Canterbury, *ad tit. domus* of Wymondley

John Edward of Upavon, dioc. Salisbury, *ad tit.* prioress of Amesbury

Simon Basset, rector of Sutton Coalfield, dioc. Coventry and Lichfield

John Glovere, dioc. Salisbury, *ad tit. domus* of Easton, order of Holy Trinity

Maurice Hammond, dioc. Salisbury, *ad tit. domus* of St John of Marlborough

William de Feriby, rector of Bayham, dioc. Coventry and Lichfield

John Stone dioc. Salisbury, *ad tit.* prioress of St Frideswide, Oxford

John Cursonn of Berwick', dioc. Norwich, *ad tit.* master of the hospital of St Giles, London

499   **887.** *Dimissorial Letters*

25 July 1357, Southwark, letters for Frater Thomas Feht, canon of Christchurch Twynham, for all holy orders,

1 October 1357, Southwark, for William Escote, rector of West Meon, dioc. Winchester, for all holy orders

23 October 1357, Southwark, for William Iston' of East Meon, dioc. Winchester, for the subdiaconate and diaconate

13 June 1357, Southwark, for M. John Noioun, rector of Havant, for all holy orders

3 November 1357, Southwark, for Thomas de Hasthorp', rector of St Olave, Southwark, for the subdiaconate

15 November 1357, for John Jardyn, rector of Ashe near Overton, for all holy orders

Memorandum that 6 December 1357, feast of St Nicholas, in the manor chapel of Southwark, the bishop ordained as acolytes William de Leveryngton', rector of Papworth St Agnes, dioc. Ely, and John Bourg', dioc. York

19 December 1357, letters for William Symon and Edward de Morton', canons of Southwick, for the diaconate and priesthood

888. ORDERS conferred by the bishop in the manor chapel of Southwark, Ember Saturday, 23 December 1357

Acolytes
John de Cadebury, dioc. Bath and Wells
Pelegrine de Podio, rector of Asson, dioc. Lescar
John de Hospitle, rector of Ricallo and of Casa Nova, dioc. Lescar
Henry Luterel, rector of Gate, dioc. Chichester
Stephen Wyke of Chertsey, dioc. Winchester

John Hayton' of Ewell, dioc. Winchester
Robert son of Robert Broun of Wyke, dioc. Exeter
John de Wycham, dioc. Norwich
John atte Churche of Upchurch, dioc. Canterbury
Frater Otho de Sancto Meremo, monk of Bermondsey
Peter de Bassefeld, John Candich', Friars Minor

889. *Subdeacons*
William de Leveryngton, rector of Papworth St Agnes, dioc. Ely
Thomas de Brigham, rector of Newington, deanery of [Monks]
   Risborough, of the jurisdiction of the archbishop of Canterbury
John Togod of Fifhide, dioc. Winchester, *ad tit.* prior of Ivychurch
Geoffrey Mone, dioc. Winchester, *ad tit.* abbot of Quarr
John Jardyn, rector of Asshe, dioc. Winchester
William Hore of Surbiton, dioc. Winchester, *ad tit.* prior of Southwark
John atte Heth' of Odiham, dioc. Winchester, *ad tit.* prior of Southwark
500   Robert Asshe, dioc. Exeter, *ad tit.* abbot of Newenham
John Amys of Gaddesby, dioc. Lincoln, *ad tit.* prior of the new house
   of the hospital of St Mary, Bishopsgate, London
John Bracyere of Ludlow, dioc. Hereford, *ad tit.* abbot of Medmenham
Thomas de Denton, dioc. Lincoln, *ad tit.* prior of Holy Trinity, London
Fratres: John de Lusteshull', Augustinian
John Dalham, canon of Newark
John Botiller, Augustinian

890. *Deacons*
Vincent de Faviis, rector of the parochial church of St Pantaleon, dioc.
   Aix [-en-Provence]
Gilbert de Noys, brother of the *domus* of Holy Trinity, Isle of Wight
Geoffrey atte Crouche of Bushey, in the immediate jurisdiction of
   St Albans, *ad tit.* prioress of St Mary de Pratis near St Albans
Roger de Wombewell', rector of Weston, dioc. Lincoln
Reginald son of Simon Choude of Hambledon, dioc. Lincoln, *ad tit.*
   prior of St Mary, Merton
Frater John de Sutton', Augustinian

891. *Priests*
John de Essex, rector of Henley, dioc. Lincoln
John Michel of Harrington, dioc. Lincoln, *ad tit.* prioress of Sopwell
M. Robert de Lemynton, vicar of Milford, dioc. Winchester
Elyas de Sutton', rector of Tunstall, dioc. Norwich
Thomas Eorl of Fareham, dioc. Winchester, *ad tit. domus* of Holy
   Trinity, London
Robert de Abboteston', dioc. Winchester, *ad tit.* prior of Poughley
Frater Walter de Thorneye, canon of St Mary, Southwark
William le Clerc son of John le Clerc of Maidstone, dioc. Canterbury,
   ad tit. abbot of Stoneleigh
Henry Coignie, perpetual vicar of White Waltham, dioc. Salisbury
Fratres: Robert Spaldyng', John Coventre, Carmelite Friars

892. *Dimissorial Letters*

1 February 1358, Southwark, letters for Fratres Roger Baron, Edward Whitchurch', John Stafford and Nicholas Redyng, for minor orders—monks of Quarr

10 February 1358, Southwark, for Wibert le Wayte, dioc. Winchester, for tonsure and minor orders as far as the subdiaconate

11 February 1358, Southward, for John Botiller of Alresford for minor orders and the subdiaconate

15 February 1358, Southwark, for Fratress Nicholas de Stoke for the diaconate, Walter atte More, John Burton and John Stelberd for the subdiaconate—monks of Netley

22 February 1358, Southwark, for John de Muleward of Bromley for the diaconate and Stephen de Wyke for the subdiaconate

23 February 1358, Southwark, for Gilbert Noys, brother of Barton, Isle of Wight, for the priesthood, Geoffrey Mone also of the I. Wight for the diaconate and Frater John Delham for the priesthood

501 **893.** ORDERS conferred by John, bishop of Rochester, by the bishop's authority, in the conventual church of St Mary, Southwark, Saturday when *Sitientes* is sung, 16 April 1357

First tonsure

James Plomer of Southwark, John de la Lee, dioc. Rochester, Elias Brokyng', John Cole and Richard atte Fenne, dioc. Winchester

Acolytes

Robert de Tykhull, dioc. York
Walter Bakere, dioc. Winchester
William Baker, same dioc.
William de Leighton, Friar Minor

Fratres: Stephen Barri, John de Abburbury and Gilbert de Bybury, canons of Osney

894. *Subdeacons*

William de Craneford, dioc. Exeter, *ad tit.* dean and chapter of Exeter, which is entered in the registry of the bishop of Exeter

Robert de Bochemeshull', rector of Hoggeston, dioc. Lincoln

M. Reginald de Lamborne, dioc. Salisbury, *ad tit.* annual rent of 5 marks due from J' Pyel, citizen of London

Thomas de Langwathby, dioc. Carlisle, *ad tit. domus* of St Mary, Southwark

John Hayton, dioc, Winchester, *ad tit.* domus of St Mary, Southwark

Fratress: Andrew Lyonns, Ralph Swanlond', Dominicans of the Guildford convent

895. *Deacons*

Nicholas de Sholdon', dioc. Canterbury, *ad tit.* prior of Leeds

John Gyles of Shorwell, *ad tit.* abbot of Quarr

Ralph Humptyng' of Weldon, dioc. Lincoln, *ad tit. domus* of St Saviour, Bermondsey

John de Plumpton', dioc. Lincoln *ad tit. domus* St Mary, Southwark

Roger de Wolvelegh', dioc. Coventry and Lichfield, *ad tit. domus* of St Mary, Nocton

John Joye of Ledbury, dioc. Hereford, *ad tit.* priory of Holy Trinity, London

Nicholas de Louthe, rector of 'Monte Alto', dioc. St Asaph, with letters from M. John de Tappan, vicar-general for Louis, bishop of St Asaph, in distant parts

Richard de Smalbergh', dioc. Norwich, *ad tit.* monastery of Chertsey

Fratres: John Lake, William Bergate, Friars Minor of the London convent

Henry de Cantuaria, John de Forde, monks of [St Mary] Graces, near the Tower of London, presented by the abbot

Thomas de Denton, dioc. Lincoln, *ad tit.* domus of Holy Trinity, London

896. *Priests*

William de Loveryngton', rector of Papworth St Agnes, dioc. Ely, with letters from M John Thursteyn, vicar-general for Thomas, bishop of Ely, in distant parts

Thomas de Brigham, rector of Newington, deanery of [Monks] Risborough, of the exempt jurisdiction of Canterbury

Richard Pipere, dioc. Canterbury, *ad tit. domus* of Dover

M. John de Middleton', dioc. Lincoln, *ad tit. domus* St Mary, Oxford

Adam de Thorp, rector of 'Queldryk,' dioc. York

Geoffrey atte Crouch' of Bushey, of the exempt jurisdiction of the abbot of St Albans, with letters from him

502 **897.** *Dimissorial Letters*

24 May 1358, Southwark, letters for John de Heyton and Frater John Dalham, canons of Newark, dioc. Winchester for the priesthood, and for Nicholas de Westcoate and John de Mussynden, monks of Chertsey, for the diaconate

11 July 1358, Southwark, for Robert de Wykford, rector of Avington, who is to study in a university beyond the Alps, that he may without difficulty seek ordination to the diaconate and priesthood by any catholic bishop on either side of the Alps

12 July 1358, Southwark, for Fratres John Chaworth, John Oxenford and John Churche, John Wordi and John Hardi, monks of Hyde, for minor orders and the subdiaconate

12 July 1358, Southwark, for Frater Oliver Gulden', canon of Christchurch, for all holy orders

2 October 1358, Southwark, for Fratres John Burghildebury, Ralph Basynge, Walter Braye and Robert Walyngford', monks of Winchester cathedral, for all holy orders and Frater Robert Beche for the priesthood

14 October 1358, Southwark, M. John de Edyndon, archdeacon of Surrey, for the priesthood

2 November 1358, Southwark, for Roger Baron, Edward Whitchirch', John Stannford and Nicholas Rydyng', monks of Quarr, for the subdiaconate

8 November 1358, Southwark, for Fratres Henry de Inglesham, William Wynton', William Forde, William Spenser and Peter de Cornub', monks of Beaulieu, for all holy orders

17 November 1358, Southward, for Edward de Brewes, canon of Christchurch Twynham, for minor orders and all holy orders

26 November 1358, Southwark, Henry de Wayte, dioc. Winchester, for all holy orders

898. ORDERS conferred by the bishop in the manor chapel of Southwark, Ember Saturday, 22 December 1358

Acolytes
John de Dighton, rector of Barking, dioc. Norwich
John Clerc of Wandsworth
John Mos of Kingston
Peter Perour, dioc. Exeter
William Denmarz of Kingston
John atte Boure of 'Scholtfeld'
John son of Robert atte Welle of Farthinghoe, dioc. Lincoln
John Preest of Windsor, dioc. Salisbury
Peter de Hardebrigg'
Walter de Colmpton, rector of Ardlougher, dioc. Meath, Ireland
Fratres: William le Chaundeler, John de Homleye and John de Walyngford' [canons of Merton]
William de Donmore, monk of Waverley
John Paul and Robert de Clopton, Friars Minor
John Legh', Dominican

503   **899.** *Subdeacons*
John Balky of Wendover, dioc. Lincoln, *ad tit.* prior of St Mary, Southwark
Richard Rolf of Tunbridge, dioc. Rochester, *ad tit.* prior of St Mary, Southwark
John Smyth of Walton, *ad tit.* prior of Newark
William de Chirchehull', dioc. Lincoln, *ad tit.* prior of Holy Trinity, London
William Bakere of Basingstoke, *ad tit.* prior of St Mary, Southwark
Simon Marchal, dioc. Meath, Ireland, *ad tit.* prior of Holy Trinity, London
Frater John Bergh', Friar Minor

900. *Deacons*
M. Nicholas de Chaddesden', portioner in the church of Waddesdon, dioc. Lincoln
Richard de Davyntree, rector of Little Shoebury, dioc. London
John atte Heth' of Odiham, *ad tit.* prior of St Mary, Southwark
Stephen Wyke of Chertsey, *ad tit.* prior of Merton
Fratres: Thomas de Evesham, brother of the hospital of Ospringe, dioc. Canterbury
Ottominus de Sancto Martino, monk of Bermondsey
Andrew Lyonns, Dominican
Richard de Berford, William Newenton, Augustinians

901. *Priests*
John Curteys, dioc. Meath, Ireland, *ad tit.* abbot of Lesnes
Robert son of Thomas le Whyte, dioc. York, *ad tit.* prior of St Mary, Merton

John Muleward of Bromley, *ad tit.* prior of [Monk] Sherborne

Edmund Soukere of Durrington, dioc. Salisbury, *ad tit.* prior of St Mary, Southwark

Henry Curteys of Denford, dioc. Lincoln, *ad tit.* prior of Stonely

John Blawere of Goodnestone, near Faversham, dioc. Canterbury, *ad tit.* prior of St Gregory, Canterbury

John Wylde of Brackley, dioc. Lincoln, *ad tit.* prior of the same St Gregory

John Wynchecombe, rector of 'Orde', of the immediate jurisdiction of the archbishop of Canterbury

Fratres: John de Farnham, Geoffrey de Bermondeseye, monks of Bermondsey

William Chelrey, monk of Rewley near Oxford, with letters from the bishop of Lincoln

Robert de Twyford', Henry Milton', William Hamond, Robert Bloundel, Friars Minor

William Marlyngford', William Verder, John Sottonn, John Wynchers, Augustinians

Nicholas de Maydenheth', Dominican

902. *Dimissorial Letters*

21 January 1359, Southwark, letters for Walter atte More and John de Denston for the priesthood, John Stelhard for the diaconate and William de Gomeshulne and Henry Christi Ecclesie for the subdiaconate—monks of 'Leccelie' premonstratensian

4 February 1359, Southwark, for John Chelworth', John de Oxneford', John Wordy and John Hardi for the diaconate and John Churche for the subdiaconate—monks of Hyde

15 March 1359, Southwark, for John atte Heth' of Odiham for the priesthood and William Bakere of Basingstoke for the diaconate, dioc. Winchester

Same date, for Walter Bakere of Burton, for the subdiaconate and John Smythe of Walton, dioc. Winchester, for the diaconate

Same date, for Fr. John Homleye, William Chaundel' and John Walynford, canons of Merton and William de Donmere, monk of Waverley and William de Wendovere, canon of St Mary, Southwark for the subdiaconate

504 **903.** ORDERS conferred by the bishop in the chapel of Farnham castle, Holy Saturday, 20 April 1359

Deacon

M. Thomas de Edyndon, warden of the hospital at Portsmouth

Priests

William Bakere of Basingstoke, *ad tit.* prior of St Mary, Southwark

John Smyth of Walton, *ad tit.* chantry of 5 marks at Ashstead, by grant of the prior of Newark

Fratres: John de Oxneford', John Hardy, monks of Hyde

Roger Vuel, Dominican

904. *Dimissorial Letters*

17 April 1359, letters for John Brey, dioc. Winchester, for first tonsure and minor orders

3 June 1359 Southwark, for Fr. Robert Baron, Edward Whitchirch', Nicholas Redyng', for the diaconate—monks of Quarr

6 September 1359, for Richard de Stoke, rector of Farnborough, for all holy orders

14 November 1359, Southwark, for Fr. Stephen de Brightwell', Geoffrey de Wynt' and Hugh de Cicestr', for all holy orders—monks of Titchfield

16 November 1359, Southwark, fr Fr. John Sculhard, Joel de Bourton', for the priesthood, William de Gomeshulne and Henry de Christi Ecclesie for the diaconate

17 November 1359, Southwark, for Robert de Wychford, rector of Houghton, for all holy orders

5 December 1359, Southwark, for Henry de Oxon', rector of St Margaret, Winchester, for minor orders and the subdiaconate

8 January 1360, Southwark, for M. Thomas de Shipton', rector of Woodhay, for the priesthood

23 January 1360, Southwark, for Fr. George Martyn, John de Estcherch' and John de Netheravenne, for minor orders, John atte Church', and John Wordy for the priesthood—monks of Hyde

23 February 1360, Southwark, for John Coumbe, dioc. Winchester for first tonsure

Same date, for John de Netherhavene, for the subdiaconate, monk of Hyde

Same date, the bishop conferred the first tonsure on Thomas atte Brugg' of North Scarle, dioc. Lincoln

11 March 1360, letters for Fr. George Bristowe, John de Christchirch for the subdiaconate, John de Netherhavene for the diaconate and John Worthy for the priesthood—monks of Hyde

Same date, for Richard Hervy for the diaconate

25 July 1360, Southwark, for William Perdie, dioc. Winchester for the first tonsure and minor orders

505 **905.** ORDERS conferred by the bishop in the manor chapel, Southwark, Ember Saturday, 21 December 1359

Acolytes

James Palmer, rector of Ansford, dioc. Bath and Wells
William de Golleye
John de Fostebury
Gilbert Betrich of Shere, dioc. Winchester
John Bromersh of Worplesdon
Richard Bauchon of Guildford
Thomas Walrond of Wraxall, dioc. Salisbury
Thomas Clere of Woodstone, dioc. Lincoln
John de Fleta, rector of Oakley near Buckingham, dioc. Lincoln
John Beauleyn of Ufford, dioc. Lincoln
Fratres: Augustine Hales, Andrew de Hatfeld, Carmelite Friars
William Duffeld

906. *Subdeacons*
John de Everdon', rector of Oxendon, dioc. Lincoln
William Annmore of Leighton Buzzard, dioc. Lincoln, *ad tit.* abbot of
  Osney
John Motte of Kingston, *ad tit.* prior of Merton
Walter Tigehale, *ad tit.* prior of St Cross, Heringham
John Roger of Allhallows Hoo, dioc. Rochester, *ad tit.* prior of Leeds
Thomas Lamb of Kington, dioc. Hereford, *ad tit.* prior of Stoneley
Fratres: Stephen de Staple, Friar Minor
William de Duffeld, Carmelite Friar
Richard de Walyngford, Dominican

907. *Priests*
Hugh atte Nashe of Wendover, dioc. Lincoln, *ad tit.* prior of St Mary,
  Southwark
Stephen Wyke of Chertsey, *ad tit.* prior of St Mary, Merton
Robert Broun, dioc. Exeter, *ad tit.* abbot of Tavistock
John Heryng' of Chisledon, dioc. Salisbury, *ad tit.* prior of Caldwell
Henry de Steynge, John Dancastre, Friars Minor
William de Rysbergh', canon of Missenden
John Overe, Dominican
William de Mordon, Carmelite Friar
John Patrik, Augustinian
Thomas de Milford, Dominican
William de Wendovere, canon of St Mary, Southwark

908. *Deacons*
Fratres: William Chaundeler, John Bloundeys, John de Walyngford,
  canons of St Mary, Merton
Salomon Russel of the city of Rochester, *ad tit.* prior of Leeds
Fratres: John Creukeer, Dominican
Henry Norton, Friar Minor
Walter Broke, Carmelite Friar, also Thomas de Huntyngdon', Thomas
  Bourgh, Carmelites
Henry Stokebrugg', Laurence de Lond', Augustinians

506 **909.** *Commission and Dimissorial Letters*
Commission to John, bishop of Rochester, to confer ordinations on the
first Saturday in Lent, in the church of the diocese of his choice, upon
those who show sufficient title with their dimissorial letters.
                              Southwark, 26 February 1360

3 May 1360, Southwark, for Fr. Peter Rose for the subdiaconate, John
  Stelhard, William Gomesthulne and Henry de Cristchirch' for the
  priesthood—monks of Netley, Cistercian
12 June 1360, Southward, for Robert Dodeford for minor orders, Edward
  Whitchirch and Nicholas Radynge for the priesthood—monks of Quarr,
  Isle of Wight

910. ORDERS conferred by John, bishop of Rochester, is his manor
chapel called the Place, in the parish of Lambeth, dioc. Winchester, by

commission from the bishop, Saturday when *Sitientes* is sung, 21 March 1360

Subdeacon
Thomas de Donyngton', rector of Haconby, dioc. Lincoln

Deacons
Robert de Shardelowe, rector of St Mildred in the Poultry, London
Thomas de Lambesfelde of Crundale, dioc. Canterbury, *ad tit.* hospital of St Mary outside Bishopsgate, London
John de Flete, rector of Oakley near Buckingham, dioc. Lincoln

Priests
John Lynton, minor (*parvus*) canon of St Paul's, *ad tit.* his own canonry
Robert de Salle, dioc. London, *ad tit.* prioress of St Leonard, Stratford-at-Bow

911. ORDERS conferred by John, bishop of Rochester, Ember Saturday in Whitweek, 30 May 1360, in the manor chapel at Place, Lambeth, by commission of the bishop

Subdeacons
Thomas de Ripple, dioc. Canterbury, *ad tit.* prior of St Martin, Dover
Fratres: Henry de Woughborne, John Wynge of the collegiate house of Ashridge, dioc. Lincoln
John de Bampton, canon of Oxney, dioc. Lincoln
William de Farville, Friar Minor

912. *Deacons*
Roger de Gyseborn', dioc. York, *ad tit.* abbot of St Agatha [Easby] near Richmond
John Clodham' of Stone, dioc. Rochester, *ad tit.* prior of Leeds
John Park', dioc. Winchester, *ad tit.* prior of Merton
William Aumory, dioc. Lincoln, *ad tit.* abbot of Osney
Thomas Walrand, dioc. Salisbury, *ad tit.* prior of Holy Trinity, London
Richard Betel, dioc. Lincoln, *ad tit.* prior of hospital of St John, Lechlade
Fratres: Robert Haveryng, Friar Minor
John de Bourum, canon of Tandridge
Henry de Elsham, canon of Osney, dioc. Lincoln

507 **913.** *Priests*
Thomas Lambeseld, dioc. Canterbury, *ad tit.* prior of hospital of St Mary outside Bishopsgate, London
Thomas Lamb, dioc. Hereford, *ad tit.* prior of Stonely
Stephen Mille of Godstow, dioc. Lincoln, *ad tit.* abbot of Dorchester
John de Flete, rector of Oakley near Buckingham
Fratres: John de Shipton', Augustinian
John Eynesham, monk of Thame, dioc. Lincoln
John de Coventree, canon of Osney
Thomas de Dynby, Friar Minor of the London convent

914. *Dimissorial Letters*
9 August 1360, Sutton, letters for Richard Arnewode, dioc. Winchester, for the diaconate

11 August 1360, Farnham, for Walter le Bakere of Broughton, for the priesthood

915. VICARIATE of Fr John, prior of Winchester and Thomas de Enham, rector of Alresford
8 September 1360, Winchester, the vicars granted letters to George de Bristoll' and John de Cristchirche for the diaconate and to John de Netherhaven' for the priesthood—monks of St Swithun
Same date, to John de Burgh', rector of Abbots Clandon, for the subdiaconate
9 September 1360, Winchester, to Richard Hervy, rector of St Margaret, Winchester, for the priesthood
10 September 1360, to M. Thomas de Shipton', rector of Woodhay, for the priesthood
13 September 1360, Winchester, to Fr John Byde, Ralph de Basynge, Walter de Braye and Robert Walyngford, monks of Winchester cathedral, for the subdiaconate
END OF VICARIATE

916. *Dimissorial Letters*
2 January 1361, Farnham, letters for Richard Poleter of Winchester city, for minor orders and the subdiaconate
6 January 1361, Farnham, for Alexander de Warham, dioc. Winchester, for the diaconate and priesthood
Same date, for Fratres Hugh de Cicestr', Stephen Brightwell' and Geoffrey de Byketon', canons of Titchfield, premonstratensian, for the diaconate and priesthood
Same date, for Richard Nowel, canon of Southwick, for minor and all holy orders
Memorandum that on the feast of the Epiphany (6 January) in the chapel of Farnham castle the bishop ordained as acolyte William de Nessyngwyk', dioc. York
29 January 1361, Southwark, letters for Fratres John Shapwyk for the diaconate and priesthood, for William Barset and Walter Abbey, monks of Hyde, for all holy orders
1 February 1361, Southwark for Fr Robert Drew, canon of Mottisfont, for all holy orders
Same date, for Edward Donebrugg', dioc. Winchester for all minor and holy orders
508 9 February 1361, Southwark, for William Pridie, dioc. Winchester for the subdiaconate
11 February 1361, Southwark, for William Gollye, dioc. Winchester, for the subdiaconate
Same date, for Henry de Baa and Robert de Thorp', dioc. Winchester, for the first tonsure
15 February 1361, Southwark, for M. John Turk', rector of Michelmersh, for the diaconate
Same date, for John Mot of Kingston for the diaconate
17 February 1361, Southwark, for Walter Tygehale for the priesthood and Stephen atte Brugge of Godalming for minor orders

Same date, for John de Burgh', rector of Abbots Clandon for the diaconate

Same date, for Fr John atte Bourne, canon of Tandridge, for the priesthood

18 February 1361, of Southwark, for Fratres Nicholas Westcote and John Mussynden' for the priesthood and for William Sutton' for minor orders—canons of Merton

3 March 1361, Southwark, for Richard Bauchon of Guildford for the subdiaconate and diaconate

8 March 1361, Southwark, for Hugh Snokeshulle, dioc. Winchester, for the first tonsure

12 March 1361, Southwark, for M. John Turk', rector of Michelmersh, and John Bourgh', rector of Abbots Clandon, for the priesthood

27 March 1361, Southwark, for Edgar Gregory of Stockbridge, for the first tonsure

11 April 1361, Southwark, for William Gollye for the diaconate and William Prydie for the priesthood

7 April 1361, Southwark for Fratres John Hyde, Ralph Basynge, Walter Braye, Robert Walyngford for the priesthood, Walter Farnhulle and William Mareschal for the subdiaconate—monks of St Swithun

20 May 1361, Esher, for Thomas le Mone of Shorwell, Isle of Wight, for the first tonsure

21 May 1361, Esher, for John Bradefeld of Hurstbourne Regis and John atte Park' of Albury, dioc. Winchester, for all minor orders

25 August 1361, [Bishops] Waltham, for Richard Fraunkeleyn, dioc. Winchester, for minor and all holy orders

12 September 1361, Farnham, for Fratres John Chaworth, John Church', George Martyn for the priesthood—monks of Hyde

13 September 1361, Farnham, for John Frye, rector of St Saviour, Winchester, for subdiaconate and diaconate

509 10 September 1361, Farnham, for William Carneyk, rector of St Alphege, and Thomas Saundres, rector of St Rumwold, Winchester for minor and all holy orders

11 September 1361, Farnham, for Thomas Gollye of 'Colcure' for the priesthood and Richard Sparewe of 'Wyke Daundely' for minor and all holy orders

16 September 1361, Farnham, for John de Doune, dioc. Winchester, for first tonsure and minor orders

17 September 1361, Farnham, for William Penne of Petersfield for minor orders

11 September 1361, Farnham, for Fratres John Berard and John Cosham for all holy orders, canons of Christchurch Twynham

16 September 1361, Farnham, for Fratres William Fossard for the subdiaconate, John de Walyngford and William le Chaundeleer for the priesthood—canons of St Mary, Merton

26 November 1361, Southwark, for Adam de Hertyngdon', rector of Heckfield, for minor and major orders

28 November 1361, Southwark, for John Bondeby, rector of Farnborough, for minor and all major orders

11 December 1361, Southwark, for M. Henry de Weston' for the sub-diaconate and Simon le Kyng for minor orders and the subdiaconate

917. *Memorandum* that Sunday, 5 December 1361, in the manor chapel of Southwark during the Mass, the bishop ordained:

Acolytes
William Wykeham, dioc. Winchester
William David, holding the predial tithes of the bishop in the manor of Northanger
John Payn, rector of Radipole, dioc. Salisbury
John de Fairfold, dioc. of Wells (*sic*)
Roger Rayson of Welford, rector of Wotton, dioc. Lincoln
Henry de Hermesthorp, rector of Wappenbury, dioc. Coventry and Lichfield

918. ORDERS conferred by the bishop in the manor chapel, Southwark, Ember Saturday, 18 December 1361

Acolytes
M. John de Wormenhale, rector of Felpham, dioc. Chichester
Robert le Clerc of Coulsdon
John Kyng' of King's Somborne
John de Bouland', rector of Arthuret, dioc. Carlisle
Thomas Grante, rector of St Nicholas, Abingdon, dioc. Salisbury
Thomas Thelwall', rector of Polebrook, dioc. Lincoln
William B,,,,,,, of Chalton, dioc. Winchester
William? Smyth of Kingston, dioc. Winchester
Robert Muskham, rector of Colby, dioc. Norwich
William de Fulborne, rector of Houghton, dioc. Norwich
Robert de Wyggeleye, rector of Wotton, dioc. Worcester
510 Simon Hereward, dioc. Lincoln
Laurence de Alwarthorp, dioc. York
John de Dronfeld, rector of South Collingham, dioc. York
John de Barton, rector of Leckhampstead, dioc. Lincoln
Robert de Neubolt, rector of South Tidworth, dioc. Winchester
Adam de Hertyngdon', rector of Heckfield
William de Fladbury, rector of Baldock, dioc. Lincoln
Thomas de Lynton', rector of Sancreed, dioc. Exeter
Robert de Lincoln, rector of Alverstoke, dioc. Winchester
Henry Marmyon of Winchfield, dioc. Winchester
John de Folkyingham, rector of half the church of West Walton, dioc. Norwich
Henry de Barnet, rector of West Stow, dioc. Norwich
Thomas de Swafham, rector of Brockley, dioc. Norwich
Thomas de Buryfeld', dioc. Salisbury, *ad tit.* prior of St Peter, Winchester
Robert de Suardeby, rector of St Botolph outside Bishopsgate, London, with letters from M. Thomas Yonge, vicar for Simon, bishop elect of London
Fratres: William Ledrede, John de Hayle and William de Keynesham—canons of Southwark

919. *Subdeacons*
Peter de Hardebrugg', dioc. Winchester, *ad tit.* prior of Holy Trinity, London
Richard Bauchon, dioc. Winchester, *ad tit.* abbot of Waverley
John Florens, dioc. Winchester, *ad tit.* prior of Newark
John Askeby, rector of Salmonby, dioc. Lincoln
Richard son of Henry Giffard of Harlestone, dioc. Lincoln, *ad tit.* abbot of Selby
John Payn, rector of Radipole, dioc. Salisbury
Thomas de Midelton', rector of Farnham [Royal], dioc. Lincoln
Stephen Clerk' of Hambledon, dioc. Lincoln, *ad tit. domus* of Snelshall
John de Stameton, rector of Oxendon, dioc. Lincoln
John de Ledecombe, rector of Hantwisell, dioc. Durham
Henry son of Richard Russel of Liddington, dioc. Lincoln, *ad tit.* prior of Louth
John de Hermesthorp', rector of Wappenbury, dioc. Coventry and Lichfield
Roger Rayson of Welford, rector of Wotton, dioc. Lincoln
Gilbert Getrich', dioc. Winchester, *ad tit.* prior of the hospital of St Mary outside Bishopsgate, London
Fratres: Robert de Braye, Henry de Baggeshut—monks of Medmenham, dioc. Lincoln
William Fossard, canon of St Mary, Merton
Thomas de Burton', canon of Bisham
Richard de Hanynton', John de Canterbur'—monks of Westminster

920. *Deacons*
M. John Corf, rector of Collingbourne, dioc. Salisbury
William de Nessyngwyk', rector of Brettenham, dioc. Norwich
Peter de Stapleton', rector of Leven, dioc. York
William Spicer, dioc. Hereford, *ad tit.* abbot of Selby
Nicholas Teenwayle of Aylesbury, dioc. Lincoln, *ad tit. domus* of Snelshall
Thomas Hervy of Towcester, dioc. Lincoln, *ad tit.* prioress of Minster in Sheppey
John de Molyngton of Hanwell, dioc. Lincoln, *ad tit. domus* of [Canons] Ashby
John Motte of Kingston, *ad tit.* prior of St Mary, Merton
Hugh de Denton', minor canon of St Paul's, with letters from M. Thomas Young, vicar-general for Simon, elect of London

511 John Bromersgh, dioc. Winchester, *ad tit.* abbot of Chertsey
Fratres: William Cherleton' and John Preston'—canons of Bisham dioc. Salisbury
William Donmere, monk of Waverley

921. *Priests*
John de Stoke of Great Marlow, dioc. Lincoln, *ad tit. domus* of Medmenham
Nicholas Waleys, rector of St Mary Abchurch, London, with letters from M. Walter de Baketon, canon of Chichester, vicar-general of Simon, elect of London

William de Cleydon', rector of Mottram, dioc. Coventry and Lichfield

James Brygge, rector of 'Busteshale', dioc. Salisbury

Walter de Almaly, rector of Thruxton in the deanery of Hereford, with letters from Adam Esgar, canon of Hereford, vicar-general of Lewis, bishop of Hereford

Frater John de Walyngford, canon of Merton

922. *Dimissorial Letters and ordination of acolytes*

27 January 1362, Southwark, letters for William Aubrey, rector of Beddington, for all minor and major orders

28 January 1362, Southwark, for Robert atte Brugge of Wickham for all minor orders

27 January 1362, Southward, for Adam Barnabe of Southampton for first tonsure, minor orders and the subdiaconate and diaconate

2 February, feast of the Purification, 1362, in his manor chapel of Southwark, the bishop ordained as acolytes Henry [de Derneford,] rector of Avington, dioc. Winchester, and William de Somerford, rector of Speen, holding dimissorial letters from the bishop of Salisbury for minor orders and the subdiaconate

14 February 1362, Southwark, for Fr William Ledrede, John Haylee and William Keynesham for all holy orders—canons of St Mary, Southwark

20 February 1362, Southwick, for M. Henry de Weston' for the diaconate and priesthood

23 February 1362, [Bishops] Waltham, for Henry Clerc of Collingbourne, rector of St Mary in Tanner Street, Winchester, for the priesthood

26 February 1362, Wolvesey, for John Kyng' of Kings Somborne and Richard Pulter of Winchester for the subdiaconate and diaconate

Same date, for Henry de Derneford, rector of Avington, for all holy orders; for William Carnek, rector of Kingsworthy, for the diaconate and priesthood; for William Crok', rector of St Peter in Colbrook Street, Winchester, for the priesthood

Same date, 26 February, Hursley, for Fr John Haselwode, Thomas Lemynton' and Thomas Seles for minor orders and the subdiaconate; for Fr Walter Farnhull' and William Marschal for the diaconate— monks of Winchester cathedral

27 February 1362, Highclere, for William de Redessede, rector of St Michael, Niton, Isle of Wight, for minor and all holy orders

512   10 March 1362, Southwark, for John Florens of Godalming and Gilbert Getrich' for the diaconate and M. Hugh Craft, rector of South Waltham, for minor orders and the subdiaconate

11 March 1362, Southwark, for John Mot of Kingston for the priesthood, and William Mogg' of Chalton for the subdiaconate

14 March 1362, Southwark, for Thomas de Alston' rector of Shalfleet, Isle of Wight, for minor and all holy orders

18 March 1362, Southwark, for Simon Kyng of Havant, for the diaconate and priesthood

923. ORDERS conferred by the bishop in the manor chapel of Southwark, Ember Saturday in the first week of Lent, 12 March 1362

Acolytes
John Bondeby, rector of Farnborough
William Aubrey, rector of Beddington
Thomas de Welford, rector of 'Sahamtony', dioc. Lincoln
Richard Kingeston', rector of Sudbury, dioc. Lincoln
Elias Aleyn of Guilden, dioc. Ely, with letters from Simon, elect of Ely
Walter Donel, rector of Balcombe, dioc. Chichester
Thomas Wytton, rector of West Hoathly, dioc. Chichester
M. William de Arderne, rector of Chesterton, dioc. Lincoln
William de la Forde, rector of Ebrington, dioc. Worcester, with letters
  from M. William de Thynghall', dean of the Arches, vicar-general of
  John elect of Worcester
John Gyffard, rector of Slindon, deanery of Pagham in the jurisdiction
  of the archbishop of Canterbury
John Lynham, rector of Bourton, dioc. Worcester, with letters from
  M. William Thynghull' (etc. as above)

924. *Subdeacons*
Dominus William de Wykeham, dioc. Winchester, canon of Salisbury
Robert de Lincoln, rector of Alverstoke, dioc. Winchester
William David, rector of Codford St Peter, dioc. Salisbury
Henry de Codyngton, rector of Bottesford, dioc. Lincoln
Robert de Muskham, rector of Colby, dioc. Norwich
Thomas de Thelwal, rector of Polebrook, dioc. Lincoln
John de Folkyngham, rector of half the church of West Walton, dioc.
  Norwich
William de Oxendale, rector of Kelshall, dioc. Lincoln
John de Boulard, rector of Arthuret, dioc. Carlisle
Henry de Barnet, rector of West Stow, dioc. Norwich
Simon Hereward, rector of St Andrew, Barnwell, dioc. Lincoln
Thomas de Swafham, rector of Brockley, dioc. Norwich
John de Barton, rector of Leckhampstead, dioc. Lincoln
William Gateman of Melbourne, dioc. Ely, with letters from Simon,
  elect of Ely, *ad tit.* prioress of Chicksands, order of Sempringham
Giles of Caldecote, rector of Farley near Romsey, dioc. Winchester
William Stephen, rector of St Anthony, London, with letters from Walter
  de Baketon, canon of Chichester, vicar-general of Simon, elect of
  London
William de Fulborne, rector of Houghton, dioc. Lincoln
Robert de Wyggeleye, rector of Wotton, dioc. Worcester, with letters
  from the prior of Worcester cathedral, by authority of the court of
  Canterbury, administrator in spirituals, *sede vacante*
John de Dronfeld, rector of South Collingham, dioc. York
Adam de Hertyngdon, rector of Heckfield, dioc. Winchester
513 Robert de Strode, rector of Withersfield, dioc. Norwich
Henry Marmyon dioc. Winchester, *ad tit.* prioress of Nuneaton

925. *Deacons*
Thomas de Middelton, rector of Farnham, dioc. Lincoln
John de Askeby, rector of Salmanby, dioc. Lincoln

John de Staunton, rector of Oxendon, dioc. Lincoln
Thomas de Folkerthorp, rector of Cosby, dioc. Lincoln
Alan Smyth of Wimpole, dioc. Ely, with letters from Simon, elect of
Ely, *ad tit. domus* of Royston
Roger Rayson of Welford, rector of Wotton, dioc. Lincoln
Fratres: William de Gildesburgh, William Crendon—brothers of
Ashridge, dioc. Lincoln
Richard de Honyton, monk of Westminster

Priests
William de Nessyngwyk, rector of Brettenham, dioc. Norwich
John Coupere of Great Alne, dioc. Coventry and Lichfield, *ad tit.* abbot
of Holy Cross, Waltham

926. *Dimissorial Letters*
29 March 1362, Southwark, letters for M. Henry de Weston, perpetual
vicar of Hayling, for the priesthood
19 March 1362, for Robert atte Brugge of Wickham, for all holy orders
30 March 1362, Southwark, for John Cordray, dioc. Winchester for all
minor orders
31 March 1362, for Robert Hardebrigg', dioc. Winchester, for the
diaconate
Same date, for William Mogg of Chalton, dioc. Winchester, for the
diaconate
1 April 1362, for John Florens of Godalming for the priesthood
4 March 1362, for Fr John de Ledrede, canon of St Mary, Southwark,
for the priesthood
12 April 1362, for William Mogg for the priesthood

927. ORDERS conferred by the bishop in the chapel of Farnham castle,
Holy Saturday, 16 April 1362

Acolytes
William Felix of Warblington
William Basynge
Fr John Pavy, Dominican of the Winchester convent

Deacons
Robert de Lincoln, rector of Alverstoke
Henry Derneford, rector of Avington, dioc. Winchester
514   William Crouk, rector of St Peter, Colbrook Street, Winchester
John de Barton, rector of Leckhampstead, dioc. Lincoln
William de Somerford, rector of Speen, dioc. Salisbury
William Aubrey, rector of Beddington, dioc. Winchester
Henry Marmyon, dioc. Winchester, *ad tit.* prior of St Mary, Southwark
John Kyng of Kings Somborne, dioc. Winchester, *ad tit.* prior St Peter
Kalendar, Winchester

928. *Priests*
John Payn, rector of Radipole, dioc. Salisbury
William Palewell', rector of Black Torrington, dioc. Exeter

Robert de Muskham, rector of Colby, dioc. Norwich
John de Folkyngham, rector of half the church of West Walton, dioc. Norwich
Richard Bauchon of Guildford, *ad tit.* abbot of Waverley
M. Henry de Weston, vicar of Hayling
William Carnek, rector of Kingsworthy
Robert de Neubolt, rector of South Tidworth

929. *Dimissorial Letters*
30 May 1362, Southwark, letters for William de Froille, for all holy orders
4 May 1362, Southwark, for John de Shirfeld, dioc. Winchester for the diaconate and priesthood
16 May 1362, Southwark, for John Umfray, dioc. Winchester, for the first tonsure and minor orders
8 June 1362, Southwark, for John Waryn, rector of North Waltham, for minor orders and all holy orders
11 June 1362, Southwark, letters for Nicholas Monk, rector of Peniton, for the subdiaconate; for Richard de Branketree, rector of Nether Wallop. for minor and all holy orders; for Melchior Wodelok', rector of Worting, for all minor orders; for Peter Hardebrugg', *ad tit. domus* of Holy Trinity, London, for the priesthood; for Richard Rouz, rector of the chapel of St Mary, Brook, Isle of Wight, for all minor orders; for John Bromersh' of Worplesdon, on oath to serve the next year at the bishop's pleasure, for the priesthood; for Gilbert Getrich', on a similar oath, *ad tit.* prior of hospital of St Mary, Bishopsgate, London, for the priesthood

930. ORDERS conferred by the bishop in the manor chapel of Southwark, Ember Saturday in Whit-week, 12 June 1362

Priests
William Wykeham, dean of the royal free chapel of St Martin-le-Grand
Robert de Lincoln, rector of Alberstoke, dioc. Winchester
William David, rector of Codford St Peter, dioc. Salisbury
Henry Derneford', rector of Avington, dioc. Winchester
Henry Marmyon, *ad tit.* prior of St Mary, Southwark

931. *Dimissorial Letters etc*
26 June 1362, Southwark, letters for Roger Oliver, dioc. Winchester, for minor orders, the subdiaconate and diaconate
9 July 1362, Southwark, for Roger de Tangeley for minor orders, the subdiaconate and the diaconate
515 18 August, Witney, for Walter de Stok', scholar of dioc. Winchester, for first tonsure and minor orders
29 August 1362, Edington, for Roger Oliver of ?Bor....street?, dioc. Winchester, for minor orders and the subdiaconate
11 September 1362, Highclere, for Fr John Drake, canon of St Denys, Southampton, for all holy orders
Same date, for John Laurence, rector of Highclere, acolyte, for all holy orders

Same date, the bishop conferred the fist tonsure on Adam Voughlere, Thomas Swen, Godfrey Swan, Roger Lynde and John Lynde, dioc. Winchester

20 September 1362, Farnham, for Peter Rose, rector of St Margaret, Winchester, for the diaconate

23 September 1362, Esher, for John Kyng of Somborne, for the priesthood; he took the oath before M. J' Corf and J' Beautre

932. ORDERS conferred by the bishop in the manor chapel of Esher, Ember Saturday, 24 September 1362

Acolytes
Fr Thomas Weston' and Richard Upton, canons of Merton

Subdeacon
John Laurence, rector of Highclere, dioc. Winchester

Deacon
John Waryn, rector of North Waltham, dioc. Winchester

Priests
John Barton, rector of Leckhampstead, dioc. Lincoln
Fratres: William Chaundeler, canon of Merton
William Cherleton and John Preston', canons of Bisham
William Aylmer, *ad tit.* of the priestly office in the chapel of St Elizabeth, collated by the bishop

933. *Dimissorial Letters etc.*
4 November 1362, letters for William Rode, rector of Shalfleet, for the diaconate; for Arnald Brocaz, rector of Whippingham, for minor and all holy orders; and John Bathyn of Longstock, dioc. Winchester for the subdiaconate and diaconate

10 December 1362, Southwark, for Walter Sellam, dioc. Winchester, for all minor orders and the subdiaconate

31 December 1362, Southwark, for Fr John Wymborne, Robert Bokeland', Thomas Newport and John Stryde, novice monks of Beaulieu, for first tonsure and all holy orders

516   14 December 1362, Esher, for William Aubrey, rector of Beddington, for the priesthood

15 December 1362, Esher, for Fr Thomas Weston' and Richard Upton for the subdiaconate; William Fossard for the diaconate, canons of St Mary, Merton

Same date, for Fr John Certeseye, canon of Newark, for the diaconate

1 January 1363, in the chapel of Farnham castle, the bishop ordained as acolytes Fratres John Hasilwode, Thomas Lymyngton', Robert Rodborne, William Bokelond, monks of Winchester cathedral, and John Crabbe, rector of Nursling

3 January 1363, Farnham, the bishop conferred the first tonsure on Richard Godchild and John le Whele

31 January 1363, Southwark, letters for John Byset, dioc. Winchester, for first tonsure

Same date, for Robert de Stokebrugg', dioc. Winchester, for minor orders

23 February 1363, Esher, for Peter Rose, rector of St Margaret in the High Street, Winchester, for the priesthood

24 February 1363, Esher, for Richard Stonhurst of Lingfield for minor orders

Same date, for William Gervays, rector of Bentworth, for all minor orders

11 March 1363, Esher, for Robert Fremantel, dioc. Winchester, for first tonsure, minor orders and subdiaconate

16 March 1363, Esher, for John Crabbe, rector of Nursling, for the diaconate; and for William Gervays, rector of Bentworth, for the subdiaconate

Same date, for Fratres Thomas de Weston' and Richard de Upton', canons of St Mary, Merton, for the subdiaconate

18 March 1363, Esher, for Thomas Prophete of Chaldon, for all minor orders

24 March 1363, Esher, for Walter Selam of Crawley, dioc. Winchester, for the diaconate

Memorandum that on Holy Saturday, 1 April 1363, in the manor chapel of Esher, the bishop ordained as acolytes John Crabbe, rector of Nursling, to the priesthood and Fratres John Gravenege, Walter Hostiler, Thomas Crokford and Nicholas Albon, monks of Chertsey

517 17 April 1363, Southwark, letters for Richard Stanhurst for the subdiaconate and diaconate

934. ORDERS conferred by the bishop in the manor chapel of Highclere, Ember Saturday in Whit-week, 28 May 1363

Acolytes
John Wylekyn, dioc. Winchester
William le Whyte, of servile condition, by special grace of the bishop as of villein status (*nativo sanguine*)
Fratres: William Fyfide, Richard Wyncestre, Thomas Chynham, John Hampton', monks of Hyde

Subdeacons
Richard Polet' of Winchester, *ad tit.* prior of St Denys, Southampton
Robert de Stokebrugg', *ad tit. domus* of Wymondley
M. Robert Rympton', rector of Corfe, dioc. Salisbury
Fratres: John Haselwode, Thomas Lemynton', Thomas More, Robert Rudborne, William Boklond', monks of Winchester cathedral
Fr John Inmore, canon of Sandleford, dioc. Salisbury

Deacons
Richard Chate, dioc. Salisbury, *ad tit.* prior of Breamore
John Burghton', rector of Highclere
Frates: Walter Farnhulle, William Mareschal, monks of Winchester cathedral

Priests
Henry Bylk, dioc. Salisbury, *ad tit.* abbot of Bindon
Walter atte Hale, rector of 'Upledecombe', dioc. Salisbury

Richard Monk, rector of Peniton
Fratres: John Cristechirche, William Basset and Walter Abbeye, monks
   of Hyde

518   935. ORDERS conferred by the bishop in the manor chapel of Esher, 23
September 1363

Acolytes
John de Lewes, rector of Dunsfold, dioc. Winchester
John Bathyn of Longstock
Richard Bakers, dioc. Exeter
Fratres: John Enggelond, Thomas Colverton, monks of Chertsey
Ralph Trefulek', John Moryng, Peter de Frensted', Dominicans
John Poygnaunt, monk of Prittlewell, order of Cluny

Subdeacons
John Combar of Romsey, rector of St Alphege in Goldstreet, Winchester
Fratres: Nicholas Albon, Thomas Crokford, monks of Chertsey
Simon de Bristoll', monk of Bermondsey
Thomas Hariere, canon of Bisham, dioc. Salisbury
Walter Somerton, George Halewyk', James Plomer, Dominicans

Deacons
Robert de Stokebrugg', dioc. Winchester, *ad tit.* abbot of Rewley near
   Oxford
Fratres: William Welynton', monk of Prittlewell, order of Cluny
William Fossard, Thomas Weston, Richard Upton, canons of Merton

Priests
Walter Selham, dioc. Winchester, *ad tit.* hospital of St Mary outside
   Bishopsgate, London
Fratres: William Keynsham, canon of Southwark
John Ben, monk of Bermondsey
William Stok', Dominican

936. *Dimissorial Letters*
9 December 1363, Esher, letters for M. Hugh de Craft, rector of South
   Waltham, dioc. Winchester, for the diaconate
28 December 1363, Highclere, for Fratres John Langred', John Haywode,
   William Ely and John Boltesham for minor orders; for Thomas de
   Lemygton', John Haselwod', Thomas Moure and Robert Rodeborne,
   for the diaconate and priesthood—monks of Winchester cathedral;
   also for Walter Farnhull' and William Yascal for the priesthood
13 February 1364, Esher, for John Combar' of Romsey, rector of
   St Alphege in Goldstreet, Winchester for the diaconate
519   21 December 1363, Overton, for Robert Stokebrugg' for the priesthood
14 February 1364, Esher, for Fr Nicholas Albon and Thomas Crokford,
   for the diaconate—monks of Chertsey; also for John Lewes, rector of
   Dunsfold, for the subdiaconate
23 January 1364, Southwark, for John Wylkyn of Winchester, for all
   holy orders

2 February 1364, Southwark, for M. Hugh Craft, rector of South Waltham, for the priesthood

1 February 1364, Southwark, for John Balle, dioc. Winchester, for minor orders and the subdiaconate

6 February 1364, Southwark, for Thomas Heyfeld of Fernham in the parish of Hurstbourne Tarrant for first tonsure and all minor orders

Same date, for Richard Fyfhide of Wallop for first tonsure and all minor orders

Last day (29) February 1364, Farnham, for Fratres William de Meldeborne and Richard de Lond', canons of St Mary, Southwark for minor orders and the subdiaconate

937. ORDERS conferred by the bishop in his manor chapel of South Waltham, Saturday when *Sitientes* is sung, 9 March 1364

Acolytes
Richard Fifhere of Winchester
John Twyford
Thomas Suel of Leckford
Adam Barneby of Southampton
Fr John Langernd', monk of St Swithun, Winchester
John Clerc of Warnford
Fr Edward, canon of Selborne
Fr John Inge, canon of Titchfield

Deacons
William Gervays, rector of Bentworth
Henry de Portsesmuth' *ad tit.* abbot of Medmenham
Fratres: John Drake, canon of St Denys, Southampton, John Haselwode, Thomas de Lemynton', Robert Rudborne, Thomas More—monks of St Swithun, Winchester
John Cole holding the office of subdeacon in the chapel of St Elizabeth

Priests
John Combar, rector of St Alphege in Goldstreet, Winchester
Richard Polenter *ad tit.* prior of St Denys, Southampton
Fratres: Walter Farnhull', William Marschal—monks of St Swithun, Winchester
Hugh de Cicestr', canon of Titchfield
Robert Brompton', Carmelite Friar

520 Memorandum that 23 March 1364, Vigil of Easter, 23 March 1364, in the manor chapel, South Waltham, the bishop ordained as acolytes Fr Richard Clanefeld and William Netheravene, canons of Mottisfont

938. *Dimissorial Letters*
6 May 1364, Wolvesey, letters for John Coule of Stockbridge, holding the office of priest in the chapel of St Elizabeth near Winchester, for the priesthood

30 April 1364, Southwark, for Henry de Portesmuth' for the priesthood

15 May 1364, Wargrave, for William Gervays, rector of Bentworth, for the priesthood

11 May 1364, Wargrave, for Richard de Stonhurst, for the priesthood; on oath to serve J' Turk, rector of Michelmersh for the year following the ordination

9 May 1364, Southwark, for Fr John de Cherteseye, canon of Newark, for the priesthood

1 May 1364, Southwark, for Fr William de Meldeborne, Richard de London' and William de Laneford, canons of St Mary, Southwark, for minor orders and subdiaconate

939. *Memorandum* that on the feast of St John before the Latin Gate (6 May) 1364, in the chapel at Wolvesey, the bishop conferred the first tonsure on Thomas de Haywode, Walter Haywode, Thomas Dayeseye, William Yonge of Bentworth and William Kingesham, dioc. Winchester

Memorandum that 10 March 1364 in the chapel at South Waltham, the bishop conferred the first tonsure on John Bakere of Romsey, Thomas Bruyn, John Doget, John Peveshale, John Blaunchard, John Felde and William Inge, dioc. Winchester

18 August 1364, Bitterne, the bishop conferred the first tonsure on William Oulak, John Denys, John atte Herne and Thomas Ridale, dioc. Winchester

20 September 1364, Esher, letters for John de Lewes, rector of Dunsfold, for the diaconate and priesthood

940. ORDERS conferred by the bishop in the chapel of Farnham castle, Ember Saturday, feast of St Thomas (21 December) 1364

First Tonsure
John de Catceshulle, William Costret and William le Muleward

Acolytes
Robert Warde of Wing, dioc. Lincoln
Fratres: John Bright, John Godalymnge and Stephen Nich', Dominicans of Guildford convent
John Honte
Fr Richard de Mersshton', canon of Newark
521 Robert de Guldeford', William Hurst, John Compton and Thomas Poteham, monks of Waverley

Subdeacons
John Stoor of Amesbury, dioc. Salisbury, *ad tit.* prioress of Amesbury, for the subdiaconate only
Fr John Inge, canon of Titchfield, Premonstratensian
Fr Edward, canon of Selborne
Fr John de Horsham, canon of Newark

Deacons
Robert de Fremantel of Kingsclere, *ad tit.* prior of Southwark

Priests
Fr John de Stokbrugg', Dominican of Guildford convent
Fr John Brightwelle, Augustinian of the Winchester convent

941. *Dimissorial Letter and First Tonsure*
2 January 1365, Farnham, letters for Fr Robert Burey, canon of Christchurch Twynham, for all holy orders

Memorandum that 12 January 1365, in the chapel of his palace at Wolveseye the bishop conferred the first tonsure: Peter Brustowe, Thomas Saunterne, Walter Pedelevere, John Bolne, John Swanton', Robert de Craneborne, Robert Vode, John atte Yerde, John Wodere, John Forster, Robert Wandlesworth', Simon Wynelrode, John Plonke, John Kyng', Henry de Ticheborne, William Norman, William Ferrour, John Bakere, John Smyth of Holyborne, Walter Chiper, Thomas Hevewyke, John Lane, John Crane (illegitimate with dispensation for minor orders), John Purbyk', Richard Lang', Henry de Ticheborne, Richard Bagge, Roger Evere, Thomas de Haleborne, John Ferrour, Thomas Elys, William Lilie, William Drake, Henry Barber, Philip Barbour, John Wyneslode—all dioc. Winchester

Richard De Chudeham, dioc. Chichester, with letters from Peter de Halstede, vicar-general for William bishop of Chichester in distant parts

William Alkeston and William Nenna, dioc. Salisbury, with letters for tonsure and minor orders

942. *Dimissorial Letters and First Tonsure*
21 February 1365, letters for Fratres Thomas Disburgh' and John Wyltechere for all minor orders; for John Englelond', William Twynere for the subdiaconate—monks of Chertsey

Same date, for Fr William Barnet, Michael de Kymeton' and William de Croyden'—canons of St Mary, Merton, for all minor orders

522 23 February 1365, Farnham, for Fratres Richard Mersston' for the subdiaconate and for John Horsham for the diaconate—canons of Newark

21 February 1365, Farnham, for Fratres Richard Wynchestre, Thomas Chynnham and John Hampton—canons of Southwark (orders omitted)

Collation of the tonsure, Sunday 16 March 1365, at South Waltham by the bishop on William Holmeggr' of Odiham, John Totteford of Alresford, William Toward of Winchester, William Roue of Bullington

943. ORDERS conferred by the bishop in the manor chapel of South Waltham, Holy Saturday, 12 April 1365

Tonsure
Fr Richard de Caneford, canon of Mottisfont
John Wych of Kingsclere
John Reynald of Andover
Edward Tynkere of Andover

Acolytes
John Pesshon of Monxton
Fr Richard de Caneford, canon of Mottisfont
Richard atte Fenne of Thames Ditton
John Beauchamp, dioc. Winchester (by dispensation of defect of birth)
Nicholas Porter, dioc. Worcester
Richard de Chideham, dioc. Chichester, with letters from Peter de Halstede, rector of Selsey, vicar-general for William, bishop of Chichester, in remote parts

Fratres John de Stannford and Thomas Denemede, canons of St Denys
William Haverynge, Chynham, and John Hampton, Friars Minor

Subdeacons
Fratres Richard Wincestre, Thomas Chynham, John Hampton, monks of Hyde
Fr Robert de Clanefeld, William Netheravene, canons of Mottisfont
Fr John Forde, John de Wotton, Friars Minor, Winchester convent

Deacon
John Stoor, rector of St Mary de Walda, city of Winchester

944. *Dimissorial Letters etc*
23 May 1365, Farnham, letters for William Widenhale, for the subdiaconate

523 25 May 1365, Farnham, for Fratres Thomas Disburgh', John Wilteschyre for the subdiaconate; for John Engelond' and William Twynore for the diaconate—monks of Chertsey
Same date, for Fr John Horsham, canon of Newark, for the priesthood
Same date, for Robert Fremantel of Kingsclere, for the priesthood, after an oath never to celebrate or minister outside the diocese without the bishop's permission
25 May 1365, Farnham, the bishop conferred the first tonsure on William Knavenhurst, William Bourdon', John Tannere and William Haukyn of the parish of Shere
3 June 1365, Wargrave, letters for Richard atte Fenne, rector of St Peter outside Southgate, Winchester, for the subdiaconate
5 June 1365, Wargrave, for John Stoor, rector of the church of Walda, Winchester city, for the priesthood
Same date, for Fratres William de Crendon', Michael de Kymeton, William Barnet for the subdiaconate, and William Fossard for the priesthood—canons of Merton
16 July 1365, Witney, for John Tropmel of the parish of Carisbrooke for minor and all holy orders
6 September 1365, South Waltham, for William Wydenhale for the diaconate

945. ORDERS conferred by the bishop in his manor chapel at Sutton, Ember Saturday, 20 September 1365

Acolytes
Fratres: John Haywode, William Ely, John Boltesham, Thomas Stoke—monks of St Swithun, Winchester
William Hanlepe, John de Lachebrok', John Purye—Carmelite Friars
Thomas de Wync', Thomas de Fordyngbrugg'—Augustinians
John atte More, John Stanlake, Philip Cornhampton'—monks of Netley

524 *Subdeacons*
Richard atte Fenne, rector of St. Peter outside Southgate, Winchester
John de Fairford', rector of Dibden, dioc. Winchester
John Pynel, dioc. Salisbury, *ad tit.* abbot of Titchfield, for this order only

Fratres: John Stannford', Thomas Denemede—canons of St Denys, Southampton

Richard Hechfeld, William de Brakkelee—Carmelite Friars of the Winchester convent

Deacons
M. Giles, rector of Farley, with the bishop's dispensation for one year accoding to the constitution *Cum ex eo*

Fratres: John Langred'—monk of St Swithun, Winchester

Richard Wynchestre, John Hampton—monks of Hyde

M. Gilbert atte Stone, rector of Orcheston St Mary, or 'Goyville', dioc. Salisbury

Giles de Bromden', dioc. Winchester, *ad tit.* abbot of Titchfield

Priests
Fratres: Thomas Meere, Robert Rudborn—monks of St Swithun, Winchester

First Tonsure conferred the same day

John Hayhond of [Crux] Easton

John Seintdenys of Sutton, born in the parish of St Margaret, Southwark, for whom his father, Henry, took the oath

John Piers of Hullavington, dioc. Salisbury

946. *First Tonsure*
2 October 1365, by the bishop in the manor chapel, Esher: Richard Bamblot, Thomas Waufy, John Proutont, John Coupere, John Proutont junior, Thomas Hayward of Leatherhead

3 October 1365, Esher, John Hernays, dioc. Winchester

Sunday, 5 October 1365, Esher, John Grewes, Thomas Thep' dioc. Winchester

3 November 1365, Farnham, John Colvill', William de Walyngford', Thomas Wodelok'

947. *Dimissorial Letters*
24 November 1365, Farnham, letters for Fratres Nicholas Albon and Thomas de Clokkesford', for the priesthood; for John Engelond' and William Twynere for the diaconate and for Thomas Desberghe and John Wylteschire for the subdiaconate—monks of Chertsey

4 December 1365, Southwark, for Fratres Nicholas de Lincoln' for minor orders and the subdiaconate; for William Meldeburn for the diaconate; and for William de Laneford for the subdiaconate—canons of St Mary, Southwark

525 15 December 1365, Farnham, for William Wydenhale of Headley for the priesthood; to scrve for the following year at the bishop's pleasure, witnesses: N'Kaerwent, J'Blebury, J'Beautree

Same date, for Fratres John Haywode, William Ely, John Boltesham, Thomas Stoke for the subdiaconate; for John Haselwode and John Langrud for the priesthood—monks of St Swithun, Winchester

17 December 1365, Farnham, for Richard atte Fenne, rector of St Peter outside Southgate, for the diaconate

21 February 1566, Wolvesey, for Fatres John Wychenham for minor orders; for Thomas Solverdon' for the subdiaconate Thomas Disburgh

for the diaconate and William Twynere for the priesthood—monks of Chertsey

948. ORDERS conferred by the bishop in the chapel of St Elizabeth near Winchester, first Saturday in Lent, 28 February 1366

Acolytes
M. Thomas de Stafford', rector of Fordingbridge
Richard Blaunchard, dioc. Winchester
Simon Curteys of Froyle
Richard Ely of Winchester
John Iwode of Basing
John Boltere of Froyle
Robert Hobbes of Cranborne
Thomas Bruyn of Romsey
William Jourde of Winchester
John Lynche of Ovington
Roger Everard
William Hervy of Exton, dioc. Lincoln
Robert Anne of Abbots Ann
John Totteford of Alresford
John Baron of Petersfield
William Drake of Alresford
Fratres: John Katerington', John Bristowe—monks of St Swithun, Winchester
William Gyles, Dominican
John Wymborne, Robert Boclonde, Thomas Nieuport, John de Warynton—monks of Beaulieu
John Wodenham—canon of Christchurch Twynham
Robert Hyndon', Simon de Gypwico—Friars Minor

949. *Subdeacons*
Richard Petruwelle, dioc. Winchester, *ad tit.* prior of St Denys, Southampton
Thomas Suel of Leckford, *ad tit.* John, provost of St Elizabeth near Winchester
John Haywode, John Boltesham, Robert Chichestre—monks of St Swithun

Deacons
John Fayrford, rector of Dibden
Dominus William Othon, rector of Bighton
William Dagnuel of Bridgenorth, dioc. Lichfield, *ad tit.* prior of Holy Trinity, Bridgenorth
Fratres: Thomas Denemede, John de Stamford,—canons of the priory of St Denys, Southampton
Robert Burcy, canon of Twynham
Peter Frymstede, Dominican

Priests
John atte Lane, rector of the chapel of Freefolk, near Whitchurch
Richard atte Fenne, rector of St Peter outside Southgate, Winchester

526

950. ORDINATIONS OF FIRST TONSURE conferred by the bishop in the chapel of his castle of Wolvesey, 1 March 1366

Thomas Colriche
John Coupere of Stoke Charity
Thomas Sparfelde
John Symth'
John Burton' of Longstock
Thomas Burgat' of Winchester
John Favel of the Isle of Wight
Stephen Brackele of Stockbridge
Roger Morewelle of Fyfield
Nicholas Seton of Stockbridge
John Carpenter of Stockbridge
Philip le Leche of Winchester
Richard Malyn of Wallop
John Pinying
Edmund de Vale
Thomas Emury of Braishfield
Richard atte Hasshe of Hambledon
Robert Burrowe of Alton
Nicholas Gervays
Richard Gervays
Robert Manecorne of Monxton
Thomas Bakere of Brading
Thomas Tebold of Abbots Ann
William Gouderer of Andover
Robert Dunsterre of Andover
Thomas de Glamarigan
John Lucas of Preston Candover
William Evesham of Odiham
Henry Frenche of Winchester
Andrew de Dene
John Piper of the Soke, Winchester
John Horsy near Porchester
Remald Lecforde
John of Halle of Hinton
John Ladde of Wherwell
John Pacforde
Peter Grinet of Catherington
William Wymbuldon' of Andover
John Budul of Barton Stacey
John Werborne of Dibden
Nicholas Lacy of Faringdon
John Davere of Whitwell
Thomas Bonere of Romsey
John Fraunkeleyn of Candover
William Jourdan of Alverstoke
John Cuppelewyk of Faccombe

951. *Dimissorial Letter*
24 January 1366, Farnham, letters for Roger de Tangele, dioc. Winchester, for the priesthood, after an oath to serve at the bishop's pleasure for the first year

952. ORDERS conferred by the bishop in the chapel of St Elizabeth, Winchester, Saturday when *Sitientes* is sung, 21 March 1366

Subdeacons
John Bartelet of Monxton, dioc. Winchester, *ad tit.* prior of Ivychurch
Fratres: Robert Hyndon, Friar Minor
John de Wodenham, canon of Christchurch Twynham
John Wymborne, Robert Boclonde, Thomas Neupoart, John Warmyngton'—monks of Beaulieu

Deacons
Richard Petruwell' of the Stoke of Winchester, *ad tit.* prior of St Denys, Southampton
John Pynel, dioc. Salisbury, *ad tit.* prior of St Denys, Southampton
Thomas Mastyn, dioc. Lincoln, *ad tit.* abbess of Tarrant (St Mary *Benedicti loci super Tarrentam*)

Priests
M. William Othyn, rector of Bighton
John Fayrford, rector of Dibden
William Dagonel of Bridgenorth, dioc. Lichfield, *ad tit. domus* Holy Trinity, Bridgenorth
Frater Robert Burcy, canon of Christchurch Twynham

953. *First Tonsure* conferred by the bishop in the chapel of his castle at Wolvesey, 21 March 1366
William Talemach' of East Tisted
John Bagge of Worthy
William Smyth of Godshill
John Gerkyn son of Robert Gerkyn
William Brocworth of Romsey
Edward Caney of Hinton
Thomas Daccombe of the Isle of Wight
John Jacob of Soberton
John Byketon of Twyford, *nativus* of the bishop, admitted by special favour
John Sutton' son of R' Sutton', illegitimate, but dispensed by the bishop
John Tannere of Winchester
John Schottere of Romsey
John Dynnyng of Winchester, illegitimate (*de soluta genitus*), but dispensed

954. DIMISSORIAL LETTERS AND FIRST TONSURE
23 March 1366, Wolvesey, letters for Fratres Richard Medstede, Thomas Echton and Walter Northwode for minor orders and subdiaconate; for William Croydon', Michael Kympton' and William Barnet for the diaconate—canons of Merton

527

29 March 1366, Hursley, for Hugh de Worston, rector of Wolferton, for the subdiaconate

30 March 1366, Hursley, for Fr John de Wodenham, canon of Christchurch Twynham, for the diaconate and priesthood

18 May 1366, Esher, for Thomas Prophete of Chaldon for the subdiaconate

528   20 May 1366, Esher, for Walter Bylby of Walton in the parish of Beddington, for first tonsure

26 May 1366, Reigate, the bishop conferred the first tonsuere on Robert Frenssh' of Tandridge and John Smyth of Godstone

28 May 1366, Esher, letters for John Bertelot of Monxton for the diaconate, *ad tit.* monastery of Ivychurch

Same date, for Fratres Thomas de Weston' and Richard de Upton' for the priesthood—canons of Merton

25 May 1366, Reigate, for Fr. John Coumbe, canon of Reigate, for minor orders

30 June 1366, Wargrave, for John Passelewe, dioc. Winchester, for minor orders and subdiaconate

15 September 1366, South Waltham, for Fatres Richard de Wynton' and John de Hampton' for the priesthood—monks of Hyde

16 September 1366, South Waltham, for Fratres William de Hurselee and John Corald for minor orders and subdiaconate—canons of Southwick

6 October 1366, South Waltham, for John Del and Adam Del and Edward Del, Richard As and Henry As, relatives of D. William Wykham, dioc. Winchester, for first tonsure

26 September, South Waltham, for John de Twyford, for all holy orders

NOTES TO PART II

First folio not numbered and blank, now pp. 271, 272.

1. Margaret, countess of Kent, widow of Edmund of Woodstock, held land in Bedhampton, 1346 (*VCH Hants* iii, 143) and in Andover (*ibid.*, iv, 347).
2. According to *Reg.* i, 1186, a Robert de Burton had been canon of Bishops Auckland and exchanged for Kempshot; according to i, 1259, Robert de Burton, lately archdeacon, d.1361.
3. Purley in Sanderstead, see *Registrum Henrici Woodlock* ed. A. W. Goodman (2 vols., Canterbury and York Society, 1940-1) 847.
5. i.e. Baldwin de Mohann, d.1348 (i, 309).
6. Sir John Darcy, lord of Knaith (i, 244, 301), son of John Darcy, baron, d.1347 (*DNB*).
10. The bishop had prisons at Southwark and at Wolvesey. For gaol delivery, see R. B. Pugh *Imprisonment in medieval England* (Cambridge, 1968) 17, 48–57, 134.
12. There had been a break into the friary at Derby in 1344 by 44 men of the town, carrying off goods to the value of 60 li., see *Reliquary,* July, 1877: 'The Friar-Preachers or Blackfriars of Derby' by C. F. R. Palmer, o.p., from a Patent Roll of 18 Edw. III. This entry would seem to indicate a renewal of grievances, with now two priests mentioned. The names common to the two lists are: William Nayl of Derby and John son of John of Chaddesden.
17. John de Burstowe. Burstow, village 2m. from Horley.
18. At this period Southampton was busy with fortifications.
21. Roger had only acquired West Shoddesden in 1340 (*VCH Hants* iv, 366, 374).
22. The husband was still alive, d.1364 (*VCH Hants* iv, 369).
23. Benedict 'Cardicensis' (Sardis or Sardica), prior of the Austin Friars, Norwich. Suffragan of Norwich and Winchester, 1333–1346 (*Stubbs*).
24. 'Kenyngton', ? Catherington (Hants.).
30. John Burgh, atte Berwe or Barrowe (*VCH Hants* iv, 92–3).
31. John Rondolf of Little Pachevesham or Randalls, a manor in Leatherhead (*VCH Surrey* iii, 295–6).
32. Haliwell, Shoreditch, London. Augustinian canonesses, daughter of William, Lord Montagu (*Complete Peerage*, IX, 83).
36. For the appropriation of Leatherhead with other land, see *VCH Surrey* iii, 300; for the seige of Leeds castle in 1321, see *VCH Kent* ii, 162, and M. McKisack *Fourteenth Century* (Oxford, 1959) 64. The Avignon date is *anno quarto,* which must be a mistake as the Croydon date is given in Roman numerals as 1345. Further detail of the appropriation is to be found in 84.
39. Lionel of Antwerp, 1338–68, second son of Edward III, duke of Clarence, boy-regent 1346-7. Translation of St Edward, 13 Oct.
46. In 1331 Nicholas de Braishfield and his wife Emma founded a chantry in Romsey abbey, fully endowed (*VCH Hants* iv, 468).
47. Thomas de Lisle, o.p., bishop of Ely, 1345-6. Blanchwel, or Blanchinel, or Blanchivel.
50. For the case of William de Inge and the archdeaconry, cf. i, 84.

51. For Benedict, bishop of Cardicensis, see 23.
52. Barnwell, augustinian priory. The Dominicans came to Thetford in 1335, taking over the old church of St Mary the Great, which had been the cathedral until the transfer to Norwich.
53. Name only in margin.
55. cf. 21.
56. The abbot of Chertsey granted Brettgrave to Guy de Bryan (*VCH Surrey* iii, 249, 275).
60. Henry Romyn held the manor of Idsworth in Chalton, a tenement of Wellsworth (*VCH Hants* iii, 106–7). Wade, probably Wade Court in Havant; Budbridge, I.Wight. Henry controlled the payment of wages to soldiers defending the Island, see *Insula Vecta,* 93–4; *VCH Hants* v, 142.
63. *Boys* in margin; *Bosco* in the entry.
65. *Jubilate,* i.e. 3rd Sunday after Easter.
66. Bulmershe, now within Reading, must have been moated and fortified.
67. cf. supra 36–8.
70. The manor, now Husseys Farm, in Froyle (*VCH Hants* ii, 504).
71. In margin: At request of the abbot of Beaulieu.
77. Robert de Hungerford held for a time the manor of Liss (*VCH Hants* iv, 84n.).
78. i.e. East Knoyle, Wilts.; *noster* because the bishops of Winchester presented to the church and so could dispense from servile condition (*The registers of Roger Martival, bishop of Salisbury, 1315-1330* ed. K. Edwards *et.al.* (4 vols., Canterbury and York Society, 1959-72) i, 29, 309; *Reg.Pontissara* ii, 420, 796).
79. Sherborne St John, cf. supra 61.
80. For the two ponds at Fleet, see *VCH Hants* iv, 6–7.
82. For Thomas West, see 767.
83. Formula for licences for consecrating portable altars, addressed to any catholic bishop.
84. The full name of Peter is found at the end of this unusual document. Earlier documents for Reigate and the church of Leatherhead, see supra 36–8, 67. The word 'appropriation' is not mentioned here, but it took place before Edyndon became bishop. The date 1344 is given in 36, with the letter of Clement VI.
85. That this is Walter Douk, see i, 264.
86. Earl John de Warenne, 1286–1347, d.30 June, buried at Lewes (*DNB*).
87. The *ad limina apostolorum* pilgrimage. Elyas Pelegrini, dean of Le Vigan, diocese of Cahors, papal tax-collector (*Lunt* 752, 737; *Lunt Acc.* 85).
88. Dorking appropriated to the priory of Reigate in 1334; also Mickleham in 1345 (*VCH Surrey* ii, 106; iii, 149).
94. 'Stubys', ?stulpes, post or pillar: Stoops, near London Bridge (*Stow* 189)
95. Thomas Pridias of Devon. There are two references to him in Truro. The Prideaux family was clearly Cornish, but later settled in Devon, acquiring property and a baronetcy (Vivian *Visitations of the county of Devon* ii, 616). The executors here are obviously

Cornish. For XIIIc. references to the family, see *Beaulieu Cartulary,* ed. S. F. Hockey, (Southampton Record Series, xvii, 1974) 256 and note, etc.

96. Date missing, probably understand *ut supra.*

98. For Matthew Redeman, see i, 1061.

100. Probate granted 8 April 1347, executor Roger, his brother (ii, 63). Almost all early councils excommunicate those who impede the execution of wills.

102. No doubt connected with the Dauntsey family and so with Dauntsey's School in West Lavington. He may be the Richard who settled his estate on himself and his wife Joan, with the remainder to his son John (d.1391) (*VCH Wilts* x, 207).

106. Archbishop John de Stratford held provincial councils almost every year, usually at St Paul's.

109. For William Jolyf, apparitor for the archdeaconry of Winchester, see 16.

110. Marginal index: *Dispensatio R.B. ut deposito regis tractoris officio,* where *tractor* is for *tractator,* one who "draws up" documents, or negotiator. The procurator is the provoker of suits.

112. i.e. the Fair Maid of Kent, d. of Edmund Woodstock, earl of Kent; she married William de Monteacuto, 2nd earl of Salisbury; the marriage was dissolved in 1349; she married Edward the Black Prince in 1361. For the manor of Woking, see *VCH Surrey* iii, 364.

113. For Margaret, countess of Kent, see 1.

114. Pewsey in Wilts. Nicholas de Sancto Botolpho, vicar of Romsey church, i.e. one aisle of the abbey church, died before Feb. 1349 (*CClR 1346–49,* 295; *ib. 1349–54* 55).

121. i.e. manor of Bandon, al. Foresters (*VCH Surrey* iv, 174).

126. Thomas de Thornecumbe, merchant of Winchester (*VCH Hants* iii, 406).

127. Drayton in Farlington, forest of Bere, manor of Pury in Bentley; Merston and Pagham are manors in Arreton, I.Wight. For Laurence de Pageham, see *VCH Hants* iii, 150; v, 146.

129. Bedenham in Alverstoke.

131. Middleton, i.e. manor of Milton (*VCH Surrey* iii, 423).

132. For John Lovekyn, see i, 264.

135. Appropriation of Kingsclere to Bisham at its foundation in 1337; it had been sold by Edward III to William, earl of Salisbury in 1336 (*VCH Hants* iv, 265).

136. John de Colonia died early in 1349, cf. 404.

137. Temple Sotherington, or Southington Temple, a manor in Selborne, was a preceptory of the Templars (*VCH Hants* iii, 7).

139. Renewal of the licence in 130.

141. Date *sic.*

144. 'cornmangere', *O.E.D.* gives 'cornmonger'.

147. The Gifford family is to be connected with the manor of Itchel in Crondall (*VCH Hants* iv, 7). The bishop was to be granted the wardship of her daughter Elizabeth (*C Fine R* vii, 143).

149. It had been agreed in 1305/6 that the vicar should receive all lesser tithes. Edward III sold the church to the earl of Salisbury for

Bisham priory; the church had been appropriated by Adam, 1337 (*VCH Hants* iv, 265–6).

153. M. Gruffudd ap Rhys and other names are from Le Neve, *Welsh Dioceses*. Kenewricus, ?Cynwrig; Penrhos, near Pwllheli. The bishop was conservator of the dominicans.

155. Bedyngton, ?Bedhampton.

158. Merdon Castle, episcopal manor in Hursley, Hants.

164. Loseley, 1½m. from Guildford.

165. Robert Jarom, cf. 145.

166. Fully translated in F. A. Gasquet *The Black Death of 1348–9* (London, 1908) 124–6; translated in part in P. Ziegler *Black Death* (London, 1969) 144; cf. *VCH Hants* ii, 32–3.

172. Edmund de Kendal was a second husband of Margaret de Norton, who died in 1346. Joan married Hugh de Brayboeuf (*VCH Hants* iii, 9–10).

179. For the journey to Calais, see i, 1227. Also, T. F. Tout *Chapters in the Administrative History of Medieval England* (6 vols., Manchester, 1920–33) iii, 228–232.

180. Something has been inserted above the first line here; there is a Thomas de Querle in i, 727.

194. Bedenham, now a farm on a peninsula at the head of Portsmouth harbour, to the north of Gosport (*VCH Hants* iii, 204).

202. Functon or Merritown (*VCH Hants* iv, 573; v, 98).

209. The manor of Ravensbury was conveyed to Henry de Strete in 1347 (*VCH Surrey* iv, 232).

216. Stephen Cambarou, bishop of 'St Poncir Thom'. i.e. of St Pons de Thomière (*S.Pontii Thomeriarum*), a bishopric formed by division of Narbonne; made *camerarius* in 1347 (E.Baluze *Vitae Paparum Avenionensium* (4 vols., Paris, 1914–27) iv, 57). Holyas, i.e. Elias Pelegrini, dean of Le Vigor, dioc. Cahors (*Lunt* 737).

217. Stephen, archbishop of Arles, i.e. Etienne Aldebrand, 1348–1350. M. Reginald became dean of Exeter in 1352.

224. cf. i, 259.

226. The vicar held the small tithes. For a fresh ordination of the vicarage in 1353, see *VCH Hants* iii, 15.

230. This entry begins with the date: 5 Feb.

232. John de Oo or Ewe, treasurer of Hereford.

241. i.e. Gosterwood (*VCH Surrey* iii, 157).

243. i.e. Fordingbridge.

245. The maintenance of the chancel was the responsibility of the rector. For the earlier arrangement with the vicar after a dispute, see *Reg. Pont.* 166.

248. Richard, archbishop of Nazareth, consecrated at Avignon (*Stubbs*, 196).

249. For the difficult relations with the Austin Friars at this period, see *VCH Hants* ii, 192. They secured papal permission to rebuild after the bishop had refused.

251. In margin: *vacat*.

255. Stockwell in Lambeth (*VCH Surrey* iv, 56–7).

258. Refers to the parliament of 1352, cf. 263.

259. Mary de St Paul, countess of Pembroke, licensed to found a charterhouse in 1346; it remained among many unfulfilled good works (*VCH Surrey* iv, 296).
262. 'the place and date as aforesaid', i.e. Farnham, probably in error.
267. As still in the C. of E. this court administers ecclesiastical law within the diocese.
269. Probably connected with the manor of Totford in Northington, Hants.
275. Items 274 and 275 are under the one date. Probably Magnesia (*Magnassien'*) a titular bishopric. Stubbs and others write: Magnatiensis, but here the *ss* is quite clear. He is Thomas, cistercian monk of Merevale. These two items presumably refer to coadjutor bishops for the diocese.
276. This consecration is not mentioned by *Emden* in a long article. He was assistant bishop at a consecration in 1362 (*Stubbs* 78, 196).
281. i.e. South Wells in Romsey, now Skidmore Farm (*VCH Hants* iv, 459).
283. Walter le Helyon of Allington in S.Stoneham (*VCH Hants* iii, 485).
284. Probably *de Peverel*; Northgate, presumably Winchester.
287. John, earl of Kent, nephew of Edward II, 1330–27 Dec. 1352.
294. Caesarius, bishop of St Maria de Rosis, suffragan, said to be a Franciscan.
291. Walter Reynolds, archbishop 1313–1327.
298. For Matthew Redeman, see i, 1061.
300. William Heywode, cf. *VCH Hants* iv, 475; the family is linked to Heywoods Farm in Stratfieldsaye, *ib.* 60.
301. John Thoresby, 1347–1352. Ellerton or Elreton on Spaldingmoor. Acton, cf. *Dugdale* vi, 977, which gives Aghton.
302. For the portion of St Laurence, see i, 611. The year is as given. Licence to appropriate dated 7 April 1351 (*CPR 1350–54* 59).
303. Margaret Molins, 1349–64.
305. Philip de Wayte held land in Soberton and in Cheriton (*VCH Hants* iii, 264; *ib.* 312). Denmead in Hambledon, probably Denmead Molins.
307, 308. Also in *Chart. Winch.* nos. 369, 368; royal licence (*CPR 1354–58*, 112).
311. In 1355 Edward III sent the Black Prince to Gascony, from where he led a successful raid up the valley of the Garonne. In 1356 he returned to Bordeaux, advancing as far as the Loire, where he won the difficult victory of Poitiers. For the settlement of Calais, see *supra* 179 and 192.
314. This item begins in the middle of a word, with no marginal index, but it must refer to the great fight at Oxford on St Scholastica's day (10 Feb.) 1355, which lasted several days between gown and town. See e.g. W. A. Pantin *Oxford Life in Oxford Archives* (Oxford, 1972) 99–104.
315. Dated *anno supradicto*.
317. ?Gomshall, Surrey. The Vachery chapel in Cranleigh is the north transept of the church (*VCH Surrey* iii, 91).
319. John de Valois (Jean II), king of France, defeated and captured by the Black Prince at Maupertuis, near Poitiers, 19 September. The

truce was signed 23 March 1357 and Edward received the Prince and the French king at Westminster, 24 May.

322. John Adryan held the manor of Farncombe in Godalming (*VCH Surrey* iii, 33) and of Brockham (*ib.* iii, 169).

324. No dates are entered for 324–6. 326: *Dat' apud S'.*; 327: *anno predicto;* 328 resumes 1357. For 324, cf. i, 1200.

328. For the background of these procurations, see *Lunt* ch.xiii. Robert Ketteringham, rector of St Gregory London; Simon de Sudbury, chancellor of Salisbury, papal chaplain; Thomas de Ryngstede, dominican, papal penitentiary and bishop-elect of Bangor; John Joufroy, bishop of Elne (Pyrénées Orient.) 1354–57; Androin de la Roche, abbot of Cluny. The archbishop set the rate at a farthing in the pound on the assessed value of the benefice (which is not stated here); for the collectors, $\frac{1}{4}$d. in 40s. and $\frac{1}{4}$d. in 60s. The archbishop's mandate was dated 18 May 1355 and the bishops were due to pay before 15 August. It will be seen that the Winchester receipt is quite late (cf. 335–338). It was the cardinal-abbot of Cluny who received the oaths of the kings of France and England at the peace of Bretigny (1360).

329. Peter atte Wode held the manor of Beauchamps in Chipstead (*VCH Surrey* iii, 192; also Wood Place in Coulsdon (*ib.* iv, 201).

333. In Cranleigh, part of the manor of Shiere Vachery, cf. 317.

336. Nicholas Capocci, bishop of Urgel, cardinal-priest of S.Vitale.

339. cf. i, 1257. John de Hampton, knight of the shire of Southampton, 1336–44, died before October 1357; Thomas held the same office (*VCH Hants* iii, 448).

343. For the family, see i, 259. Sterborough Castle, 4m. NE. of East Grinstead, Surrey.

346. Date omitted.

357. In French. Date *iour des almes.*

359. i.e. N. and S. Talworth in Long Ditton (*VCH Surrey* iii, 521).

360. Robert de Ledrede, the king's sergeant-at-arms; his chapel is now an ale-house (*VCH Surrey* iii, 275).

362. The titles of the personnel of the nunciature are omitted here. For details, see 328.

368. Kulmynton here; *Le Neve:* Kilvington, dean, 1354–61.

373. Yateley, served from Crondall.

383. cf. *CCIR 1349–54*, 554. Robert de Ledrede died intestate; Thomas de Rothall ordered to administer his goods.

386. A family called Stangrove held land in Bletchingley from the XIIIc. in Stangrave; also held the manor of Crowhurst (*VCH Surrey* iv, 275).
For Robert de Stangrave, see i, 487.

392. John de Noion (cf. Noyon, France) in the papal taxation service. He held a benefice in the diocese, cf. i, 1081.

393. i.e. Henry Woodlock.

397. *marescalia domini regis.*

401. cf. 315.

407. Roger Hussee, lord of Barton Stacey, had fought in Scotland and in France (*VCH Hants* iv, 418).

408. Reginald de Cobham held the manor of Gatwick (*VCH Surrey* iii, 184).
412. For the question of the subsidy, see *Lunt*, c.III, v, 95–103.
414. The clergy proposed an aid of 100,000 florins as a voluntary subsidy. As there had been no papal income tax for 34 years, there was opposition; the funds had instead been directed to the king's military expeditions. See 422.
419. cf. 333.
420. Arnald de Auxio, bishop of Poitiers.
422. This concerns papal taxation, see *Lunt* 95–103.
423. i.e. Robert de Keteringham.
427. cf. 425
433. Papal provisions for benefices, 433–8.
436. 'and Wells' omitted.
438. Adam had earlier been absolved from a suspension, 389.
439. Thomas 'Lambergensis', suffragan bishop of London, 1362 (*Stubbs* 197).
443. *VCH Hants* ii, 506, gives the date of the death of John Bardolf as 1371.
444. i.e. Edward.
454. Androin de la Roche, abbot of Cluny, see 328.
 Sir William de Notton, excommunicated in 1358 for passing judgement on the bishop of Ely for knowingly harbouring a murderer. Cited to appear at the papal court, he failed to appear and so was excommunicated. The bishop of Ely died at Avignon in 1361; Innocent VI died 12 Sept. 1362; Urban V elected 28 Sept. 1362; Sir William de Notton died 1363 (for the whole story, see *DNB*. under *Thomas Lisle*).
455. cf. *CClR 1360–64,* 479.
456. cf. 257.
457. cf. 258; mandate reissued.
458. Mandate reissued. Ralph, bishop of London, must be an error, cf. 459.
459. Mandate reissued.
461. The name of the patron, Jarponvile, and for the consequences of non-residence, see i, 1635–9; for Robert de Sulkeshull, see i, 1624.
462. The duke's mother was buried there. The priory suffered severely from the Black Death (*VCH Hants* ii, 174).
469. Stoneham Abbatis.
475. Arnald of Auxio, bishop of Poitiers and Albano, not archbishop (Baluze, *Vitae Paparum Avenionensium* iv, 426).
476. *Dat' et cet.*
477. By concession of the bishop: the latin seems to be *decima nosipsos concedente.*
483. *?hut tigurrium.*
490. Edmund Avenel, knight of Crux Easton (Crokestone), (*VCH Hants* iv, 312).
491. cf. 276.
492. Elizabeth, widow of John Plantagenet, 3rd. earl of Kent (*VCH Hants* iv, 347).

493. William de Melbury held the manor of Southavon in Sopley (*VCH Hants* v, 130) and the manor of Ibsley.
494. i.e. Roche Court, now N. Fareham, 1 mile N. of Fareham. Geoffrey Roche, lord of Steventon (*VCH Hants* iv, 171) and lord of Ellisfield.
498. This benefactor often mentioned, see Index. stockfish, i.e. dried cod.
500. Philippa Mortimer (de Mortuo Mari) countess of March, daughter of Lionel, second son of the king.
502. Alien priories rather than parish churches.
505. Two folios have been cut out following fo.53*, but there is no evidence that they were ever used or numbered.
506. cf. *CPR* iii, 26.
508. Three brother bishops.
512. These 12 dispensations are sometimes numbered; some grants are by another grantor.
513. Probably Abbotts Ann.
514. John Gaucelinus (Baluze *Vitae Paparum Avenionensium* iii, 322).
515. Edyndon was master of St Cross, 1335–45.
518. See *Lunt,* 640–643. Stephen was to become pope Innocent VI. Anibaldus de Ceccano.
522. Simon Islip, cons. 20 Dec. 1349.
523. John de St Paul, archbp, 1350–66.
524. 'to further orders', earlier he is 'priest'.
525. John Sheppey, 1353–1360.
526. Archbp., 1352–1373.
527. Elevated to York, 1352. Pope Clement VI died 6 Dec. 1352.
529. Probably in error for Worminghall, Berks.
532. Michael Northburgh, 1355–61; Michael Malconhagh, 1355–58. The spelling of the *Reg.* is more probable than *Stubbs.* After *Rosis,* there is a gap, ending with *episcopis.* Withern in Galloway.
533. In 1529 Henry VIII took from Wolsey the lodging of the archbishops of York at York House, near Westminster and changed its name to White Hall (*Stow* 365, 401).
535. Thomas Percy, 1356–69: fifth son of the second baron Percy of Alnwick. Provided to Norwich, though only aged 22 years, ordained deacon, 4 April 1355, at Esher (see 858).
536. *in mon' Andren' Morinen' dioc;* i.e. Thérouanne (Pas de Calais) was the *civitas* of the Morini. Guy, bishop of Porto (Italy).
544. Adam Houghton, bp., 1362–1389. *Ricardo* written in, in pencil.
545. Simon Langham, translated to Canterbury, 1366. John Barnet, translated to Bath, 1363 (*Stubbs* 78).
548. St George in Velabro.
549. William Bragose, cardinal-priest of St Laurence.
550. John de Bukingham, bp., 1363–1398.
552. La Hoke, i.e. Hook in Titchfield, near Warsash. They built the chapel, installed bells and held services. When ordered to desist, they protested in Titchfield church; when summoned to appear at the cathedral, they refused and were put under interdict (*Wykeham's Reg* ii, 281, 283, 300).
553. cf. 249. The site had been obtained in 1341 and the papal licence to transfer in 1343, with a second licence to proceed without the

bishop's permission (*C.Pap.L* iii, 85, 191). Finally the site was forfeited and granted to the city (*CClR* 15 May 1352), (*VCH Hants* ii, 192; A.Gwynn *The English Austin Friars* (London, 1940) 77–8). Oliver de Bohun is mentioned *VCH Hants* iii, 65, 148.

555. There is a gap for the remainder of the page.
556. A note here says that the formula for commissions to stewards is to be found on the sixth page following; the admission of stewards begins with 572.
558. St Giles fair, 1 Sept.
559. John Trilleck, bp. of Hereford, 1344–61.
560. William de Overton seems to have held much episcopal land (*VCH Hants* iii, 279, 334).
566. Rigaud of Assier, 1320–23. This document is not in his *Reg.*
568. In French.
571. A big smudge over the year, but Farnham and January suggest 1349. Henry Woodlock, 1305–1316.
572. Items 572–7 are in French.
583. *hospicius,* perhaps 'almoner'.
587. Items 587–9 are in French.
594. The name Brocaz appears several times in the *Gascon Registers, 1308–19,* ed. G. P. Cuttino (1976). *contrarotulator,* a comptroller, the keeper of a counter-roll.
599. Michael de Gastina of dioc. of Evreux, see *Insula Vecta,* 28, 99.
609. 'Rector' here, of course, is the receiver of the rectorial tithes, not the priest-in-charge.
    Raymond de Fargis, cardinal-deacon of S. Maria Nova. Annibaldus Gaetani de Ceccano, cardinal-bishop of Tusculum, treasurer of York (this is an earlier date than in *Le Neve*). Most of the pensions can be found in the *Taxatio.*
610. It is better to read 611 before 610.
612. i.e. 610.
614. For R'Sadington, chief baron of the exchequer, see i, 49.
615. *'which is entered in his registry'* is underlined.
618. No date.
619. Three items of almost identical content. In French.
621. Philip IV. 1346 is the year of Crécy. No year is given in the date.
625. *'modicum',* ?humble. Interesting reference to a school at Maidstone.
627. cf. 593.
631. cf. 598.
635. Probably Weston Corbet: *Farlegh',* Farleigh Wallop or Farley Chamberlayne.
639. Note: prior, also rector; Highclere was appropriated to Bisham by Adam de Orleton. The family fortune of the Pole family was made in the wool trade; William was the leading English financier to Edward III.
640. For Thomas West, see i, 767; ii, 82.
643. *Hunt',* ? Huntingdonshire.
645. Prior Thomas de Wiltshire, cf. 655, 657, 660; *CClR 1346–49,* 364, under date of 12 July 1347; *CPR 1345–8,* 287–9, 331, 427. For the story of Bisham, see *Introduction.* The personal names are Gascon; the place-names are all in the region of Bordeaux. The *CClR* adds

the name of Fr. Arnald de Piolio, of the Augustinian convent, Bordeaux. Reginald de Pontibus had a brother, Arnald, Friar Minor at Bordeaux, to whom with Fr. Arnald Salmerii, guardian of Rions, administration of the will was granted (*CClR*).

650. Marginal note says this was paid.

652. According to A.B. Emden *A Survey of Dominicans in England,* (Dissertationes Historicae of the Dominican Historical Institute, xiii, Rome, 1967) 395, Arnald de Lym belonged to the Winchester convent and was ordained deacon 18 Dec. 1312. He left the Guildford convent and later desired to be reconciled (*C.Pap.L.* ii, 530) cf. 47, dated Nov. 1346. He received a general pardon from the king, 28 Jan. 1347 (P.R.O., Rot. Cart. et Pat. apud Cales, 21 Edw.III, m.14). Petition to Parliament (*Rolls of Parl.*, ii, 186b), 3 March 1347, from the prior of the London convent. Adam, bp., had decided that Arnald was not a monk but a dominican. The royal brief resulted from Arnald's account of his ill-treatment. Granted a general pardon from any transgressions, 17 Nov., 1347 (*CPR 1345-8*, 524). Later the monks of Hyde were ordered to produce the apostolic letters permitting Arnald to return to the Order of Preachers.

658. *Reg.* gives the year as 1366.

662. See, for example Ziegler *Black Death,* 238, 247-8; this was followed by the Statute of Labourers in 1357.

669. cf. 664 and its date.

673. Holy Trinity, London: Trinity Priory of Christchurch Aldgate (*Stow* 111).

674. Ralph Stratford, bp.

678. cf. *Cal Fine R* vii, 123.

681. 'Dodyngton' is entered as of the I.Wight. No such place-name is indexed for this diocese.

682. William de Tothale, prior of the Hospitallers, d.1318 (*Dugdale,* vi, 799). The general chapter for England was held at the preceptory of Melchbourne, Beds. The founder of St Cross entrusted the hospital to the Knights Hospitallers. After much dispute, the Order handed over the management to the bishop in 1185, but kept the muniments until 1379 (*VCH Hants* ii, 194).

685. The first word on p. 424 is *Uppingham,* for Whippingham, I.Wight. Some years later a similar confusion in London caused the fines of the alien rector of Whippingham to mount up to 47s.(*Insula Vecta* 99).

686. For the enemy attacks from 1338 on Portsmouth, see *VCH Hants* iii, 187.

687. *Warenn'* is *Warner* in 685 and 686.

690. Bernard Brocaz, often granted leave of absence etc. in the *Reg.* The name derives from Brocaz, dép. Landes. For the family, see Montagu Burrows The *Family of Brocas of Beaurepaire and Roche Court,* (London, 1886): a family destined to hold high rank in the county (*VCH Hants* iii, 212f). Cf. 594.

691. When *Quasimodo* is sung, i.e. first Sunday after Easter.

693. Claim for dispossession: *arrainasset quandam assisiam nove disseisine.*

698. cf. *Reg. Com. Seal* 8. 'Lestuves', for the Stews in Southwark, see *Stow* 360f.

699. *Reg. Com. Seal* 7, under the name Carter.

701. Northington, in *Reg.* 'Northampton'. 'Burg'. ?Burghclere, or Overton Burg and Overton, probably two manors.
Six sheets have been cut out after fo. 77, but these may be unused ends of the gathering, because a new foliated section begins next.

702. Bishop of Sardica, see i, 71n. Dimissory letters: indicating that the holder may proceed to holy orders. The ordinands brought these letters to the bishop; this fact has normally been omitted here.

703. From this point the diocese of origin of the ordinands has not been indexed. *Ad titulum*. Title at ordination means the provision of maintenance once a man has been ordained. Some ecclesiastical superior will promise a benefice, or the man may have means to support himself (*patrimonium*). All these possibilities are to be found among the subdeacons. cf. *Introd*. Chantry of Ashford, not in *VCH Surrey,* but a chantry of Ashstead was set up by the prior of Newark in 1261.

704. *Chart. Winch.* mentions the priors and congregations of St Peter and of St Mary Kalendar, as holding tenements and having chaplains. cf. Nos. 112, 149, 470. Prior of St Mary Kalendar is now considered as the superior of a confraternity or guild (*Med. Rel. Houses*). See *Reg. Com. Seal,* 318n. Calke, ?*Calceto.*

705. *Keresley* ?Kerselowe. *penes registrum* etc frequently recurring phrase, referring more likely to the registry rather than a book, the register. For chantry of Ashstead, see 703.

706. *domus* seems at first to be used for small houses, later as a general term. Ossulveston or Ouston priory. Hospital of St James, to the west of Charing Cross (*Stow* 401). Ivychurch: *mon' Ederosi.*

708. St Martha, i.e. Chilworth, Surrey.

709. 'Abbot' of Ossington, in error: preceptory of Knights Hospitallers.

710. Woodhampton?. Penton Grafton or Penton Mewsey, Hants. Tarrant, formerly *locus benedictus super Tarent* or *locus benedictus Reginae super Tarentam* (T. Tanner *Notitia monastica* (revised edition, Cambridge, 1787) 107). Ashridge, house of Bonhommes, Herts.

711. Worthy Mortimer, i.e. Headbourne Worthy, Hants. Ludeshulle, i.e. Litchfield. For this difficult reading of Welsh names, see 705n.
Thomas Honstanton or Houstanton.
Mulnestrete, i.e. Milne Street (P.H. Reaney *Place-Names of Cambridgeshire and the Isle of Ely* (London, 1943), 48; Royal Commission on Historical Monuments *An Inventory of the Historical Monuments in the City of Cambridge* (2 vols., London, 1959), xliv–xlv, xlviii, li, 99. The street stood midway between the High Street and the river, with the King's Mill and the Bishop's Mill, with the church of St John Zachary. Trinity, King's and Clare colleges now occupy the area.

712. St Leonard's, Eastcheap, was with St Vedast's, Foster Lane, among the 13 churches which formed the deanery of the Arches (I. J. Churchill *Canterbury Administration* (London, 1933), i, 63n.

717. Eldon in King's Somborne. For two churches there, see *VCH Hants* iv, 480, i.e. Upper Eldon.
721. St Vedast, Foster Lane, see 712n.
722. St Mary, Thetford, will be the Cluniac priory.
723. 'Rodepeyton', dioc. St Davids?
724. Ieoneldon, ?Yeldon, Beds. *loco regali juxta Exon'*, should read *Oxon'* i.e. Rewley abbey. See *Register of John de Grandisson,* ed. F. C. Hingeston-Randolph (3 vols., London 1894–9) ii, 1014, recording these three ordinations. *Domus* of St Michael, probably Warwick.
726. Sheepbridge, Great and Little, in Swallowfield (*VCH Berks* iii).
729. *Reg.,* 31 April.
736. Richard, bp. of Ossory.
737. Mapledurham in Buriton, Hants.
738. Portsmouth: hospital of St John Baptist and St Nicholas, i.e. Domus Dei.
739. ? Winterborne Steepleton, Wilts.
741. There does not seem to be a Dadington or Doddington in the diocese. That this is an error for dioc. Lincoln and so either Lincs. or Northants., see 744.
742. The years are as in the *Reg.*
744. St Mary's Hall, Oxford, to become Oriel College, see *History of the University of Oxford* i, ed. J. I. Catto, (Oxford, 1984) 302. Cold Overton, in *Reg.* Overton Quatremars.
745. *domus de Combermere,* i.e. the cistercian abbey.
746. Stoke by Eye, i.e. Stoke Ash, Suffolk.
748. Tunbridge, dioc. Chichester ?. Neuton, i.e. Niton, see 757.
749. *presented to* . . . . . *Bramfield,* crossed out. *extra barra Veteris Templi,* in a different hand. For the hospital of St Giles in the Field, see *Stow* 392. Shipton Beauchamp?
751. *Lega.* If this were Canonsleigh, Devon, it should read Prioress.
757. College of St Mary in the Fields, see N. Tanner *The Church in late Medieval Norwich, 1370–1532* (Toronto, Pontifical Institute of Mediaeval Studies, Studies and Texts, 66; 1984).
757. Stratford atte Bowe of Chaucer, Prologue: today Stratford le Bow (Mdx).
762. For the chapel of the grange of Bovery, Beuffre and its disappearance, see S. F. Hockey *Beaulieu, King John's Abbey,* (Beaulieu, 1976) 59n5, 199, 211.
765. Sulby (Welford), Northants, *Reg. Solve.* The premonstratensian monastery was St Mary. *Coneren'* is presumably Connor, today dioc. Down and Connor, but Culrath does not appear in gazetteers of Ulster. St Radegunds, Bradsole, Kent.
767. Northborough, *Reg.* Northbury, Burstow, Surrey, dioc. Canterbury, in the deanery of Croydon. Staple, chapel in Adisham, Kent. *Reg.* Weighton, probably Watton, Norf.
770. Westundeworth? Westworth in Upham, Hants. Tiron is dioc. Chartres, *Reg.* reads Evreux.
771. The church in Fleshmonger St will be St Peter's.
774. Wield, *Walda,* but the church is of St James. *Wickham Scures:* the Scures family held Wickham until 1381 (*VCH Hants* iii, 234).

781. *Kynggate, Winchester,* ? St Nicholas.
791. ? Clougoneford, dioc. Hereford.
792. Christchurch, London or Trinity Priory, Aldgate. Wymondham, Leics, not the priory, Norfolk. For Moulton, Norfolk, in deanery of Bocking, see I. J. Churchill *Canterbury Administration* i, 64n.
 Thomas de Lisle, bishop of Ely, 1345–1361 was at the papal court in 1348 and again during the Black Death (*DNB*).
797. Both the priors of Hamble and of Andwell are given in the *Reg.* as procurators of Tiron, which must mean that one of them was procurator in England. Winchingham (Norfolk), or Witcham (Camb.). Wokingham?, dioc. London. Hudicote Boys, dioc. Worcester?.
 Brothers of St Cross, i.e. Crossed Friars in Hart Street (*Stowe* 126, 133, Crouched Friars; *VCH London* i, 514–16)
798. Alan of Walsingham, prior of Ely, from 1341 (*Le Neve*).
799. St Mary Bothaw (Bothagh'), one of the 13 churches in the deanery (*Stowe* 205).
801. *magna* belongs to Childerly, now dropped; cf. ii, 806.
802. For St Cross, see ii, 797.
803. *juratus per W' de Farlee. juratus* occurs six times against names on pages 465 and 466, but only here is the name given by whom he was sworn in.
805. Shefford West, *Reg.* Schifford Magna.
807. For St Cross, London, see n. 807 above.
809. For hospital of St John, Oxford, see *History of the University of Oxford* i, 158, 176, 226.
 Gayton, prob. Gayton le Marsh, Leics.
811. For Good Easter, Essex, see J. H. Denton *English Royal Free Chapels, 1100–1300* (Manchester, 1970).
814. Wateley: ? Whatley (Som), more probably Wheatley in Binstead, Hants (*VCH Hants* iii, 488). Newton Valence, cf. ii, 825.
 Reginald Brian, bishop of St Davids, 1349–1352 (Le Neve, *Welsh Dioceses,* 64).
818. John Thoresby, bishop, 1350–52.
823. Newark, *Reg.* reads just *Novo.*
826. Monk of Chertsey, see ii, 805.
827. *Sitientes,* i.e. Saturday before Passion Sunday.
829. Treiorwerth, Anglesey ? Trelewarth.
834. 18 Sept. Gervase Abraham, *Reg.* reads St Margaret, but see ii, 832–3.
844. College de Vaux (*de Vallibus*) founded by bp. Giles of Bridport, 1262, for 20 scholars who had migrated from Oxford (*VCH Wilts* iii, 369–85; *History of University of Oxford* i, 127 and n. 2).
855. Papal confirmation dated 12 Feb. 1352. he being also canon of Salisbury and Lincoln, holding the church of Ringwood and the hospital of St Cross (*C.Pap.L.* iii, 460; *C.Pap.Pet.* i, 225)
858. For Thomas bp. of Norwich, see ii, 535.
862. Laurence de Leck, prior, 1352–7; William Bateman or de Norwyco, bp. 1343–55 (*Le Neve*).
863. Bishop's Lynn became King's Lynn in 1537.

888. Lescar (Basses-Pyrénées) near Pau, episcopal see until the Revolution. Ricallo and Casa Nova have not been recovered.
889. Aquem', in dioc. Aix-en-Provence (Bouches du Rhone). Church not recovered.
893. The date must be 1358; *Reg.* reads lvii.
895. Louis (Ludovicus in *Reg.*) Llywellyn ap Madog ab Elis (1357-75). "in distant parts" will refer to his complicated succession to the see.
896. Queldryk, absent from modern gazeteers, is to be found in *Taxatio* under Archdeaconry of Cleveland.
    For St Mary Hall, Oxford, see *History of the University of Oxford* i, 227, 302.
898. 'canons of Merton' in a much later hand. 'Schotfeld', prob. Shotford, Norf. or Suff.
901. Orde, ?Oare, deanery of Ospringe.
902. Leccelie, the only likely premonstratensian house will be Langley, Norf.
903. 5 marks, cf. ii, 738
906. Stoleye, ? Norf.
907. The *Reg.* puts the priests before the deacons, causing confusion. After John Heryng the *Reg.* reads: Fr. William Chaundeler, John Bloundis, John de Walyngford, canons of Merton, with a corrective note: *isti fuer' ord' diac' ideo vacant h'*. They appear as deacons in 908.
915. The bishop left for Calais Aug. 24, returned Nov. 6.
917. Predial tithes, i.e. from the produce of the soil.
919. Hantwisell (Hantwysiel), absent from the gazeteers, recovered from *Taxatio*
921. Busteshale, prob. for Bustlesham. Lewis de Charlton, bp. 1361-9. Esgar, or Osger (*Le Neve*).
923. John Barnet, bp. of Worcester 1362-3.
927. St Peter Kalendar, by confusion with St Mary Kalendar.
934. *nativo sanguine, servilis condicionis,* a dispensation was required for a bondsman, giving proof of manumission (Decretals of Gregory VI, III, i, c.18)
941. In this long list of 39 names, Henry de Ticheborne appears twice. William de Lynne, bp. of Chichester 1362-68.
953. *Nativus,* for the requirements of canon law, see above 934.

* * * * * *

At the death of William de Edyndon the bishopric was granted to Nicholas de Kaerwent, John de Blebury, M. Walter de Sevenhampton, M. John Corf, Walter Heywode and Thomas Hungerford, rendering to the exchequer 200li. each month of the voidance, 8 Oct.1366 (*C.Fine R*, vii, 339), but see also *CPR 1364-67*, 353 and *CPR 1367-70*, 15. where the holding of the temporalities is granted to William of Wykeham.

CONCORDANCE
FOLIATION – PAGINATION

This table relates the foliation of the sixteenth, seventeenth and eighteenth centuries in both volumes of Edington's register to the pagination used in this edition.

fo.	p.1	fo.20	p.42	fo.41	p.83
	2	21	43		84
fo.1	3		44	42	85
	4	22	45		86
2	5		46	43	87
	6	23	47		88
3	7		48	44	89
	8	24	49		90
4	9	25	50	45	91
	10	25	51		92
5	11		52	46	93
	12	26	53		94
6	13		54	47	95
	14	27	55		96
7	15		56	48	97
	16	28	57		98
8	17		58	49	99
	18	29	59		100
9	19		60	50	101
10	20	30	61		102
10	21		62	51	103
	22	31	63		104
11	23		64	52	105
	24	32	65		106
12	25		66	53	107
	26	33	67		108
13	27		68	54	109
	28	34	69		110
14	29		70	55	111
	30	35	71		112
15	31		72	56	113
	32	36	73		114
16	33		74	57	115
	34	37	75		116
17	35		76	58	117
	36	38	77		118
18	37		78	59	119
	38	39	79		120
19	39		80	60	121
	40	40	81		122
20	41		82	61	123

fo.61	p.124	fo.86	p.174	fo.111	p.224
62	125	87	175	112	225
	126		176		226
63	127	88	177	113	227
	128		178		228
64	129	89	179	114	229
	130		180		230
65	131	90	181	115	231
	132		182		232
66	133	91	183	116	233
	134		184		234
67	135	92	185	117	235
	136		186		236
68	137	93	187	118	237
	138		188		238
69	139	94	189	119	239
	140		190		240
70	141	95	191	120	241
	142		192		242
71	143	96	193	121	243
	144		194		244
72	145	97	195	122	245
	146		196		246
73	147	98	197	123	247
	148		198		248
74	149	99	199	124	249
	150		200		250
75	151	100	201	125	251
	152		202		252
76	153	101	203	126	253
	154		204		254
77	155	102	205	127	255
	156		206		256
78	157	103	207	128	257
	158		208		258
79	159	104	209	129	259
	160		210		260
80	161	105	211	130	261
	162		212		262
81	163	106	213	131	263
	164		214		264
82	165	107	215	132	265
	166		216		266
83	167	108	217	133	267
	168		218		268
84	169	109	219	134	269
	170		220		270
85	171	110	221		271
	172		222		272
86	173	111	223	1	273

fo.1	p.274	fo.26	p.324	fo.51	p.374
2	275	27	325	52	375
	276		326		376
3	277	28	327	53	377
	278		328		378
4	279	29	329	53+	379
	280		330		380
5	281	30	331	54	381
	282		332		382
6	283	31	333	55	383
	284		334		384
7	285	32	335	56	385
	286		336		386
8	287	33	337	57	387
	288		338		388
9	289	34	339	58	389
	290		340		390
10	291	35	341	59	391
	292		342		392
11	293	36	343	60	393
	294		344		394
12	295	37	345	61	395
	296		346		396
13	297	38	347	62	397
	298		348		398
14	299	39	349	63	399
	300		350		400
15	301	40	351	64	401
	302		352		402
16	303	41	353	65	403
	304		354		404
17	305	42	355	66	405
	306		356		406
18	307	43	357	67	407
	308		358		408
19	309	44	359	68	409
	310		360		410
20	311	45	361	69	411
	312		362		412
21	313	46	363	70	413
	314		364		414
22	315	47	365	71	415
	316		366		416
23	317	48	367	72	417
	318		368		418
24	319	49	369	73	419
	320		370		420
25	321	50	371	74	421
	322		372		422
26	323	51	373	75	423

fo.75	p.424	P	459	GG	494
76	425		460	HH	495
	426	Q	461		496
77	427		462	II	497
	428	R	463		498
A	429		464	KK	499
	430	S	465		500
B	431		466	LL	501
	432	T	467		502
C	433		468	MM	503
	434	U	469		504
D	435		470	NN	505
	436	V	471		506
E	437		472	OO	507
	438	W	473		508
E$^+$	439		474	PP	509
	440	X	475		510
F	441		476	QQ	511
	442	Y	477		512
G	443		478	RR	513
	444	Z	479		514
H	445		480	SS	515
	446	AA	481		516
I	447		482	TT	517
	448	BB	483		518
K	449		484	UU	519
	450	CC	485		520
L	451		486	VV	521
	452	DD	487		522
M	453		488	WW	523
	454	EE	489		524
N	455		490	XX	525
	456	FF	491		526
O	457		492	YY	527
	458	GG	493		528

Indexes

The subject index which follows refers to both volumes 1 and 2 of Bishop Edington's register; the index of personal names and placenames refers to the second volume alone. Acitations in the form 85n., for example, relates to the text in note 85, placed in the note section between the calendar and the index.

The medieval spelling of placenames is given in brackets when this differs from the modern. Suspensions remain.

For the religious orders: ben. for Benedictines and cist. for Cistercians; for the friars, dom. for the Dominicans, fm. for the Minors and carm. for the Carmelites.

References to counties are to the historic counties, not to the modern administrative counties.

SELECTED SUBJECT INDEX

229

1297, 1347, 1368, 1534, 1536, 1553, 1571, 1625, 1660, 1669; ii, 134, 302, 428, 650-1
, exchange of, i, 1039
Precentorship, i, 165, 292
Presentations, to benefices, *passim*
, changed, i, 64, 775
, disputed, i, 54, 65-8, 70, 98, 155, 475, 482, 574, 651, 771, 836, 980, 988, 1163, 1630, 1655, 1657, 1715, 1743
, renounced, i, 617, 1213
, sought, ii, 43
, to priory, i, 242, 1304, 1456, 1556
Priories, alien, *see* Alien.
Prison, ii, 117, 124, 455
Processions, i, 47-8; ii, 26
Procurations of archdeacons, i, 68, 1691
of papal nuncios, i, 39f, 81; ii, 228ff, 328, 335-8, 347-356, 362-370, 518, 628
Procurator, episcopal, ii, 14, 29, 87, 110
Provision, i, 1, 3, 10-13, 16, 68, 306, 334, 337, 343, 345, 362, 367-8, 389, 661, 883, 900, 909, 923, 949, 1084, 1649; ii, 433-8, 442, 509ff, 515
, of prior by nomination, i, 909, 914, 923, 943, 949, 969
Public notary, appointments, i, 63, 78-9; ii, 15, 19, 520, 539-540, 555
Purgation, ii, 89-90, 114-5, 117, 124-5, 133, 455, 460

Ransom, ii, 422
Reconciliation of church, ii, 49, 223, 248
, of churchyard, i, 71; ii, 23, 197, 201, 253, 294, 491
Reeves, accounts of, ii, 560
Registers, i, 11, 178, 334; ii, 93, 615
, order to search, i, 54
Registrar, i, 106; ii, 110, 272
Renunciation of papal licence, ii, 553
, of presentation, i, 1213
Resignation, i, 145, 171, 190, 253, 262, 661, 705, 931, 1084, 1111, 1173, 1192, 1196, 1220, 1224, 1238, 1242, 1245, 1420-1, 1434, 1499, 1501-2,

1532, 1542, 1607, 1641, 1679, 1733, 1738, 1740, 1751-2
Robbery, ii, 66, 455
Rome, *see limina.*

St Swithun's farthings, i, 84; ii, 50, 212, 234, 613
Sanctuary violated, ii, 269
Schools, ii, 625
Siege of castle, ii, 36
Sequestration, of crops, ii, 101
, of fruits of rectory, ii, 611
, of goods of archdeacon, ii, 50, 610ff
of rector, ii, 477-8, 638-9, 641
, of tithes, ii, 317
, unclassified, ii, 101, 207, 447, 451, 466, 502, 504, 691
Sequestrator, i, 36, 84, 101; ii, 9, 148, 193
Stipends, excessive, ii, 456
, increased, i, 1692, 1705
Study, dispensations for, 1 year, *passim*
, 1 year renewed, i, 1569
, 2 years, i, 34, 1182
, 3 years, i, 1602
, 7 years, i, 135, 205, 811, 875, 1062
, disputed, i, 1602
Subsidy on clerical income, ii, 414-6, 422, 462
Surveyors, stewards, *see* Manorial officials.
Suspension lifted, ii, 389, 428, 501, 521
Synodals, i, 84, 1636; ii, 157, 212, 219, 234

Tapisser, ii, 605
Taxation of clergy, papal, i, 39-40, 65, 477; ii, 421ff, 477, 651
, royal, i, 68; ii, 597, 614-6, 619-21, 624, 633, 635-7, 641, 665-7, 670-2, 676-81, 685, 687
, other, ii, 100
Templars, ii, 626
Thanksgiving ordered, ii, 319-320
Theft, ii, 99-100, 186, 455
Tithes, i, 66-7, 223, 860, 896, 941, 1197, 1218, 1636, 1659, 1691, 1748;

INDEX OF PERSONAL NAMES AND PLACENAMES

Baughurst (Bagehurst), Hants, 702, 709, 739, 742
Bayeux, dioc., 237
Bayham (Begham), Sussex, 766, 880, 886
Baynard, Eleanor, 195
Baynel, John, 710
Bayson, John, 799
Baysyngstok', Dominic de, ben., 652
Beauchamp, John, 943
Beaulieu, abbey, Hants, 71n, 243, 707, 711, 737-740, 763, 770-2, 777, 834, 897, 933, 948, 952
    , chapel of Beufre, 762, 830
Beauleyn, John, 905
Beaumond, John, 846, 857, 862
Beutre, John de, 15, 19, 63, 77, 80, 234, 251, 328, 356, 539-40, 544-5, 550, 931, 947
    , Roger de, 781, 792, 798, 803
Beche, Nicholas and Margaret de la, 66
    , Robert, ben., 845, 866, 872
Bec-Herluin, abbey, France, 609
Beckhurst, Thomas, 703
Becke, Robert, 875
Becwell, John, 766
Beddington (Bedyngton), Surrey, 121 609, 922-3, 927, 933, 954
Bedeford, Robert de, 802, 807
    , Roger de, ben., 860
Bedefordia, John de, dom., 885
Bedel, Nicholas, 762
Bedenham (Badeham) in Alverstoke, Hants, 129, 194
Bedhampton, Hants, 155, 492, 770, 774, 789
Bedwas (Bedewas), Mon, 878
Bedyngfeld, Peter de, 764
Beegh', Begh', William, 770, 776, 780
Beel, John, ben., 800, 805, 810
Beighton (Beghton'), Norf, 757
Bekensfeld, Andrew de, 781, 787, 793
Bekford', Peter de, ben., 652
Bekke, William, 823, 827, 829
Belle, John, 845
    , William, 728, 737, 809, 815, 826
Bellerby, John de, 744
Bello, John de, dom., 728
Belper (Beau Repair), Derb, 797, 810
Ben, John, ben., 935
Benedict, bp. of Cardicensis, 23, 51, 702, 708, 713-4, 725, 729, 736, 741
    , XII, pope, 515
Beneit, Benet, Bennet, Robert, 835, 869

, Walter, 803, 836, 860, 873
Benham, William de, 777
Benmond, John, 528, 846
Bennebury, John de, 840, 845
Bense, John, ben., 238
Benstede, John, 769
Bentworth (Bynteworth), Hants, 933, 937-9
Benyt, see Beneyt.
Berard, John, aug., 916
Berbury, John, 878
Berdewell', Richard de, 794
Bere, Hants, 127
Bereford, John de, 109, 708, 760
    , William de, 760
Bereham, John, dom., 879, or Bercham.
Berendon. Peter de, 799
Berford, Richard de, 900
Bergate, William, fm., 895
Bergh', John, fm., 899
    , Nicholas atte, son of John atte, 769, 775
    , Thomas, carm., 908
Berkeleye, in W. Horsley, 341
Berkeswell (Baukwell), Warw, 706
Berkham, John de, 768
Berkhamstead, Little (Parva Berkamstede), Herts, 702, 704, 716, 724, 835
Berkshire, sheriff of, 646, 661
Berkstede, John de, fm., 737
Berkyng', Adam de, aug., 743, 749, 766, 773
    , Roger de, 808
Berlee, John, 728
Bermondsey, priory, 51, 433, 609, 703, 705, 709, 710-1, 726-8, 734, 736, 791, 796-7, 810-1, 821, 868, 888, 894, 900-1, 935
    , ch. of St M. Magdalen, 609, 770, 773, 831, 860-2
    , place, 446
Bermondeseye, Geoffrey de, ben., 901
Bernard, John, dom., 327, 732, 737
    , Nicholas, 791, 797, 807
    , Richard, 280, 817
Bernes, Roger de, 772
Bernham, Robert de, 859
Beronden', Peter de, 781, 787, 793
Bers, Peter del. 645, 655, 657, 660
Bersey, John, carm., 724
Bertegrave in Epsom, Surrey, 56, 160
Bertelot, John, dom., 735, 954